Interpreting at Church:

A Paradigm for
Sign Language Interpreters,
4th Edition

Leo Yates, Jr.

Notes taken from the HOLY BIBLE: NEW INTER-
NATIONAL VERSION®. NIV®. Copyright © 1973,
1978, 1984 by International Bible Society. Used by
permission of Zondervan.

The "NIV" and "New International Version" trade-
marks are registered in the United States Patent and
Trademark Office by International Bible Society.

ISBN-13: 978-1519367617

ISBN-10: 1519367619

Printed in the United States of America

––––––––––––––––––––––––––––––––

Library of Congress Control Number: 2006910139

Printed by CreateSpace,
An Amazon Company
7290 B Investment Dr.
North Charleston, SC 29418
Phone: 866-356-2154

Acknowledgments

To the church, which I love, and the interpreting profession for which I care deeply, this book is dedicated to the two. If it were not for my beloved parents, Leo and Betty Yates, I would not be who I am. It was they who cultivated my life, spiritually and professionally. Family members Sarah and Cindy have shown me much encouragement, the kind that helped me to write this book. Without the editing by Kimberly Fisher, this book would not be in print.; I am deeply thankful. Dictionaries do not hold enough words to express my appreciation for the support of friends and colleagues who reviewed this book. They are Karl Kosiorek, Kathleen Austin, Aretha Scruggs, Rev. Giovanni Arroyo, Bishop Peggy Johnson, Jeanne Maddox, Barbara Sully, Rev. Joo Kang, Linda Brown, Jennifer Bell, Tina Burke, and Sarah Gumina. Their comments, advice, and criticisms served to sharpen the focus and clarity of this book. I am forever indebted to the Deaf models who share their language with book readers. My seminary education from the Master of Divinity program at Wesley Theological Seminary is invaluable; it has enriched my book and my life immensely. Most of all, may God receive my eternal thankfulness for inspiring me and calling me to write this book.

About The Author

Leo Yates, Jr. holds two national certifications (CI & CT) from the Registry of Interpreters for the Deaf (RID). He has interpreted professionally in the church and the community for over twenty years. Leo holds a Bachelor's of Science degree, majoring in Business Administration. In addition, he earned his Master of Divinity degree from Wesley Theological Seminary and a Master of Science in Clinical Counseling degree from Bellevue University. Leo is a Deacon in The United Methodist Church and served previously as the pastor of two Deaf churches in Maryland. Also, Leo was an RID committee member who helped to write the current Standard Practice Paper: Interpreting in Religious Settings. Before entering into the interpreting profession, Leo co-owned a retail business in the Maryland area. Leo is appointed as a professional counselor at University of Maryland Medical Center in Baltimore, MD, while working part-time as an associate pastor at a church in the Baltimore-Washington Conference of the United Methodist Church. Leo is a staff interpreter at Foundry United Methodist Church in Washington, DC. He also serves on The United Methodist Committee on Deaf and Hard-of-Hearing Ministries. Furthermore, Leo and his twin sister, Sarah (also an interpreter) are children of Deaf parents. He enjoys mentoring interpreters and presenting religious interpreting workshops.

Also available from Leo Yates, Jr. are <u>Pocket Reference of Religious Signs</u> and <u>Deaf Ministry: Ministry Models for Expanding the Kingdom of God</u>.

Table of Contents

Introduction i
Chapter 1 – Advancement of the Profession 1

History of RID 1

Professional Accountability.....................................2

Certification 3

The Law Pertaining to Deaf People........................7

Ethical Standards..9

Interpreting & Transliterating...............................10

Quality Assurance Screening.................................12

Summary..13

Chapter 2 – Ethical Issues 15

The Need for an Interpreter 15

Balancing Faith and Profession 17

Boundaries 20

Multiple Roles..22

Interpreter Compensation 23

Dress Attire for Interpreters 26

Participating in the Service.................................... 27

Skill Development.. 28

Demand-Control Schema 29

Decision Making 31

RID Article 37

Summary 41

NAD-RID CODE OF PROFESSIONAL
CONDUCT.. 43

Chapter 3 – Dynamics of Church Settings 49

Different Contexts 50

Educating the Congregation 52

Logistics for Interpreter Placement 54

Compensation 55

Hard of Hearing and Late-Deafened Parishioners
.... 56

Captioning.. 58

Deaf-Blind Parishioners 59

Group Process... 63

Worship.. 65

Types of Christianity 66

Denominational Worship Styles 69

The Presbyterian Worship Service 71

The Lutheran Worship Service 72

The Episcopal Worship Service 73

The United Methodist Worship Service 74

The United Church of Christ Worship Service ...75

The Baptist Worship Service 75

The Catholic Worship Service 77

The Pentecostal Worship Service 78

Cross-Cultural Venues 79

Tensions within Churches 81

Summary 82

Chapter 4 – Accepting the Interpreting Request ..89

Standard Practice Paper 90

Interpreter Interview 95

Considerations Before Accepting 96

Accepting the Assignment 97

Worship Space 99

Choice of Language 102

Meeting the Speaker 103

Conclusion of the Service 104

Summary 105

Chapter 5 – Intricacies of Interpreting 107

Mastering Language Skills 107

Sign Language 108

General Knowledge 112

Interpreting Models 113

Interpreting Process 116

Simultaneous and Consecutive Interpreting 118

Language Register 119

Linguistic Expansion 121

Expansion Techniques 123

Errors and Omissions 126

Monitoring 127

Mentoring 129

Team Interpreting 132

Professional Development 136

Considering Humility 137

Summary 137

Chapter 6 – Analysis & Application 139

Lectionary 140

Commentaries 140

Scripture 142

Parallel Bible 143

Study Bible 148

Music 153

Analyzing and Signing Music 155

Sermons 159

Prayers 161

The Lord's Prayer 163

Creeds 164

Apostle's Creed 165

Summary 166

Chapter 7 —Weddings & Funerals 169

The Dying Process...................................... 169

Funerals.. 171

Fees.. 172

Preparation... 173

Interpreter Placement................................... 176

Funeral Liturgy... 177

Funeral Terms 180

Weddings 181

Interpreter Placement................................... 182

Negotiation 184

Fees.. 184

Legal Component... 185

Wedding Liturgy... 186

Wedding Phrases... 188

Summary 190

Conclusion **191**
References...**195**
Appendix A – Organizations **201**

Appendix B – Church Internet Sites 207
Appendix C – Suggestions for New Interpreters 213
Appendix D – Standard Practice Paper: Multiple
Roles in Interpreting 219
Appendix E – Advocacy 223
Appendix F – RID Views Article 229
Appendix G – RID Views Article #2 237
Appendix H – Wedding Liturgy 243
Glossary of Interpreting Terms 251
Glossary of Theological Terms 257
Glossary of Church Terms 269
Religious Sign Dictionary 277
Index 339

Introduction

Interpreters working in church settings, sometimes called religious interpreters, open a gateway for communication in these specialized settings. Interpreters/practitioners enable minority language users to be included when a discourse is audible and signed. Because of the presence of and work provided by sign language interpreters, language and culture no longer has to be a barrier between Deaf and hearing people in religious settings.

This book, slanted toward interpreting in Christian churches, provides insight for new interpreters working in church settings. Newcomers and other interested readers will be exposed to Christian idiosyncrasies that begin the exploration of interpreting in a Christian setting. Academic education, collaboration with experienced professionals, research, and hands-on experience has been integrated; these four methods are the essence of this book's content.

Faith is the primary motivation for writing this book, yet with a deep respect for the interpreting industry, it is written with a professional emphasis for incoming interpreters working in Christian venues. The vocation of interpreting is a profession, which is underscored by the paradigm used for this book. Readers are strongly encouraged to explore other materials, as well, in order to expand their knowledge of interpreting in various church contexts.

Religious Interpreting

Industry professionals generally call persons who

provide interpreting services *interpreters* or *practitioners*. From time to time, the term "signer" may be referenced; however, interpreters are encouraged to educate consumers with the proper title. When one provides interpreting services, it is much more than signing. It involves consultation, preparation, delivery of services, and follow-up in the setting where the interpreter works.

Religious interpreting has a place in society, as it assists in the spiritual transformation of a congregation and provides inclusion in a populated religious setting. Whether a Deaf congregation is providing American Sign Language (ASL)-to-English interpretation for hearing participants or a hearing congregation is providing English-to-ASL interpretation for Deaf participants, religious interpreters are needed to make communication possible between two languages. An inclusive setting within the church is essential where the congregation can be open to diverse cultural and linguistic alternatives.

The decision to have an interpreter present for Christian worship services is one of many steps in the transcendent process that enables congregations to invite others who might have a different modality of language and cultural experiences. "Everyone is important, and all people are welcome here" is the view people should perceive. When the church provides professional interpreters for church services and programs, the doors widen with linguistic ambiance and hospitality for those whose language capabilities might otherwise place them in the minority. The professional interpreter, who provides religious interpreting or transliterating services, helps to fill a fundamental human need and enables seekers to develop their faith further in their faith communities.

"It is a calling," is what some say motivated them to learn sign language. Others may be influenced by a fascination that stems from seeing interpreters at work, or from having an encounter with a Deaf person at church that sparked an interest in learning the language. Another typical story is that of befriending a Deaf individual during childhood. Whatever the motivation, interpreters in faith-based settings are a crucial link in the chain of communication.

Interpreters provide communications access at a worship service, one reason they are valued in Christian settings. Faith, believing in a higher power, and experiencing spiritual renewal are still important for most faith communities. Religion may be less emphasized today than it was a century ago, but religious themes, ideas, and influences still saturate society. When a crisis occurs, whether personal or public, people feel compelled to seek guidance, hope, and support from the Church. Millions of visitors, for example, attended church following the catastrophic events of 9/11. Some visitors became church members, while others received what they needed and left again. Interpreters help to bridge hearing and Deaf communities, both parts of the Church.

Deaf Churches

Like other language minority groups, many Deaf people congregate in a church setting for spiritual and fellowship reasons. Generations ago, Deaf people who attended Deaf residential schools usually had some type of church exposure, usually on Sunday mornings or

Sunday afternoons, when a minister or priest came to the school campus. Others attended hearing churches, without having an interpreter, with family members. Some Deaf people had good church experiences; others did not. In matters of faith, each experience was different.

Worship services to the Deaf community were perceived as a ministry for the church. Centuries have gone by since the Episcopal Church organized the first Deaf congregation in the United States; next was the Catholic Church, soon followed by the Lutheran Church. Not far behind these three denominations came the Methodist Church and the Baptist Church, both of which had established Deaf worship services by the turn of the twentieth century.[i]

Deaf worship services, where the dominant language is ASL, sometimes adapt liturgy (a prescribed format for worship) to better suit congregations. For instance, contemporary praise services popularize the worship service with music, whereas some Deaf congregations may give less emphasis to music and more to drama, an extension of ASL storytelling. Because ASL is a visual and spatial language, it is not uncommon for Deaf worship services to include dramas more frequently than hearing worship services do, perhaps during Scripture readings or as sermon illustrations. A number of Deaf congregations incorporate a drum during a song that is being signed so that vibrations ripple through the worship space, a cultural practice that may be somewhat annoying or distracting for hearing people but enhances the experience for Deaf worshipers.

Most Deaf congregations will welcome hearing

visitors. A hearing person learning to sign can expect common questions from Deaf church members, such as the following:

- ❑ Your first and last name?

- ❑ Are you Deaf, hard of hearing, or hearing?

- ❑ Are there Deaf people in your family?

- ❑ Why are you learning sign language?

- ❑ Who is teaching you the language and culture?

It is normal for a hearing person to feel intimidated because of not knowing the language; most first-time visitors to any church, Deaf or hearing, usually feel awkward. An interpreter can assist the minority language user to feel more at ease because communication can take place between the parties. As an interpreter facilitates communication, hearing people can clear up common misconceptions about Deaf people.[1]

Cultural aspects that differ from hearing culture can be observed within Deaf congregations. Whether a Deaf church member shares with others an anecdote about a Video Relay Service (VRS) call with a child or announces to others the upcoming homecoming event at the Deaf school, Deaf culture is a major influence in the dynamics of a Deaf congregation. Deaf culture, with similar experiences, common language, and shared

---

[1] Common misconceptions: (a) Can Deaf people drive? (b) How do Deaf parents know when their child is crying? (c) Will their children be Deaf?

traditions, often differentiates a Deaf congregation from a hearing congregation.

Questions for the Future

In Roger Hitching's book, <u>The Church and Deaf People</u>, Hitching includes an interview with Chaplain Shrine, a Deaf chaplain in the Church of England. Shrine indicates three potential concerns for the Deaf church.

1. Its members are aging, which suggests that many Deaf churches will die out in the next twenty years or so. Younger people are not joining.

2. The church has a poor image in the Deaf community, where it is often regarded as irrelevant, old-fashioned, and stuck on English and hearing ways of doing things.

3. The Deaf church is generally ignored and marginalized by the wider church.[ii]

Shrine's concerns are valid. Historically, Deaf churches were geographically located near Deaf clubs. Most Deaf clubs, which were more prominent in the early and mid-twentieth century, have folded, and with more Deaf children being mainstreamed, in part because of having cochlear implants, in public schools, there is a potential need for more interpreters in churches in the near future.

With the present need for qualified interpreters in religious settings, and a future need for additional interpreters, there might be a possible crisis for the

Church at large. Granted, the interpreter may be seen as a bridge for hearing and Deaf populations, but the Church is the concrete for that bridge. There is a need for further cooperation, education, and involvement by church officials. It is they who facilitate conditions and provide qualified interpreting services to congregations.

Hu - "get to the top"

ENDNOTES

[i] Costello, Elaine. Religious Signing: A Comprehensive Guide for All Faiths. New York: Bantam Books, 1986.

[ii] Hitching, Roger. The Church and Deaf People: A Study of Identity, Communication and Relationships with Special Reference to the Ecclesiology of Jürgen Moltmann. Cumbria, CA: Paternoster Press, 2003, 27.

Chapter 1 – Advancement of the Profession

Standards exist to which interpreters must adhere, and it is important for new interpreters to know these standards. Chapter one includes some of the knowledge interpreters should have about the profession, including a partial account of the development of the profession. Interpreters, regardless of what setting they are working in, ought to be familiar with the progression and advancement of the interpreting profession.

History of RID

Before the establishment of the Registry of Interpreters for the Deaf (RID), most interpreters either had Deaf family members or were associated with the Deaf community. Perhaps they worked at the residential Deaf school or an area church. These early interpreters performed informal interpreting services, typically as a favor. Other venues for interpreting included meetings, special doctors' appointments, legal proceedings, and churches.

Pre-RID interpreters knew English and sign language, and this was thought to be the only prerequisite necessary to interpret for friends, family members, or colleagues. It is important to note that before the RID was formed, no interpreting education programs (IEPs) existed. There was no official registry of interpreters, and ASL was not considered an official language.

In June of 1964, at Ball State University (formerly Ball State Teachers College), a group of people with a common interest in formalizing the profession met during a teachers' conference where they were interpreting. Those present agreed that it would be necessary to have the following:

- ❑ A registry of "qualified" interpreters

- ❑ A set of standards (ethics)

- ❑ Interpreter education

- ❑ Testing and licensure

- ❑ Promotion of awareness for interpreting services

By the end of the conference, these Deaf and hearing participants established the Professional Registry of Interpreters for the Deaf. In 1972, the organization was incorporated, its goals and mission were further refined, and the name was slightly changed to become the RID of today.[iii]

Professional Accountability

Sign language interpreting is considered a profession. Qualified and licensed interpreters provide professional services to Deaf, deaf-blind, hard of hearing, late-deafened, and hearing people. Like other professions such as medicine or teaching, the interpreting profession has four attributes that establish it as a legitimate profession. These are as follows:

- ❑ Specialized knowledge and skills

❑ Fulfillment of a fundamental human need

❑ Accountability structure

❑ Placement of another's interests before one's own

These attributes underscore professionalism in the interpreting setting. The interpreter must market him- or herself as a legitimate professional in the Deaf and hearing communities and assume responsibility for the work in order to interpret in the faith community.

Through RID, interpreters remain accountable when they participate in the Certification Maintenance Program (CMP) for certified members and the Associate Continuing Education Tracking (ACET) for non-certified members. These essential programs were established helps to ensure that interpreters remain proficient and updated with regard to changes in the profession. It is mandatory for certified interpreters to participate, while participation for associate members is optional. For the sake of accountability, associate members should also take part in the program because it helps to be exposed to best practices, to be associated with the profession, and help keep track of their professional development.[iv]

Certification

Unless the practitioner is a *generalist interpreter* (having a minimum amount of competence in various settings), he or she usually works in a specific field such as mental health, religion, education, law, government, or medical. The *specialist interpreter* has advanced education, additional knowledge and/or training in a specialized setting. Because there is no specialist certificate offered at this time, it is not uncommon for interpreters to have a post-secondary education, degree, or training in their specialization. The prerequisite for RID certification is a bachelor's degree, unless one is eligible for the Alternative Pathway track (see RID's website for additional information).

As in other professions, licensure requirements have evolved since the inception of RID. Some certifications that are no longer offered, yet are still accepted in the profession, are:

❑ Comprehensive Skills Certificate (CSC)

❑ Interpretation Certificate (IC) [partial certificate of the CSC]

❑ Transliteration Certificate (TC) [partial certificate of the CSC]

❑ Master Comprehensive Skills Certificate (MCSC)

❑ Specialist Certificate: Performing Arts (SC: PA)

❑ Specialist Certificate: Legal (SC:L).

❑ Certificate of Interpreting (CI)

❑ Certificate of Transliteration (CT)

❑ National Interpreter Certificate Advanced (NIC Advanced)

❏ National Interpreter Certificate Master (NIC Master)

❏ Oral Transliteration Certificate (OTC)

Deaf and hard of hearing interpreters, working as relay interpreters and/or interpreting for deaf-blind individuals, were awarded the Reverse Skills Certificate (RSC), but that certification is replaced by the Certified Deaf Interpreter (CDI). The National Association of the Deaf (NAD) used to offer national certifications, which were the NAD III (Generalist), NAD IV (Advanced), and the NAD V (Master). Those interpreters who continue to hold these certifications have registered them through RID. The certifications offered to practitioners are the National Interpreter Certificate (NIC) and the Certified Deaf Interpreter (CDI), which is offered through the Center for the Assessment of Sign Language Interpretation (CASLI), an RID supported LLC.

Many interpreters are what the profession considers generalists. A generalist works as a practitioner in the community, either as a contract employee (freelance interpreter) or as a staff interpreter. As a staff interpreter, the practitioner may be employed by an interpreting agency or an organization. Freelance interpreters commonly contract their services with an interpreting agency or directly with the business or organization. When working in multiple settings (e.g., VRS, church, government, medical, etc.), many generalists are adaptive and possess a general knowledge in various disciplines.

New and seasoned interpreters seeking certification will be offered the National Interpreter Certification (NIC). The computerized test is taken first; upon passing, the candidate for certification takes the interview and performance testing concomitantly. Successful candidates achieve the NIC. At one time this certification had three levels – the NIC, NIC Advanced, and NIC Master, but transitioned to the single-level NIC, in part for clarity and to streamline the scoring process.[v] This licensure was developed in a collaboration between the National Association of the Deaf (NAD) and RID.[2] The two organizations forged a partnership called the NAD-RID National Council on Interpreting (NCI).[vi] Prior to this collaboration, each organization tested and awarded its own certifications. NAD and RID agreed to establish a joint task force to study and implement a new certification system. They recommended redesigning the testing process to include a psychometric test that examines the interpreter's knowledge (computerized or written test), ethical standards (interview portion), and performance.

After research and study, it is RID's view (and that of the profession) that interpreters holding certification most likely will provide a higher quality of service that is demanded of interpreters. Certification preparation materials can be also acquired through RID.[3]

---

[2] Before this collaboration, NAD had its own process for awarding certification. Holders of NAD certification were awarded a NAD III (Generalist), NAD IV (Advanced), or NAD V (Master). NAD certified members maintained their certification status and CMP when they transferred to the RID CMP system. NAD no longer awards certification.

[3] Testing information can be located by going to RID's website: http://www.rid.org/rid-certification-overview/nic-certification/.

Another avenue for practitioners who work in an educational setting (K-12) is to achieve the Ed: K-12 by passing the Educational Interpreter Performance Assessment (EIPA), which is offered by the Boys Town National Research Hospital. A candidate passing the written test and earning a 4.0 or higher on the EIPA can become certified member of RID (not RID certified) when joining the association; in which time RID will oversee the Ed: K-12 holder's CMP. RID's website has further
mation.[4]

When an interpreter has been awarded certification, this shows the individual's qualifications, that he or she has been examined, tested, and awarded certification, and that the quality of services by the professional meets RID's qualifications. A certified interpreter is to discern if he or she has the proper skills for an assignment, thus providing assurance to consumers in churches of professional qualifications. Most congregations are less likely to require interpreters to have certification; however, all interpreters (including those who work only in churches) are encouraged to establish professional development goals, which may include the process of earning certification.

The Law Pertaining to Deaf People

Before an interpreter takes the interview and performance test, the candidate is required to take a 150-question computerized test (an alternative paper

---

[4] More information about EIPA interpreters becoming certified members of RID can be read at http://www.rid.org/rid-certification-overview/ed-k-12-certification/.

and pencil test is offered). Besides testing the interpreter's general fund of knowledge and familiarity with the tenets of the Code of Professional Conduct, one segment of the computerized test specifically examines the interpreter's understanding of current legislation and its impact on communications access for those with hearing loss.

Federal law mandates the prohibition of discrimination against those with disabilities. Guidelines[vii] from the Department of Justice stipulate:

❑ *American with Disabilities Act (ADA):* The ADA prohibits discrimination on the basis of disability in employment, State and local government, public accommodations, commercial facilities, transportation, and telecommunications. It also applies to the United States Congress.

   o Title I requires employers with 15 or more employees to provide qualified individuals with disabilities an equal opportunity to benefit from the full range of employment-related opportunities available to others.

   o Title III covers businesses and nonprofit service providers that are public accommodations, privately operated entities offering certain types of courses and examinations, privately operated transportation, and commercial facilities. Public accommodations are private entities who own, lease, lease to, or operate facilities such as restaurants, retail stores, hotels, movie theaters, private schools, convention centers, doctors' offices, homeless shelters, transportation depots, zoos, funeral homes, day care centers, and recreation facilities including sports stadiums and fitness clubs.

○ Title IV addresses telephone and television access for people with hearing and speech disabilities. It requires common carriers (telephone companies) to establish interstate and intrastate telecommunications relay services (TRS) 24 hours a day, 7 days a week. Title IV also requires closed captioning of federally funded public service announcements.

❑ The *Individuals with Disabilities Education Act (IDEA)* (formerly called P.L. 94-142 or the Education for all Handicapped Children Act of 1975) requires public schools to make available to all eligible children with disabilities a free appropriate public education in the least restrictive environment appropriate to their individual needs.

Complete descriptions of these guidelines, plus several others, are accessible through the Department of Justice. Notable, however, is that the ADA *does not apply* to religious institutions or churches. Sadly, the church has the discretion whether or not to provide and pay for an interpreter. The Deaf person's spiritual growth may be underdeveloped, and centuries of exclusion may continue because of lack of communications access at local churches.

Ethical Standards

The ability to make ethical choices is necessary, not only for full-time interpreters, but for part-time interpreters as well. The Code of Professional Conduct (formerly known as the Code of Ethics) delineates seven tenets for the professional.

1. Interpreters adhere to standards of confidential communication.

2. Interpreters possess the professional skills and knowledge required for the specific interpreting situation.

3. Interpreters conduct themselves in a manner appropriate to the specific interpreting situation.

4. Interpreters demonstrate respect for consumers.

5. Interpreters demonstrate respect for colleagues, interns, and students of the profession.

6. Interpreters maintain ethical business practices.

7. Interpreters engage in professional development.

A full version with explications of the Code of Professional Conduct (CPC) tenets is accessible from RID's website, as well as at the end of chapter two.

During the interview portion of the National Interpreting Certification test, the interpreter must demonstrate the ability to adhere to ethical standards by giving possible solutions to circumstances that compromise one or more of these tenets. To ensure that the quality of interpreting services is at least adequate, if not better, RID has put in place the Ethical Practice System (EPS) to receive complaints.

Interpreting & Transliterating

One section of the performance test rates the interpreter on language assessment. During this assessment, the interpreter must produce the right language for the Deaf or hard of hearing individual and determine whether to interpret or transliterate the message from the *source language* into the *target languages* (e.g., interpreting from English into ASL).

Between 1989 and 2005, candidates for certification (those who passed the written test) had a choice between two sign language certifications (the CI and CT) offered through RID. Many practitioners chose to take both tests. When successfully completed, the certification test validates the person's ability to meet the minimum professional standards required of interpreters. A candidate who is able to interpret from ASL to spoken English as well as from spoken English to ASL would be awarded the CI. Candidates taking the CT had to exhibit the ability to transliterate between an English-based sign language and spoken English as well as transliterate between spoken English and an English-based sign language.[viii] These two certifications replaced the CSC, and in turn are now replaced by the National Interpreter Certification (NIC).

There are a number of reasons for implementation of the NIC. One reason is that the candidate should be able to not only meet but exceed the minimum standards. Included in the NIC test is a scoring process, which differentiates itself from the last test that was pass/fail. New interpreters must take one test that incorporates both interpreting and transliterating in order to be awarded certification. Interpreters must be able to demonstrate their ability to interpret and transliterate to meet the diverse language needs of consumers. The Deaf community is populated with both ASL and Signed English users, which means qualified interpreters are also needed in the church setting.

Quality Assurance Screening

Several states offer a Quality Assurance Screening (QAS), an alternative diagnostic assessment that indicates the interpreting and transliterating levels of working practitioners. A written and performance-based test is administered for those who are screened. The QAS is a state-recognized (not nationally-recognized) assessment for interpreters. The following is a brief description of Virginia's screening[ix].

A screening level may be awarded for either skill area (Transliterating or Interpreting) depending upon the competencies demonstrated. Therefore, it is possible that a candidate could be awarded one level for interpreting and another level for transliterating.

Level I:	50%
Level II:	65%
Level III:	80%
Level IV:	95%

Some of the competencies that are assessed include:

1. Voice to Sign Skills (spoken English to Sign Language)
    - ❏ Clarity of signs
    - ❏ Accuracy of message
    - ❏ Accuracy and appropriateness of fingerspelling
    - ❏ Vocabulary
    - ❏ Consistency of sign system when transliterating
    - ❏ Appropriateness of mouth movements when transliterating
    - ❏ Spatial orientation when interpreting
    - ❏ Use of ASL structure and syntax when interpreting

2. Sign to Voice Skills (Sign language to spoken English)
    - ❏ Clarity of speech

- ☐ Appropriateness of intonation and inflection
- ☐ English vocabulary and grammar
- ☐ Appropriate use of processing time
- ☐ Accuracy of the message
- ☐ Ability to incorporate fingerspelled words
- ☐ Smoothness of presentation
- ☐ Ability to convey the speaker's affect

3. Both Voice to Sign and Sign to Voice (Interactive) Skills (Simulated interpreting/transliterating situations):
   - ☐ Expressive capabilities
   - ☐ Receptive capabilities
   - ☐ Ability to recover smoothly from errors
   - ☐ Ability to maintain a comfortable flow
   - ☐ Accuracy of message

For some interpreters working in educational settings, they will test for the QAS or the Education Interpreting Performance Assessment (EIPA).[5]

Summary

The target audience of this book is those who interpret in Christian settings and those interested in becoming interpreters for this specialized setting. Interpreters, in whatever setting, have responsibilities; it

---

[5] Some states offer the Education Interpreting Performance Assessment (EIPA), which was specifically developed for interpreters who work in the educational setting. It has not been accepted by all fifty states. As of 2016, educational interpreters with an EIPA level IV or higher and who join RID are considered certified members of RID (not RID certified). More information can be read at www.rid.org/rid-certification-overview/ed-k-12-certification.

is not enough simply to know how to sign and provide interpreting services. RID was established in order to formalize the interpreting profession. With training, testing, credentials, and accountability in place, RID has organized and promoted interpreting services in the United States.

ENDNOTES

[iii] "About RID." Registry of Interpreters for the Deaf. Retrieved from www.rid.org/about.html.

[iv] "CERTIFICATION MAINTENANCE PROGRAM." Registry of Interpreters for the Deaf. Retrieved 6 Aug. 2006 www.rid.org/cmp.html.

[v] "NIC…Moving Forward Together" Registry of Interpreters for the Deaf. Retrieved 26, Nov 2011. www.rid.org/NICNews/index.cfm.

[vi] "National Council on Interpreting (NCI)." Registry of Interpreters for the Deaf. Retrieved 8 Aug. 2006. www.rid.org/nci.html.

[vii] "A Guide to Disability Rights." U.S. Department of Justice: Civil Rights Division. Feb. 2006. Retrieved 6 Aug. 2006 www.usdoj.gov/crt/ada/cguide.htm#anchor65610.

[viii] "Explanation of Certificates." Registry of Interpreters for the Deaf. Retrieved 6 Aug. 2006. www.rid.org/expl.html.

[ix] "VDDHH QAS Packet of FAQ." Virginia Department for the Deaf and Hard-of-Hearing. Retrieved 8 Aug. 2006. www.vddhh.org/downloads/VQASPacket/FREQUENTLYAS KEDQUESTIONS.doc.

Chapter 2 –
Ethical Issues

An important part of the interpreter's role is to know, understand, and adhere to the Code of Professional Conduct (CPC). Interpreters' responsibilities include interaction with the public and handling unfamiliar scenarios in an ethical manner. Chapter two addresses familiar scenarios that are typically encountered in religious settings, details some of these scenarios, suggests some possible solutions, and provides resources for those new to the field. For further exploration, read the Code of Professional Conduct in its expanded document.[6]

The Need for an Interpreter

Work for an interpreter in a religious setting can be exciting and fulfilling. A need exists that only the interpreter can fill. Perhaps a Deaf worshiper needs an interpreter, and someone comes forward willingly to interpret, or a hearing congregant feels compelled to help because he/she knows the manual alphabet (fingerspelling) or some signs. When a Deaf worshiper meets a willing congregant, there tends to be a sense of relief that someone from the congregation can sign.

As a member of the congregation, the hearing person might feel obligated to help; after all, Scripture suggests that people have a responsibility to help those in need. However, when a person steps into the shoes

---

[6] The full version of the CPC is at the end of this chapter.

of an interpreter, an additional responsibility must be shouldered. Interpreting is much more complex than helping; it includes preparation, analysis, ethical responsibility, professionalism, sign production, cultural mediation, and so forth. The interpreter's role is to be taken seriously and held accountable. The helper, despite the best of intentions, might compromise someone else's faith by accidentally deleting or misinterpreting information. How does one deal with this situation when there is no professional available to interpret?

A well-meaning fellow worshiper can do a number of things. First, be hospitable! Approach, introduce yourself, befriend, and sit with the Deaf person. Second, explain limited signing experience to the Deaf person. Third, since most congregations use a worship bulletin, point to where the congregation is in the service so that the Deaf person can follow the bulletin. If a hymn or song is being sung, point to the stanza and move the index finger along the words being sung. Last, introduce the Deaf person to someone in charge at the church. Advocate that the church provide an interpreter the following week. Almost anyone would appreciate this help.

Resources to find an interpreter are available, though in some geographical areas, they may be limited. Approved interpreters (both RID and NAD) are easier to find today because the RID's Internet website has an online registry where agencies and interpreters can be located by city and state.[7] Technological advancement allows Video Remote Interpreting (VRI) from a remote location with services through DSL and cable high-

---

[7] RID's registry is located at www.rid.org.

speed connections. By way of the Internet and more people entering the profession, interpreters are more accessible today than a decade ago.

Balancing Faith and Profession

ETHICAL QUANDARIES

Qualified?

Multiple Roles

Volunteer or Be Paid?

Faith Bias

Boundaries

Mistakenly Disempower

Some churches are more flexible in terms of level of expertise when it comes to obtaining an interpreter, as the cost for providing interpreting services can be prohibitive for a small or under-funded congregation. This flexibility enables new interpreters the opportunity to work within the church. Is this wrong? No, not if the interpreter's work is proficient and done in a professional manner. It is helpful to keep in mind that public confidence in the interpreter increases when the interpreter (1) has language competency (e.g., possess a command of both the source and target language), (2) the quality of interpreting is adequate (e.g., only makes a few mistakes), (3) is ethical (e.g., keeping information and situations confidential), and (4) is professional (e.g., dependable and objective).

Customarily, the pastor, minister, or priest is the staff person most thought of in churches; however, other roles or positions are commonly present in some churches. Of these roles, many of them have ethics from their specified disciplines. Other church staff disciplines with their code of ethics include, but are not limited to, pastoral counseling (The American Association of Pastoral Counselors), Christian education (Association of Christian Schools International), and parish nurses (International Parish Nurse Resource Center). With the religious interpreter (the practitioner who only works in church settings) in mind, having a code of ethics that RID recommends and upholds (the CPC) can offer the religious interpreter industry-wide standards, collaboration with other practitioners in the field, and a network.

[handwritten margin note: Why Religious Interp?]

Interpreters frequently face ethical dilemmas as they provide services to consumers. Some CPC tenets are easier to follow than others; however, the interpreter must not only be aware of disturbing conditions as they arise, but must also deal with them in accordance with the tenets of the CPC. These tenets are to be followed at all times, even in settings where services are offered *pro bono*. Some people of deep and passionate faith may experience an inner struggle when faced with issues of confidentiality, for example, but the consumer's personal issues must be held in trust and boundaries be maintained.

As an example, at a religious interpreting workshop a participant shared a story with the group about a practitioner who interprets regularly in the community and at her church. This practitioner divulged confidential information to the congregation about a Deaf consumer she had interpreted for that past week. The interpreter told the congregation she had interpreted an appointment at an abortion clinic. She asked the congregation to forgive her for doing that. She also requested prayers for the Deaf woman involved and disclosed the Deaf woman's name to the congregation. The roomful of workshop attendees gasped in shock when they heard that someone had done this; everyone agreed this matter should never have been made public. This story is a prime example of the need to keep certain information confidential. It is imperative that an interpreter be able to make good decisions about what to say and what not to say.

Interpreters need to consider their own tolerance threshold when they agree to an assignment outside of their own faith tradition. For example, some people of the Baptist tradition do not find it acceptable for women to be preachers. If an interpreter is not comfortable in a setting where women are permitted to preach, then the interpreter should decline the assignment. It is not appropriate for the interpreter to share personal opinions with the consumer about female preachers; the interpreter must remain impartial.

On RID's website, there are a number of documents that give guidance for specific settings.[8] One such document is the RID Standard Practice Paper for Interpreting in Religious Settings.[9] This document recommends that the interpreter research a church or denomination's theology and doctrines before deciding to accept an assignment. Some people do not find it

---

[8] On the Internet, go to www.rid.org/aboutinterpreting/standard-practice-papers.
[9] The SSP: Interpreting in Religious Settings can be accessed at www.rid.org/about-interpreting/standard-practice-papers and is on page 91 in this book.

easy to step outside of their own faith tradition, and it is the interpreter's personal responsibility to judge whether an assignment is acceptable.

Boundaries

An obstacle for some interpreters is to maintain boundaries and remain in the interpreter role. It is highly possible that the Deaf person may mistakenly transfer the pastor's authority to the interpreter. This can happen because the interpreter shadows (sometimes stands next to) the minister and affects the minister's body language. Because the interpreter is able to communicate in the consumer's own language, this can contribute to the possibility of transference. Whatever the reason for transference, it is the interpreter's responsibility to stick to his or her role.

It is not unheard of for Deaf worshipers to share personal problems or issues with the interpreter. Being sensitive to the consumer is understandable, but a word of caution is needed here. Interpreters must be able to make appropriate judgments as to where the line is crossed. The switch from interpreter to pastoral counselor can occur quickly and without realization. It is advisable to request that both the interpreter and consumer go together to speak to the pastor about the worshiper's issue. This will enable the interpreter to remain in the professional role of interpreting for the worshiper and pastor. The pastor, not the interpreter, has the training and credentials for pastoral care and counseling, and it is important to allow the minister to perform these duties.

Though not all interpreters have difficulty setting limits and keeping boundaries, these are a problem for some. Sometimes personal circumstances prevent interpreters from maintaining boundaries; if this is the case, it is essential to be aware of triggers. One book that addresses this issue is titled <u>BOUNDARIES</u>[10]. This book highlights behaviors to be aware of and suggests solutions one can use. It is possible to be liked and still keep healthy boundaries, but it takes awareness and practice.

Sermons can be seen as speeches of exhortation. Most preachers want their sermons to be inspirational so a lesson or application will be remembered. Sermons can be dry, humorous, tear-jerking, or even emotionally transforming. During emotional moments, interpreters need to be able to distance themselves somewhat so they are not pulled in along with the audience. This can be a real challenge, because the interpreter has to remain in the interpreting role while listening to illustrations and stories that are meant to affect the soul.

Like other professionals who work in the church, interpreters have a right to worship as well. The need to worship is understandable, and if the interpreter is not spiritually fed because of the work performed, he or she may want to follow in the footsteps of other professionals, such as clergy, some of whom worship outside their own church setting in order to be fed spiritually.

---

[10] The book <u>BOUNDARIES</u> (2002) is by authors Dr. Henry Cloud and Dr. John Townsend. <u>BOUNDARIES</u> is a relatively inexpensive book; it can be purchased at many bookstores. To view video presentations based on the authors' book, go to http://www.cloudtownsend.com/video-advice/.

Multiple Roles

Faith-driven interpreters enjoy interpreting in religious settings. In fact, it is not uncommon for some interpreters to have multiple roles within the church.[11] An interpreter might teach an ASL class to hearing parishioners, lead a Bible study, or shoulder responsibility for other church programs. Multiple roles can create uncertainty, however, about which role takes priority over the others. In the event of uncertainty, it is helpful to remember that communication is a fundamental human need, and the interpreter's prime duty is to meet that need between parties.

Before a conflict arises, interpreters and others involved should examine where the interpreter may have a conflict. If Deaf and hearing people are participants in a venue where the practitioner's other role takes precedence, such as teacher or facilitator, the interpreter should speak to the Deaf consumer prior to the event. Some people attempt to please both language users by using sim-com (signing and speaking at the same time); however, it is not usually recommended. This communication method typically has English as the dominate language, thus neglecting grammatical features of ASL. Some Deaf people do not mind when hearing people use sim-com, but others do. In cases where ASL users prefer sim-com not be used, an option is to host a second event for the hearing people. Working out communications needs is not an easy task at times, and it is best to work out the logistics *before* a

---

[11] The Standard Practice Paper: Multiple Roles in Interpreting is located in Appendices (Appendix D).

conflict occurs.

Interpreter Compensation

A common in-house debate among interpreters working in religious settings is whether services should or should not be performed gratis. RID's Standard Practice Paper for Interpreting in Religious Settings briefly addresses this subject. Whether to provide services *pro bono* is ultimately up to the practitioner.

Trying to manage the costs for interpreter compensation, especially when costs were not budgeted for, can be a challenge for church interpreter coordinators, even more so for small membership churches. It is not uncommon that the threshold of quality tends to fluctuate when utilizing volunteer interpreters. When this occurs, it's best to consult with the primary users of the interpreter. Ethically, compromising someone's spiritual life should not be an option and the primary user's input ought to be a part of the hiring or evaluation process to ensure minimum quality.

Some issues to consider, however, are the following:

❏ If an interpreter refuses payment, it may set a precedent (and an assumption) that all professional interpreting services will be free.

❏ If the interpreter accepts the payment, this allows the interpreter to make the choice to endorse the check and put it in the offering plate. The interpreter could use the donation as a tax deduction for contribution to a charitable organization.[12]

❑ Interpreting professionally is an interpreter's livelihood. It should be respected as such. Just as another ministerial staff member would be compensated, so should the interpreter.

❑ Even if the regular interpreter does not wish to be paid, church leaders responsible for the annual budget should add a line item for interpreters.[13] If the regular interpreter needs to be off, there will be funding available to hire a substitute.

❑ A fundamental question to consider is whether the interpreter should be compensated when consumer(s) miss the service (and should the interpreter still interpret regardless)? Professional standards dictate that interpreters are still to be paid since the block of time was contracted for interpreting services.

---

[12] Interpreters must report compensation to the IRS. Typically, interpreters are hired as independent contractors (freelance interpreters). Interpreters should receive a 1099 – MISC form from the church. For more information, go to www.irs.gov/pub/irs-pdf/p1779.pdf to access it online.
[13] PROFESSIONAL STANDARDS: The interpreter is customarily paid for a two-hour minimum, even if the service is only an hour (this includes time for preparation). A service that is complex or lasting over sixty or ninety minutes should have a team of interpreters. If consumers do not show up for the service, the interpreter is still to be paid. Also, an interpreter holding certification is paid more per hour compared to an interpreter without credentials. These are standards throughout the profession.

Clearly, it may not be easy for small churches to pay an interpreter, especially if it wasn't budgeted for. These considerations can guide further discussions to address the issue. Also, the Business Practices: Billing Considerations by RID (under the Standard Practice Papers section on RID's website) can provide guidance as well. The bottom line is that it is entirely up to the interpreter whether or not to accept payment; there is no right or wrong answer.

Practitioners who bill churches for their interpreting services will want to keep a copy of the invoice (for their own records) that is sent. One method for generating invoices is in Microsoft Word or Excel. After printing the invoice, a notation (on the electronic copy) of the date the invoice was sent is recommended. Rates that are normally charged are dependent upon having certification, experience, education, interpreting setting, and region (economics - supply and demand). Typical rates range $15 to $75 per hour, which varies according to being employed (staff) or contracted, certified or not certified, and setting. A sample invoice is provided.

		INVOICE
Jane Smith, NIC	Date:	02/24/20xx
433 Anywhere St.	Invoice:	100
Marion, NY 10007	For: Interpreting Services	
Phone: 455-555-0191		

Bill To:
First Church
Attn: Bookkeeper
101 Main St.
Marion, NY 10007

	Description	Amount
2/24/20xx	Interpreting Services for 11am Worship Service (2 hour minimum)	$50.00
2/17/20xx	Interpreting Services for 11am Worship Service (2 hour minimum)	$50.00
		Total $100.00

Please make all checks payable to Jane Smith. Payment is due upon receipt.

Dress Attire for Interpreters

People come dressed for worship in a variety of ways these days. In a traditional setting, the interpreter dresses in business attire. At a minimum, female interpreters should wear a blouse with dress slacks or a skirt and avoid the use of nail polish; male interpreters should wear a dress shirt and tie with dress slacks. Interpreters need to dress in solid colors that contrast their skin color to allow for visual clarity. Avoid flashy pendants or jewelry, for they may be visually distracting. These recommendations emphasize a professional look for interpreters.

If interpreting a contemporary praise service, it is preferable to dress similarly to what most people are wearing; however, to lean towards dressing more conservatively is usually more professional. Again, use solid colors that contrast skin color. A good rule of thumb is to observe what the clergy wears and dress similarly. When there is still uncertainty, a quick email or a brief phone call to the church is certainly acceptable. Determining the dress code will assist the interpreter to fit in better. Keep in mind, the dress code (e.g., business, business casual, or casual) will depend on the request (e.g., worship, a meeting, or a church bazaar).

Participating in the Service

In most settings, the interpreter is not a participant and remains a neutral party; however, this is not always the case when interpreting a church setting. If the interpreter is a member of the congregation, he or she may participate in some fashion. For example, the interpreter could request prayers, give a financial donation, or accept a sacrament (e.g., Holy Communion). The CPC tenets do not speak directly to these examples, however, so the interpreter should speak beforehand with the consumers, both deaf and hearing, to see if participation would be viewed as a conflict.

In 2004, a religious interpreters' conference was held in Columbia, Maryland, during which an afternoon Deaf panel discussion addressed the topic of interpreter participation. There were, in addition to the Deaf panel, 250 interpreters present for this forum, all of whom were in consensus that it is permissible to consult with the consumer about participation, if participation would not interfere with the facilitation of communication. This, however, is not always the professional norm, so it is best to approach this issue on a case-by-case basis.

Skill Development

Tenet number seven of the Code of Professional Conduct stipulates that the interpreter is to continue professional growth. This is crucial for novice interpreters entering the profession. Ideally, enrollment in an IEP[14] is the way to develop skills and knowledge; the alternative, for those unable or unwilling to enroll in an IEP, is to attend RID-approved conferences, seminars, and workshops. Alternatively, mentorships at church have gained popularity. Independent study is not out of the question, because the learner can gain insight and learn from colleagues. Furthermore, internet sites such as Signs of Development and Leadership Institute for Interpreters provide webinars that offers workshops on various topics.[15]

A mentor can help a new interpreter to establish professional goals and monitor progress. The mentor can also identify skills that need improvement. New interpreters need role models in the field. A number of interpreting agencies offer internship or mentorship opportunities. Furthermore, some sub-chapters of RID may be able to make referrals. Sub-chapters can be located on RID's website.[16] In addition, Signs of

---

[14] University of Northern Colorado offers an online interpreting program and certificate programs. Information about the programs can be read at www.unco.edu/doit/.

[15] Signs of Development's website is www.signs-of-development.org and Leadership Institute: for Interpreters' website is www.leadershipinstitute.biz.

[16] Affiliate chapters can be located at www.rid.org.

Development offers diagnostic assessment and virtual mentoring.[17]

Expansion of one's lexicon is only part of the learning necessary to be an interpreter, and true proficiency comes only when the entire gamut of the interpreter's role is learned. If unsure where to begin the learning process, a good start would be to study the criteria that RID uses for examination of interpreters for the NIC. RID sub-chapters usually offer workshops; there is a list of workshops by state on the RID website. Furthermore, RID sells resources that can be added to personal libraries.

Demand-Control Schema

As practitioners working in the field, issues or dilemmas can frequently occur. The Demand-Control Schema (DC-S) is an ethical framework that is taught to interpreting students in IEPs and offered to practitioners continuing professional development at various trainings throughout the country. The DC-S was adapted and further developed by Dr. Robert Pollard and Robyn K. Dean and is based on Robert Karasek's Demand-Control theory (1979). The demand component has four demand categories: (1) environmental (i.e., the setting, preparatory materials, lighting, or the terminology specific to the setting), (2) interpersonal (i.e., assumptions, interactions with consumers, or personality conflicts), (3) paralinguistic (e.g., an accent impeding the communication or regional signs not

---

[17] More information about PACE Mentoring (Performance Assessment for Career Enhancement) can be read at www.signs-of-development.org/website/paceM.html.

recognized), and (4) intrapersonal (i.e., internal stresses such as anxiety, hunger, or tiredness).[18]

DEMANDS	**CONTROLS**
Environmental	Pre-Assignment
Interpersonal	Assignment
Paralinguistic	Post-Assignment
Intrapersonal	

When demands such as situations or stresses arise, interpreters can use controls (pre-assignment controls, assignment controls, and/or post-assignment controls) to analyze and deal with the demand, either before, during, or after in order to better prepare for next time. A simple example: sheets of music for the anthem to be sung during a worship service were not given to the interpreter (environmental demand), which might cause anxiety (intrapersonal demand). Controls for these demands can include: (1) a pre-assignment control - the interpreter can contact the choir director before the service requesting the music, (2) an assignment control - possibly relocating by the choir (if possible) to share the music when the anthem is sung or being fed by a team interpreter (hopefully reducing any anxiety), and (3) a post-assignment control – reminding the choir director after the worship service that the music is needed for future services. It is strongly recommended to study and attend a DC-S training, in person or through an online webinar, and regularly use this ethics framework.[19]

---

[18] Permission is granted by Robyn K. Dean for citing the Demand-Control Schema framework.
[19] Information for this and further reading and training information can be read at www.urmc.rochester.edu/deaf-

Decision Making

When considering a situation that causes an ethical concern, the interpreter has a few things to keep in mind when deciding the best course of action. The philosophical approach (see Interpreting Models in chapter 5), the CPC tenets, and who is affected should all be taken into account. The following (the WH – HO – SO model) is a framework for working through issues and helps the interpreter to consider solutions.

Who	What	Where
Who and how many persons are affected?	What is causing the circumstance? What tenet(s) refer to this issue? [Read the full version of the CPC.]	Where is the dilemma taking place?
When	**How**	**Solutions**
When does or did the situation occur? Is there a pattern?	How is the situation occurring? Is it based on feeling or fact?	What are one or more solutions addressing the issue? [Sometimes the SPP or a textbook is helpful.]

In a sense, the interpreter will want to think critically about the issue. There are times when consulting with a neutral colleague or mentor is recommended.

wellness-center/training-education/demand-control-schema-interpreting-work/.

If one's intuition is involved, work through the reasoning rather than basing the dilemma or solution on just intuition. Keep in mind that sometimes our own emotional clutter can interfere with our decision making; if this is the case, it is best to distance ourselves emotionally as best we can in order to choose an approach and/or solution.

Real Life Scenarios

Working interpreters will confront ethical dilemmas. One way to deal with ethical matters is to think through how to handle problems ahead of time. The following are real-life scenarios that have occurred.[20] How might an interpreter answer these?

1. *Working at a church for quite some time (but not anywhere else), you have come to know the Deaf woman who attends the church. After sharing with you that her primary doctor has referred her to an oncologist (cancer specialist), she asks you if you can go with her to interpret at the consultation. Her reason for asking is that the specialist will not provide an interpreter. What do you do?*

Who	What	Where
Who and how many persons are affected?	What is causing the circumstance? What tenet(s) refer to this issue? [Read the full version of the CPC.]	Where is the dilemma taking place?
The Deaf woman,		At the church

---

[20] For additional scenarios and case studies, readers may want to read <u>Encounters With Reality: 1001 Interpreter Scenarios, 2<u>nd</u> Ed.</u> (2009) by Brenda Cartwright and <u>Decisions? Decisions? A Practical Guide for Sign Language Professionals</u> (1999) by Janice H. Humphrey.

myself (the interpreter), and the doctor & his staff.	The doctor's refusal for providing an interpreter. Also, my inexperience. Tenets 2 & 6 (maybe 3)	where the Deaf woman told me, also at the doctor's office.
When When does or did the situation occur? Is there a pattern?	**How** How is the situation occurring? Is it based on feeling or fact?	**Solutions** What are one or more solutions addressing the issue? [Sometimes the SPP or a textbook is helpful.]
This is the first time I was asked to interpret for her outside of church. Also, it will occur at the doctor's office. I may be setting a prece- dent and future interpreting requests may occur more often.	Because the doctor isn't following the ADA and full access to communication isn't happening. Also, the Deaf woman asked me, pulling me into the situation.	Decline the request. Nancy Frishberg's book speaks to this. Find another interpreter, maybe ask an agency. Suggest asking the primary doctor to refer the Deaf woman to another oncology practice who will provide an interpreter. Tell the Deaf woman to keep any notes if she goes without an interpreter.

Being somewhat new, I would not want to take a chance that I could interpret wrong information—this is out of the scope of my interpreting experience. If I had a mentor, I would refer the request to my mentor. Some interpreting agencies or state commissions might be willing to provide *pro bono* services for circumstances such as this. Also, I would encourage her to keep any written notes by the doctor.

2. *A Deaf couple has been coming to the worship service, though the husband has come less often than the wife. After three missed Sundays, the Deaf wife shares with you that her husband has left her, and she is not only depressed, but is struggling to make ends meet. What do you do?*

If I were confronted with this situation, I would express my sympathy, tell her I would pray for her, and then suggest we go see the pastor or other church leader. This circumstance falls in the realm of pastoral care. This relates to the CPC 2.5 and 2.6.

3. *The pastor's teenage daughter has taken two sign language classes (ASL 1 & 2), and has expressed interest in learning how to interpret. The one weekend you need off to go to a family reunion, you are unable find a replacement. The pastor's daughter happily volunteers to cover for you. Do the Deaf consumers go without having an interpreter? Does the daughter try to do her best under the circumstances?*

As much as I would not want to hurt the young girl's feelings, I would let her know that she is not ready for something like this, that she could be overwhelmed, and I do not want to put her in that predicament. I would check with a church official to see if we can make a request to an interpreting agency. This relates to CPC 2.3, 2.6, and 4.1.

4. *A Deaf family who comes to worship each week has family from out-of-town come for a visit. The visitors come with the Deaf parishioners to church. Two of the three children are*

*disruptive during the worship service. Do you break role and
tell their Deaf parents?*

Since I am a CODA (Child of a Deaf Adult), I have
a tendency to be more sensitive towards hearing
people's perceptions of Deaf people. Because of
this, I would break role and let the Deaf parents
know the kids are being disruptive. This also falls
under the responsibility of cultural mediation. This
relates to CPC 4.2 and 4.4.

5. *A minister is thrilled that a Deaf person has joined the
   church. The minister thinks it will be a good idea to teach a
   sign language class so hearing members can communicate with
   the Deaf person. What do you do?*

The first thing I would do is affirm the pastor and
tell the pastor that is a great idea. Furthermore, I
would suggest we ask the Deaf parishioner if he or
she can teach it, or recommend a Deaf person to
teach the class. If I were available to interpret the
class, I would volunteer my time. This relates to
CPC 4.4 and 6.3.

6. *The Deaf parishioner comes to church and shows you her new
   hearing aids. Afterwards, she goes to sit with the other Deaf
   people. During the service, the parishioner's hearing aid begins to whistle loudly, but she does not do anything. You
   notice hearing parishioners beginning to stare. Do you break
   role and inform the Deaf woman?*

I would break role and let her know her hearing aid
is whistling and that people are beginning to stare.
In addition, it is a cultural courtesy to tell her. This
relates to CPC 2.2 and 4.2.

7. *After interpreting at a church for six months and being paid the entire time, the bookkeeper (the one who writes the check) informs you that the church can no longer afford to pay you. What do you do?*

   This is a tough one. It would really depend on my monthly budget and if I could afford to do without the extra compensation. If I were strapped financially, I would have to look elsewhere for work. Perhaps, I could negotiate and see if the church might afford my services twice a month, if I did the other days *pro bono*. There is not one right answer for this. This relates to CPC 6.2.

8. *In the beginning of March, you begin interpreting at a hearing church. Each week you submit an invoice to the church. After two months, you have still not been paid. How do you handle this?*

   In a professional manner, I would call the church to find out who I should speak with and then ask that person if he or she received my invoices - that I am concerned because no payments have been received. If the church was having financial difficulties, I might negotiate new terms for compensation. This relates to CPC 4.2 and 6.5.

9. *After interpreting at church for about two years, the Deaf family you have been interpreting for is purchasing a new home. The couple asks if you can come and interpret at the settlement. What do you do?*

   Another tough scenario. If I were familiar with real estate, had experienced the settlement process, and had legal language proficiency, I might do it. For me, my intuition might play a role, but professional judgment is still necessary in one's decision-making. If I felt that I should not do it, I'd refer the Deaf couple to another interpreter. This relates to CPC 2.0 and 3.2.

10. *Already having a strong faith, you began interpreting at your home church three years ago. A Deaf man began coming to your church for the first time six months ago. He didn't go to church as a child, and he has not been baptized. The pastor comes up to you before the service and asks you if the Deaf parishioner would like to be baptized. What do you do?*

I would deflect the question and suggest speaking to the Deaf parishioner directly, and I would add that I would be happy to interpret for them. This relates to CPC 2.5 and 4.4.

Most of these scenarios do not have only one right answer. It is up to interpreters to make ethical decisions, even at the risk of straining relationships within the church.

RID Article

The following is an article that was first published in the *RID Views* (an interpreting magazine) in 2011 regarding the role of ethics in church settings. It is included here to emphasize the importance of ethics in the interpreter's work and encourage churches to consider their consumers' (congregants) needs.

Religious Interpreting: The Role of Ethics
By Leo Yates, Jr., MDiv., CI & CT

Recently, I was interviewed by an author who was writing a book about spoken language interpreting. The author, who is less familiar with sign language interpreting, asked about ethics and religious interpreters, wondering if religious interpreters had any type of ethics. This led me to think that if this author is uncertain, perhaps others are as well. It had me question, how firm are ethics established in religious settings?

Classes of Interpreters

In the counseling field, there are classes of counselors: mental health counselors, addictions counselors, vocational counselors, etc. From the many years I have interpreted in churches, I explained to the author, that there are generally two classes of interpreters who work in churches:

* Class One: RID/professional interpreters

* Class Two: Religious interpreters

Class one interpreters are the RID and/or professional interpreters who work in various settings, including religious venues. This class one type interpreter is what the industry calls either a *generalist interpreter* (having the ability to work in multiple settings with a certain amount of competence) or a *specialist interpreter* (having specialized or advanced education and/or knowledge in a specialized setting). The class two practitioner is the interpreter, commonly called a religious interpreter, who feels a spiritual calling or desire to learn ASL and interprets primarily in his or her faith community. Religious interpreters typically have apprenticeship type training, which is commonly provided by deaf church members and established interpreters in their faith community. Another class two type interpreter is the practitioner who learns by way of independent study, with little or no professional development. The category of class two interpreters is based on my observations from many years of working in church settings and from meeting practitioners at conferences and seminars I either presented at or attended. Both, class one interpreters and class two interpreters, provide much needed services to the faith communities they work in.

From there, I shared with the author that, from my professional perspective, ethics and accountability is necessary, it is a needed standard for those who work in all settings, including religious settings. When having ethics, interpreters then have better credibility and integrity. Also, by incorporating ethics and standards into one's work, these help promote confidence in the interpreter by both deaf and hearing consumers. The level of confidence and trust will typically increase or decrease when the interpreter (1) has language competency (e.g. possess a command of both the source and target language), (2) the quality of interpreting is adequate (e.g. how well the message is interpreted, only makes a few mistakes), (3) is ethical (e.g. keeping information and situations confidential), and (4) is professional (e.g. dependable and objective). Ethics is fundamental to public confidence and the ethos for all interpreters in religious settings should include ethics.

Part of my reasoning for the need of ethics comes from the work of other various staff that is affiliated with church settings. Customarily, the pastor, minister, or priest is the staff person most thought of in churches; however, other roles or positions are commonly present in some churches. Of these roles, many of them have ethics from their specified disciplines. Other church staff disciplines with their code of ethics include, but are not limited to, pastoral counseling (The American Association of Pastoral Counselors), Christian education (Association of Christian Schools International), and parish nurses (International Parish Nurse Resource Center). With the class two interpreter in mind, having a code of ethics that RID recommends and upholds can offer the religious interpreter industry-wide standards, collaboration with other practitioners in the field, and an association with the profession.

Other Ethical Considerations

There seems to be a misperception from some of those in the profession about religious interpreters. This appears to be, in part, from not following professional standards (e.g. interpreting a 3 hour service by one's self instead of having a team). Similarly, this resonates with the mental health profession and how addictions counseling has a separate classification, even bordering on mental health counselors looking down on addictions counselors (Mustaine, West, Wyrick, 2003). Both types of counselors are healing agents and both are needed to serve the public. The utilization of ethics for the religious interpreters can help some of those in the interpreting profession to find more value in the work of religious interpreters; they too have an important part in serving the public.

Like other settings, those coordinating interpreting services for churches are typically unfamiliar with the practice and what standards are commonly held. Through education, continued promotion of standard practices, and inviting collaboration through a new membership section for interpreters who work in religious or spiritual settings, this can further the inclusion for religious interpreters. This premise also holds true for the interpreter coordinators in church settings. Furthermore, when interpreter coordinators are aware of these standards, they can then come to a better decision for who is requested (or hired) to interpret. Trying to manage the costs for interpreter compensation, especially when costs were not budgeted for, can be a challenge for church interpreter coordinators, even more so for small membership churches. It is not uncommon that the threshold of quality tends to fluctuate when utilizing volunteer interpreters. When this occurs, it's best to consult with the primary users of the interpreter. Ethically, compromising someone's spiritual life should not be an option and the primary user's input ought to be a part of the hiring or evaluation process. When having the basic knowledge of standards and ethics, the interpreter coordinators in church settings can be better informed in their hiring/recruiting practices.

When religious interpreters are a part of the RID umbrella, they can be exposed to industry practices. What RID and/or professional interpreters can learn from religious interpreters is their experience (e.g. cultivating interpreting teams), their best practices (e.g. their craft, innovative practices like with music), and knowledge (e.g. religious signs and lexicon expansion) they have for the work in this specialized setting. In addition, learning about their spiritual calling or desire for their work can be informative and encouraging (even inspiring) for the class one type interpreter.

In conclusion, sharing common ground between religious interpreters and RID/professional interpreters is our desire to provide services to our communities, both deaf and hearing. Cultivating this common ground is the insistence for keeping ethics in the heart of our work. Ethics, I believe, can be the bridge that brings these two classes of interpreters together. Most importantly, ethics will further mutual respect for both classes of interpreters. At the conclusion of the interview, I told the author, yes, religious interpreters not only ought to have ethics, but should have them as a part of their work.

References

American Association of Pastoral Counselors. (1993). *AAPC Code of Ethics*. Retrieved on November 11, 2011 from http://aapc.org.

Association of Christian Schools International. (2009). *Establishing a Code of Ethics*. Retrieved on November 11, 2011 from www.acsi.org/Resources/PublicationsNewsletters/Christian SchoolEducation/tabid/681/itemid/4229/Default.aspx.

International Parish Nurse Resource Center. (2004). *Modules of the Basic Parish Nurse Preparation Curriculum*. Retrieved on November 11, 2011 from www.parishnurses.org.

Mustaine, B., West, P., & Wyrick, B. (2003). Substance abuse counselor certification requirements: Is it time for a change? *Journal of Addictions & Offender Counseling, 23*, 99-108.

Summary

An unfamiliar religious setting is a challenge to the new interpreter. Chapter two exposes the newcomer to some of the ethical dimensions of religious interpreting. This chapter is by no means all-encompassing, but it alerts the newcomer to issues that may arise during the course of work and encourages an ethical and professional mindset that interpreters should have. RID provides additional guidance through published Standard Practice Papers, the CPC, the *Journal of Interpretation*, and the *RID VIEWS* (quarterly publication). Blogs and vlogs by interpreters and stakeholders relating to ethics are also more readily available on the internet that is thought provoking and insightful.

NAD-RID CODE OF PROFESSIONAL CONDUCT

Tenets

1. Interpreters adhere to standards of confidential communication.

2. Interpreters possess the professional skills and knowledge required for the specific interpreting situation.

3. Interpreters conduct themselves in a manner appropriate to the specific interpreting situation.

4. Interpreters demonstrate respect for consumers.

5. Interpreters demonstrate respect for colleagues, interns, and students of the profession.

6. Interpreters maintain ethical business practices.

7. Interpreters engage in professional development.

Applicability

A. This Code of Professional Conduct applies to certified and associate members of the Registry of Interpreters for the Deaf, Inc., Certified members of the National Association of the Deaf, interns, and students of the profession.

B. Federal, state or other statutes or regulations may supersede this Code of Professional Conduct. When there is a conflict between this code and local, state, or federal laws and regulations, the interpreter obeys the rule of law.

C. This Code of Professional Conduct applies to interpreted situations that are performed either face-to-face or remotely.

Definitions

For the purpose of this document, the following terms are used:

Colleagues: Other interpreters.

Conflict of Interest: A conflict between the private interests (personal, financial, or professional) and the official or professional responsibilities of an interpreter in a position of trust, whether actual or perceived, deriving from a specific interpreting situation.

Consumers: Individuals and entities who are part of the interpreted situation. This includes individuals who are deaf, deaf-blind, hard of hearing, and hearing.

1.0 CONFIDENTIALITY
Tenet: Interpreters adhere to standards of confidential communication.
Guiding Principle: Interpreters hold a position of trust in their role as linguistic and cultural facilitators of communication. Confidentiality is highly valued by consumers and is essential to protecting all involved.

Each interpreting situation (e.g., elementary, secondary, and post-secondary education, legal, medical, mental health) has a standard of confidentiality. Under the reasonable interpreter standard, professional interpreters are expected to know the general requirements and applicability of various levels of confidentiality. Exceptions to confidentiality include, for example, federal and state laws requiring mandatory reporting of abuse or threats of suicide, or responding to subpoenas.

Illustrative Behavior - Interpreters:
1.1 Share assignment-related information only on a confidential and "as-needed" basis (e.g., supervisors, interpreter team members, members of the educational team, hiring entities).
1.2 Manage data, invoices, records, or other situational or consumer-specific information in a manner consistent with maintaining consumer confidentiality (e.g., shredding, locked files).
1.3 Inform consumers when federal or state mandates require disclosure of confidential information.

2.0 PROFESSIONALISM
Tenet: Interpreters possess the professional skills and knowledge required for the specific interpreting situation.
Guiding Principle: Interpreters are expected to stay abreast of evolving language use and trends in the profession of interpreting as well as in the American Deaf community.

Interpreters accept assignments using discretion with regard to skill, communication mode, setting, and consumer needs.

Interpreters possess knowledge of American Deaf culture and deafness-related resources.

Illustrative Behavior - Interpreters:

2.1 Provide service delivery regardless of race, color, national origin, gender, religion, age, disability, sexual orientation, or any other factor.

2.2 Assess consumer needs and the interpreting situation before and during the assignment and make adjustments as needed.

2.3 Render the message faithfully by conveying the content and spirit of what is being communicated, using language most readily understood by consumers, and correcting errors discreetly and expeditiously.

2.4 Request support (e.g., certified deaf interpreters, team members, language facilitators) when needed to fully convey the message or to address exceptional communication challenges (e.g. cognitive disabilities, foreign sign language, emerging language ability, or lack of formal instruction or language).

2.5 Refrain from providing counsel, advice, or personal opinions.

2.6 Judiciously provide information or referral regarding available interpreting or community resources without infringing upon consumers' rights.

3.0 CONDUCT

Tenet: Interpreters conduct themselves in a manner appropriate to the specific interpreting situation.

Guiding Principle: Interpreters are expected to present themselves appropriately in demeanor and appearance. They avoid situations that result in conflicting roles or perceived or actual conflicts of interest.

Illustrative Behavior - Interpreters:

3.1 Consult with appropriate persons regarding the interpreting situation to determine issues such as placement and adaptations necessary to interpret effectively.

3.2 Decline assignments or withdraw from the interpreting profession when not competent due to physical, mental, or emotional factors.

3.3 Avoid performing dual or conflicting roles in interdisciplinary (e.g. educational or mental health teams) or other settings.

3.4 Comply with established workplace codes of conduct, notify appropriate personnel if there is a conflict with this Code of Professional Conduct, and actively seek resolution where warranted.

3.5 Conduct and present themselves in an unobtrusive manner and exercise care in choice of attire.

3.6 Refrain from the use of mind-altering substances before or during the performance of duties.

3.7 Disclose to parties involved any actual or perceived conflicts of interest.

3.8 Avoid actual or perceived conflicts of interest that might cause harm or interfere with the effectiveness of interpreting services.

3.9 Refrain from using confidential interpreted information for personal, monetary, or professional gain.

3.10 Refrain from using confidential interpreted information for the benefit of personal or professional affiliations or entities.

4.0 RESPECT FOR CONSUMERS

Tenet: Interpreters demonstrate respect for consumers.

Guiding Principle: Interpreters are expected to honor consumer preferences in selection of interpreters and interpreting dynamics, while recognizing the realities of qualifications, availability, and situation.

Illustrative Behavior - Interpreters:

4.1 Consider consumer requests or needs regarding language preferences, and render the message accordingly (interpreted or transliterated).

4.2 Approach consumers with a professional demeanor at all times.

4.3 Obtain the consent of consumers before bringing an intern to an assignment.

4.4 Facilitate communication access and equality, and support the full interaction and independence of consumers.

5.0 RESPECT FOR COLLEAGUES

Tenet: Interpreters demonstrate respect for colleagues, interns and students of the profession.

Guiding Principle: Interpreters are expected to collaborate with colleagues to foster the delivery of effective interpreting services. They also understand that the manner in which they relate to colleagues reflects upon the profession in general.

Illustrative Behavior - Interpreters:

5.1 Maintain civility toward colleagues, interns, and students.

5.2 Work cooperatively with team members through consultation before assignments regarding logistics, providing professional and courteous assistance when asked, and monitoring the accuracy of the message while functioning in the role of the support interpreter.

5.3 Approach colleagues privately to discuss and resolve breaches of ethical or professional conduct through standard conflict resolution methods; file a formal grievance only after such attempts have been unsuccessful or the breaches are harmful or habitual.

5.4 Assist and encourage colleagues by sharing information and serving as mentors when appropriate.

5.5 Obtain the consent of colleagues before bringing an intern to an assignment.

6.0 BUSINESS PRACTICES

Tenet: Interpreters maintain ethical business practices.

Guiding Principle: Interpreters are expected to conduct their business in a professional manner whether in private practice or in the employ of an agency or other entity. Professional interpreters are entitled to a living wage based on their qualifications and expertise. Interpreters are also entitled to working conditions conducive to effective service delivery.

Illustrative Behavior - Interpreters:

6.1 Accurately represent qualifications, such as certification, educational background, and experience, and provide documentation when requested.

6.2 Honor professional commitments and terminate assignments only when fair and justifiable grounds exist.

6.3 Promote conditions that are conducive to effective communication, inform the parties involved if such conditions do not exist, and seek appropriate remedies.

6.4 Inform appropriate parties in a timely manner when delayed or unable to fulfill assignments.

6.5 Reserve the option to decline or discontinue assignments if working conditions are not safe, healthy, or conducive to interpreting.

6.6 Refrain from harassment or coercion before, during, or after the provision of interpreting services.

6.7 Render pro bono services in a fair and reasonable manner.

6.8 Charge fair and reasonable fees for the performance of interpreting services and arrange for payment in a professional and judicious manner.

7.0 PROFESSIONAL DEVELOPMENT

Tenet: Interpreters engage in professional development.

Guiding Principle: Interpreters are expected to foster and maintain interpreting competence and the stature of the profession through ongoing development of knowledge and skills.

Illustrative Behavior - Interpreters:

7.1 Increase knowledge and strengthen skills through activities such as:
- pursuing higher education;
- attending workshops and conferences;
- seeking mentoring and supervision opportunities;
- participating in community events; and
- engaging in independent studies.

7.2 Keep abreast of laws, policies, rules, and regulations that affect the profession.

Chapter 3 - Dynamics of Church Settings

Interpreting in an unfamiliar church setting might make the practitioner a little leery. Whether the congregations are made up of mostly older church members or are young, thriving, multi-cultural congregations including a variety of people of different ethnicities, ages, backgrounds, and cultures, churches have dynamics just like family dynamics. Parts of the underlying culture can include environment (the church location), values (is the church more member-driven or doctrine-driven), and rituals. Each congregation is different, and the interpreter will need to work in accord with these cultural distinctions. As stated, each congregation has unique dynamics. There might be similarities with other congregations, but every church will have observable distinctions. Each congregation has a history, its own culture and sub-cultures, and its own expectations and preferences, which set it apart from other churches. Social, intellectual, or moral influences affect the dynamics as well. Qualities that help make the interpreter successful in settings with changing dynamics are flexibility, diplomacy, and good manners. The knack to communicate one's needs to make the church setting more conducive to interpretation activities is also essential. The ability and willingness to adapt in various contexts enables the interpreter to be comfortable and more accessible for interpreting assignments in his or her faith tradition.

Different Contexts

MULTIPLE PLATFORMS

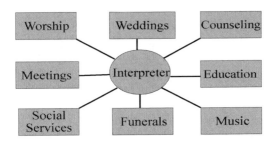

Interpreting in church settings can offer a variety of interpreting genres; however, interpreting services by the practitioner predominately take place in the context of worship. For hearing churches with a thriving Deaf ministry, Deaf consumers may participate in other programs and services offered by the church, such as:

❑ Performing arts such as music and drama

❑ Pastoral care and counseling

❑ Weddings (possibly including pre-marriage counseling and the reception)

❑ Funerals and memorial services

❑ Retreats (e.g., a day long, overnight, and weekly retreats are common)

❑ Committee meetings (e.g., finance or leadership)

❑ Special worship services (e.g., Ash Wednesday or Good Friday)

❑ Sunday School (e.g., children or adult) or Bible study

❑ Church-related programs (e.g., fundraiser or youth trips)

❑ Social services (e.g., food pantry, referral services, self-help groups, and case management assistance)

Newer interpreters will need to be mentored and have additional experience in order to interpret in pastoral counseling settings, weddings, funerals, and committee meetings. Some contexts (e.g., weddings) will require additional preparation than others.

It is recommended that professional interpreters who work in settings that have liability risks purchase professional liability insurance. If the practitioner interprets regularly in pastoral counseling settings, the interpreter should consider the need for insurance coverage. In fact, most priests and ministers carry professional liability insurance for protection purposes. RID has an arrangement with an insurance agency to sell insurance to RID interpreters (another good reason to be a member).[21] Practitioners can obtain a referral to the insurance agency by contacting RID. Professional

---

[21] DHH Insurance provides liability insurance policies to RID members. Their website is www.DHHInsurance.com .

liability coverage is in the best interest of the interpreter.

Educating the Congregation

When an interpreter comes to the sanctuary for the first time, he or she is often unfamiliar with the dynamics of the congregation. Most churches that encounter a Deaf individual or family for the first time are unacquainted with resources available to them. It is necessary at times to switch hats in order to educate consumers (e.g., church leaders) about interpreters.

From interpreter to educator, the practitioner will work to make the environment accessible to the parties involved. RID provides general information about the profession of sign language interpreting. A copy of their publication[22] given to those working with the interpreter for the first time might be helpful and prevent undermining or undervaluing the interpreting services. Hearing people who have never interacted with Deaf people may also need to be advised what to expect.[23]

From time to time, interpreters may be the only link to finding community resources. Church leaders who inquire will need to be made aware of what

---

[22] Standard Practice Paper: Professional Sign Language Interpreting is available at http://www.rid.org/about-interpreting/standard-practice-papers/.

[23] For instance, interpreters can explain cultural distinctions and language differences.

resources are available in the community. Resources that might be helpful to know and share are:

- ❑ Department of Rehabilitation Services (V.R.) locations

- ❑ Area interpreting agencies[24]

- ❑ Area churches that have Deaf ministries (for consultation)

- ❑ Textbooks on Deaf culture and sign language

- ❑ Information on the American Disabilities Act (ADA) for advocacy purposes[25]

- ❑ The state relay service (711)[26] and video relay service

Education comes with the territory. Churches are sometimes at a loss in knowing that a newcomer who is Deaf needs accommodations such as sufficient lighting, removing visual distractions or barriers, and reserved seating. One form of Deaf empowerment is to ask the

---

[24] When searching RID's search engine, look up the search by state. The website is www.rid.org.

[25] For more information on the ADA can be read at www.ada.gov/cguide.htm.

[26] For Deaf members who are active in the church, a TTY or a video phone in the church office may be necessary so out-going calls can be made. Also, IP Relay on the Internet is an alternative for deaf members who can access the Internet through a computer.

Deaf consumer (if present) to do the educating so as to allow the practitioner to remain in the interpreting role.

Logistics for Interpreter Placement

Generally, the interpreter will want to consult with the consumers, both Deaf and hearing, regarding placement. Often the interpreter stands near the front of the sanctuary, close to either the pulpit or the lectern. However, the interpreter may need to make adjustments and relocate when there is interference such as a procession or liturgical dance. Furthermore, the interpreter will want to be placed away from lighting that illuminates from directly behind, such as a window.

Another consideration for placement is where the consumer is seated. Ask the Deaf consumers where they would like to sit so they may be able to clearly see the interpreter. Often, it is near the front of the sanctuary. The Deaf consumer can inform an usher or someone in charge to reserve these seats. Likely, the practitioner will interpret this request. It is not at all surprising if there are no seats reserved, as consumers are responsible for their own seating arrangements. If you are filling in for another interpreter, inquire where the consumers usually sit (seats may already be reserved). This will ensure the consumers can adequately see the interpreter. While it is important that the consumer be able to see the interpreter, it is equally important for the interpreter to be able to hear the speakers. The interpreter should be prepared to discuss other logistical arrangements (e.g. length of the service and use of sound systems) when needed.[27]

Compensation

Before the first assignment begins, the payment arrangements (paid or not) should be established between the practitioner and the church. The interpreter has a right to receive compensation; moreover, a fair and reasonable fee should be arranged in a professional manner. For some interpreters a verbal consent is acceptable, while for others a signed agreement is preferable. If a signed agreement seems too formal, submitting invoices (weekly or monthly) is another alternative.

Most Christian congregations are dependent upon weekly offerings in order to meet budget requirements. There are many congregations that have experienced a decline in membership, which affects budgetary matters. Because of this, some congregations may find it a challenge to pay competitive rates for interpreters. Interpreters may need to negotiate, in a professional manner, what is acceptable. Some interpreters charge a

---

[27] If the service were traditional, it is suggested to stand close to the pulpit so Deaf parishioners can see both the preacher and the interpreter. When interpreting in a contemporary praise service that incorporates multimedia, and if the multimedia is used quite frequently, stand near the screen. If there is a praise band which is located near the deaf congregants, then the interpreter can relocate to where the band is and not be stationary. Out of respect for the consumers, still ask what their preference would be for where the interpreter should be located.

reduced rate, while others charge their regular rate. Chapter two includes additional considerations.

Hard of Hearing and Late-Deafened Parishioners

The best interpreters have a diverse set of skills and knowledge. Interpreters engage with Deaf, hard of hearing, late-deafened, deaf-blind, and hearing consumers. Statistics[28] show more people are hard of hearing and late-deafened than culturally Deaf. The interpreter may need to assess an environment to meet the needs for hard of hearing or late-deafened individuals who rely on speech reading or total communication. The interpreter will want to look at the acoustics and layout of the room or sanctuary: See if:

❑ There is sufficient light on the speaker.

❑ A copy of the sermon can be given.

❑ Seats close to the speaker are reserved.

❑ Assistive listening devices (ALDs) are available for consumers who use them.

An audit checklist is at the end of this chapter, which provides additional consideration for churches to be more accessible for individuals who are hard-of-hearing and/or late-deafened.

---

[28] Statistics of hearing loss distinctions can be located on the website of The League for the Hard-of-Hearing (http://www.chchearing.org/about-hearing-loss/facts-about-hearing-loss).

Three common types of assistive listening devices that are typically used are:

❑ **FM System** - FM Systems work like a miniature radio station. The transmitter has a microphone and sends FM waves to a receiver. In the United States special frequencies are set aside for users of FM systems so that there is no interference from outside FM transmissions.

❑ **Infrared System** - An infrared system uses invisible beams of light (like one's remote control). Infrared light waves are transmitted by an array of LED's (light emitting diodes) that are located on a panel. The receivers have a detector that senses the infrared light and converts the signal to sound.

❑ **Induction Loop** –Induction loop technology by magnetic induction is a basic principle of electronics. It works with an electrical current that is amplified and passed through a loop of wire. As a result, a magnetic field is generated around the area of the wire. The magnetic field that is created varies in direct proportion to the strength and frequency of the signal (or sound) being transmitted.[x]

Normally, only one system is used. As technology continues to evolve, new revolutionary equipment will probably be invented. The practitioner can keep up to date on technology by remaining in touch with an organization such as *Hearing Loss Association of America* (formerly the *Self Help of the Hard of Hearing*) or the *Alexander Graham Bell Association for the Deaf and Hard-of-*

Hearing.

Further information about the hard of hearing and late-deafened population can be found at the *Hearing Loss Association of America* website[29], *Association of Late-Deafened Adults*[30], or the *Alexander Graham Bell Association for the Deaf and Hard of Hearing*[31] website. A plethora of information and resources are available.

Captioning

Another avenue for greater communications access is Computerized Access Realtime Translations (CART).[32] A stenotype machine, a notebook computer, and realtime software are used to produce text, which is projected onto a screen.[xi] CART services are generally more expensive than interpreting services. A less expensive alternative to CART is Computerized Assisted Notetaking (CAN), in which a person types plainly onto a computer (usually a laptop). The CAN technician can sit next to the consumer or project the text onto a screen. In addition to services, videotapes and DVDs display ought to have closed captioning for viewers.

---

[29] Hearing Loss Association of America has a website. It can be accessed at www.hearingloss.org.
[30] Association of Late-Deafened Adults has a website at www.alda.org.
[31] The Alexander Graham Bell Association for the Deaf and Hard-of-Hearing promotes spoken language and hearing technologies. The organization's website can be accessed at www.agbell.com.
[32] To locate a CART service provider, log onto the National Court Reporters Association (NCRA) website at www.ncra.org.

Deaf-Blind Parishioners

Deaf-Blind people are often overlooked. They are frequently missing from the pews, but they too are meant to be part of the church. People with hearing and vision loss need accommodations just like the rest of the Deaf and/or hearing community. The term 'Deaf-blind' can be somewhat misleading, because of the misconception that a person is fully blind and fully Deaf - this is not always the case. Deaf-Blind individuals vary in hearing and visual loss, which means there is not one specific method for provision of accommodations. The practitioner will want to meet with the deaf-blind individual beforehand in order to learn what accommodations are needed.

Communication, stimulation, and companionship are essential to human beings. Deaf-Blind people need this as well. Some helpful tips to keep in mind:

❑ Touch is especially important for deaf-blind people. It is their link with the world. It can show you are nervous, withdrawn, friendly, tired, or bored. You may be uncomfortable "holding hands" during pauses, but it is best to wait for the deaf-blind person to break contact. It keeps that link and makes it easier for the deaf-blind person to get your attention.

❑ Communication options: POP (print on palm), tactile, CV (close vision), distant signing, tracking, limited space/tunnel vision, tactile finger-spelling, sim-com (if the person still has some residual hearing), as well as others.

❑ Begin slowly with a new person until they are used to you and you see how best to communicate. This is particularly true since most interpreters working with deaf-blind individuals are also working as support service providers (SSP), their guide, as well.

❑ Remember the deaf-blind person cannot see head nods, facial expressions, and other grammatical markers. Additional signs must be added.

❑ When you know the person better, touch will also include an occasional squeeze, stroke, pat on the back, walking close, or a hug of greeting and farewell.

❑ If the person's hands are heavy, it may mean he or she is tired or having difficulty understanding. Be aware of a need for a break in the conversation or interpretation.

❑ Help other people who are new to the deaf-blind world learn how to communicate with them. Do not be surprised if people, even Deaf people, are reluctant to communicate by touch.

❑ All people like an interpreter with the right attitude - someone who is flexible and who is there to make communications go smoothly.

❑ Be careful that clothing contrasts skin color. Some deaf-blind people are even more sensitive to bright colors than sighted Deaf people. Take off rings or bracelets, and keep fingernails trim, and free from visually distracting fingernail polish. Do not wear strong perfumes or colognes, including some scented hand lotions.[xii]

Some Deaf and most hearing people feel awkward or uncomfortable as they communicate with a Deaf-blind person, but the interpreter can lead the congregation to be open and inclusive with Deaf-blind parishioners.

Reasons for hearing and vision loss vary among individuals. Granted, some people inherit their sensory loss, but for many there are causes for it. Just like the rest of society, Deaf-blind individuals want to keep their independence, and with technology and other forms of assistance, much of their independence can be retained. Empowerment of Deaf-blind persons within a congregational setting can be achieved when most or all of the information and environment is accessible, perhaps by providing Braille materials, reading materials in large print, or by making the church's website accessible for those with disabilities.[33] Since each Deaf-blind person is different in terms of sensory loss, open communication is a must.[34]

The term 'Deaf-blind' describes a condition that combines in varying degrees both hearing and visual loss. Two sensory losses multiply and intensify the impact each would have alone and create a severe

---

[33] Two resources on the Internet are www.helenkeller.org and www.nidcd.nih.gov.

[34] RID's Standard Practice Paper: Interpreting for Individuals Who are Deaf-Blind is helpful. It can be accessed by going to www.rid.org/.

disability, which is different and unique. All Deaf-blind people experience problems with communications, access to information, and mobility. However, their specific needs vary enormously according to age, onset, and type of deaf-blindness.

Though listing the full range of reasons why a person may be Deaf and blind is not in the scope of this book, readers are nevertheless encouraged to study further about this area of deafness. A few terms to be familiar with are:

Legal Blindness - this is not a medical term but a legal one. It means that someone has 20/200 vision or worse in both eyes using the best pair of glasses. It can also refer to someone who has better than 20/200 vision but whose visual field is 20 degrees or less. The top number in the ratio refers to the distance the patient is in feet to the eye chart; the bottom number refers to the size of the letters or numbers.

Macular Degeneration - this is the leading cause of central vision loss among older individuals. One of the usual presenting symptoms is that there is a problem with reading. The individual then seeks out care thinking that new glasses are needed. Upon examination, it may be found that the central region of the retina, the macula, has been damaged. There are several types of macular degeneration, the first being called the "dry" Type. This is characterized by a thinning of the macular tissue without any fluid build-up in the retinal tissue. Ninety percent of all macular degenerations are of this type. The "wet" type occurs when new blood vessels grow under the macula and leak fluid and blood into the surrounding area. This can cause significant damage to the retina resulting in a central blind spot. Currently, no treatment exists for this problem, but promising treatments are being explored. Low vision optical aids can sometimes help. While this problem is more common in people over age 55, it can happen in childhood; then, it is usually called Stargardt's Disease.

Glaucoma – this is an eye disease that occurs when the tiny channels that allow fluid to drain from the eye become clogged. The result is a buildup of pressure inside the eye. This increased pressure causes damage to the optic nerve, and in time loss of vision may occur. Glaucoma usually develops without any warnings or symptoms and slowly does damage. Without treatment, glaucoma will lead to total blindness. Another type of glaucoma, acute angle-closure glaucoma, may produce noticeable blurred vision and pain either in the eyes or head. Regular eye exams are needed to routinely test for glaucoma. This condition is managed with eye drops, laser therapy, or surgery. There is no cure for glaucoma. Glaucoma is a major cause for blindness worldwide.

Usher Syndrome - this is the most common condition that involves both hearing and vision problems. A syndrome is a disease or disorder that has more than one feature or symptom. The major symptoms of Usher syndrome are hearing impairment and retinitis pigmentosa, an eye disorder that causes a person's vision to worsen over time. Some people with Usher syndrome also have balance problems. Usher syndrome is inherited or passed from parents to their children through genes.[xiii]

Group Process

Interpreters work in various contextual settings. Interpreting for consumers at worship services is generally the norm; however, interpreters work with groups as well. Churches, like other organizations, make decisions at committee and board meetings. Churches have administrative divisions, which run the church like a business in some ways. When requested to work at a meeting, interpreters will want to obtain an agenda, minutes, and any updates to be discussed beforehand; if needed, it is appropriate to request additional information. Some professionals refer to this as *pre-conferencing*. The quality of services is enhanced when prepared.

Committee members will meet in such places as the church, a person's home, or over a meal at a nearby restaurant. Parking lot conversations (where committee members strategize or complain) occur but are less likely to need an interpreter. Though group settings usually have fewer participants compared to a worship service, they are generally more interactive. The Deaf consumer's involvement will determine how often an interpreter is needed for a committee meeting.

In a mostly hearing setting, Deaf consumers generally sit across from the interpreter. On the other hand, in a mostly Deaf setting, hearing consumers sit close to the interpreter.

Almost without exception, a chairperson or minister will be appointed to lead or facilitate the meeting. Generally the practitioner sits close to the primary speaker, enabling the consumer to observe the speaker's body language or expressions even while focusing on the practitioner's interpretation. However, there are exceptions to the norm, and it is important to note the consumer's preference for location.

For groups not used to having an interpreter, one should establish a precedent from the very start. When the meeting is of a serious nature (i.e. financial, or about the minister), assurance may be needed that the interpreter will keep all conversations confidential. Ask committee members or guests to take turns when speaking when people are constantly talking over one another, so that the interpreter does not omit any information accidentally. "You can speak directly to Mr. Jones" is a common instruction interpreters share with first-time users to help lessen the likelihood of the "Tell him..." scenario. Team interpreting is helpful for meetings going over an hour (group work is more taxing), or for tension-filled meetings. Also, when helpful, it is appropriate for the interpreter to have notes (names, topic and subtopics, reoccurrence of unfamiliar terms and/or acronyms, etc.) to look at.

Bible studies and Sunday school classes are typically handled in the same manner. Curricula and agendas will be needed ahead of time for preparation purposes. Many hearing churches are delighted when Deaf people wish to be part of the congregation. However, when they provide for interpreting services and plan financial budgets to pay interpreting fees, the members of the board may overlook interpreting costs for mid-week services or church-related programs.

Worship

Christian worship services originated from Jewish worship; the Early Church adapted the service for its own use. The Gospels and the Acts of the Apostles depict early Christians, then still very much a part of Judaism, as frequenting both the Temple and syna-gogues, as well as worshipping in private homes. "Breaking bread" (the Eucharist/Holy Communion) was the center of Christian worship.

In general, worship for both the Eastern (Ortho-dox) Churches and the Catholic Church (the Western Church) is based on regular celebration of the "Lord's

Supper," celebrated by a priest with more or less participation from the present congregation. Worship services in these traditions share bread (mostly bread/wafer and wine), and make it more prominent in the service, although they also include prayer, reading Scripture, singing a song, and listening to some form of teaching or sermon.

Many mainline Protestant traditions celebrate Holy Communion (the Eucharist) monthly or quarterly, while worship is centered on a sermon, which may resemble a lecture or a passionate exhortation. Worship in these contexts also includes spoken prayer (either extemporaneous or prepared), liturgical recitations (litanies), Scripture, and music (hymns or songs of praise). Taking up an offering (collection of donated money) is common for all congregations and typically collected after the sermon.

Types of Christianity

This section of the chapter briefly explains the three major categories of Christianity. Because history influences the dynamics of church traditions, it is beneficial to read how Christianity has evolved over past centuries.

Many Christian churches are classified by denomination. Protestant denominations split from the Catholic Church because of arguments over doctrine. This wasn't the first schism; in fact, it had happened before with the Great Schism. In the 11th century, the split between the Eastern and Western Church occurred. It was mostly based on personality conflicts between the Bishops of Rome and Constantinople, doctrinal differences, and papal authority. This unfortunate split was fuelled by cross-cultural miscommunications and despicable behavior by Crusaders in the Western Church. Christians in the Western Church were led by a pope, and called Roman Catholics. Most Christians in Eastern Europe, Russia, and parts of the Middle East belong to Orthodox Churches.[xiv]

In the 15th century the invention of the printing press made it easier for more people to read and study the Bible. Up until this time, the Western Church's Bible was written in Latin. This, and opposing doctrines, led many thinkers over centuries to develop new ideas and to break away from the pope to start the Protestant Reformed churches. The most important of these thinkers were Martin Luther, Ulrich Zwingli, and John Calvin. Furthermore, disagreements among Protestant thinkers caused additional fractions among denominations. Some of the first Protestant denominations, though there are now thousands, were the Anabaptists, Lutheran, and Presbyterian (reformed) Churches. In England, a similar protest against the pope, first political and later religious, led to the Church of England (the Anglican Church), which considers itself a Protestant church as well.[xv]

One example of how Protestant denominations differ from the Roman Catholic and Orthodox Churches is that they do not classify the following five rituals as sacraments.[35]

---

[35] The Episcopal Church and the Anglican Church are both considered Protestant denominations, yet they do consider these five rituals as sacraments.

❑ Holy Orders (ordination of clergy)

❑ Sacrament of Reconciliation (confession)

❑ Confirmation (becoming a permanent church member)

❑ Anointing the Sick

❑ Matrimony (marriage)

Many Protestant denominations do not have an exclusive male priesthood and differ by not expressing the same adoration for Mary, the mother of Jesus. All three Christian sects (Eastern Orthodoxy, Catholicism, and Protestantism) consider Holy Baptism and Holy Communion / Eucharist to be the primary sacraments (or ordinances). According to the Catholic Church and the Orthodox Church, Christians are to live by Scripture *and tradition*, whereas Christians in Protestant Churches are to live by Scripture alone.[xvi]

Furthermore, the Bible's content differs slightly between the Roman Catholic Church and Protestant Church. The Roman Catholic Church canonized the intertestament books, also known as the Apocrypha (samples are the Book of Maccabees and the Book of Wisdom). The intertestament books were written during the four hundred year period between the Old Testament and the New Testament. Protestants may exclude the Apocrypha from the Protestant version of the Bible, but still consider them important books, partly because they help Christians understand the context of Judaism in the time of Jesus' life.

In Christianity, the term *interdenominational* refers to the combining of two or more denominations' traditions, while *non-denominational* is when a church has not formally aligned themselves with an established denomination or formal institution. Non-denominational churches have their own internal methods for developing policy and worship without interference from denominational organizations, which have their own policies and worship practices. Members of non-denominational churches often consider themselves simply "Christians," and many feel comfortable visiting other denominations with compatible beliefs.

On the other hand, some non-denominational churches consciously reject the idea of a denominational structure as a matter of doctrine and insist that each congregation must be autonomous. They sometimes point out that in early Christianity, there were no denominations. Today non-denominational churches do not recognize any ecclesiastical authority (e.g., the pope) above the local congregation.

Denominational Worship Styles

With there being thousands of denominations worldwide, it is impossible to describe all the shades of worship styles and their denominational contexts within the scope of this book. In this section; however, a range of denominations are touched on which highlights the variety of worship styles parishioners may experience, along with additional resources for the interpreter.

Worship styles are characterized by: culture, a range of charisma, the degree of evangelicalism (keeping with the gospel and its teachings), a level of enthusiasm, denominational history, geography (e.g., urban or rural), beliefs and doctrine, ethnicity, and for some, by experience/struggle. Worship services in a denomination or church setting can often be stylized further by tradition and cultural-identity, as seen in deaf worship services and in the black church. The black church, which is not a specific denomination, is predominantly made up of African American congregants and has a special contextual style of worship. Two such denominations that incorporate this style are The African Methodist Episcopal Church (AME) and The African Methodist Episcopal Zion Church (AME Zion). The following excerpt explains this concept further.

"According to Professor Jonathan Walton (Harvard Divinity School), for more than 300 years, the black church in America has provided a safe haven for black Christians in a nation shadowed by the legacy of slavery and a society that remains defined by race and class. Inspired by the story of Exodus, African Americans can think out, pray out and shout out their anger and aspirations, free from the unstated yet powerful constraints that govern dialogue with the larger white society. In the pulpit and the pews, in choir lofts and Sunday schools, the black church continues to offer affirmation and dignity to people still searching for equality and justice, still willing to reach out for a more inclusive, embracing tomorrow."[xvii]
* To read more about the black church, go to www.pbs.org/godinamerica/black-church/.

The following are brief descriptions that provide a bird's eye view of what an interpreter might expect when working in these worship settings.

The Presbyterian Worship Service

Presbyterian worship services are distinguished by the centrality of Scripture. This comes from the denomination's reformed tradition, which was spearheaded by John Calvin in order to bring reform to the Catholic Church as part of the Protestant Reformation. Bible readings and sermons that explain and apply its teachings are a central focus of the service. The Presbyterian Church (USA), the largest Presbyterian denomination in the U.S., suggests in its constitution that the service be arranged around five actions centered on the Word (Scripture): gathering around the word (meeting as a congregation), proclaiming the word (reading Scripture and preaching), responding to the word (as in through offerings), the sealing of the word (Sacrament), and bearing and following the word into the world. Many congregations will stand, a gesture of respect, when the Gospel is read. A worship service includes singing, prayers, affirmation of faith (e.g., The Apostles Creed), preaching, and the Sacraments. Clergy are commonly addressed as reverend. The denomination's recommended Bible translation to use is The New Revised Standard Version (NRSV), but other translations may be read from. The Book of Common Worship and hymns from The Presbyterian Hymnal are mostly used. The lectionary is often followed.
* Information for this and more worship information can be found at http://gamc.pcusa.org/ministries/worship/ and many Presbyterian hymns are online at www.hymnary.org/hymnal/PH.

The Lutheran Worship Service

The two largest Lutheran church bodies in the U.S. are the Evangelical Lutheran Church in America (ELCA) and the Lutheran Church - Missouri Synod (LCMS), with the LCMS being the more conservative. Named after Martin Luther, its spiritual father who sought Catholic reform, this denomination has similarities to Catholicism in terms of revering tradition and rituals. The basic pattern of importance for worship among Lutherans is the *gathering*, encountering God's *Word* (Scripture readings and sermons), sharing of a *meal* (Eucharist), and being *sent* into the world. For Lutherans, worship is fundamentally about what God is doing and the people's response to God's actions. Worship is an encounter with God, who saves. Generally, a Lutheran service has prayers that are sometimes litanies (reading responses), hymns sung by the congregation, celebration of the Eucharist, Scripture readings that can include kneeling in many Lutheran congregations, and a sermon or meditation. Typically, three or four Scripture lessons from both the Old Testament and New Testament are read. Also, some Lutheran congregations permit non-Lutherans to partake in the Eucharist. The minister is addressed as reverend or father (e.g., Rev. Mike or Fr. Mike). The Evangelical Lutheran Worship and the Lutheran Hymnal are both used. Also, the lectionary is mostly followed.
* Information for this and more worship information can be found at www.elca.org/Growing-In-Faith/Worship.aspx and many Lutheran hymns can be found at http://www.lutheran-hymnal.com/online/tlh_online.html.

The Episcopal Worship Service

The Episcopal Church is a part of the Anglican Communion. For some, the Episcopal service strikes a balance between a Catholic service and a mainlined Protestant service. In general, many Episcopal worship services tend to be "High Church" (more formalized and traditional), with prescribed rituals and readings, bishops and priests, vestments (priestly garments), saints' days (memorializing saints), and elaborately decorated churches. These, of course, are similar to a Catholic service.

Episcopal (Anglican) rituals are expressed through a collection of rich liturgies (prayers and services). Therefore, the service has a strong emphasis on liturgy, both historical and contemporary. Generally, the congregation stands when the clergy processes in and out from the sanctuary. The Eucharist (Communion) is the climax of the service, which is similar to Catholic Mass. Commonly experienced in a standard worship service are hymn singing, Scripture readings (usually an Old Testament reading, New Testament reading, and the Gospel reading), a meditation or sermon, special prayers, reciting of the Nicene Creed, and most often a confession is recited and the pardon (forgiveness) read from a priest. The priest is addressed as reverend or father/mother (e.g., Rev. Taylor or Fr. Taylor). The New Revised Standard Version (NRSV) is the official Bible for readings, but other versions may be used. Liturgies from the Book of Common Prayer and hymns The Hymnal 1982 are mostly used. The lectionary is mostly followed.

* Information for this and more worship information can be found at www.episcopalchurch.org and many

Episcopal hymns at
http://oremus.org/hymnal/82.html.

The United Methodist Worship Service

Sharing the same roots with the Episcopal Church
(both have Anglican roots), the Methodist service can
have an Anglican familiarity to it. This is because John
Wesley, its founder, was an Anglican priest. Depending
on congregational culture, it will be either more formal
(high church) or less formal (low church) in nature and
fall in the range of being conservative, moderate, or
liberal in thinking and attitude. This influences whether
the service has a traditional, contemporary, or blended
style. Some Methodist congregations emphasize
Scripture and preaching, while other congregations have
Holy Communion as a shared focal part of the service.
Many Methodist services popularize hymn singing and
stress grace throughout worship. Litanies and affirmation of faith (e.g., The Apostle's Creed) are common in
Methodist services, more so when Holy Communion is
celebrated. Clergy are commonly addressed as pastor or
reverend (e.g. Rev. Peggy or Pastor Peggy). The New
Revised Standard Version (NRSV) is the official
translation, but other versions may be utilized. The
United Methodist Book of Worship for liturgies and the
two hymnals, The United Methodist Hymnal (traditional hymns) and The Faith We Sing (contemporary songs)
are mostly used. The lectionary is often followed.
* Information for this and more worship information
can be found at www.umc.org (click on the "Resources" tab) and most Methodist hymns and songs at
www.hymnsite.com/.

The United Church of Christ Worship Service

Many of the UCC services have an ecumenical tapestry throughout worship, borrowing from various traditions. Like most Protestant services, worship includes prayer, singing of either traditional hymns or songs (or both), Scripture readings, a sermon, and the Sacraments (Communion and/or baptism). Services among UCC churches can vary and have a traditional, blended, or contemporary style. This denomination does not, however, recite affirmations of faith (e.g., The Nicene Creed). For some UCC congregations, the service intentionally incorporates inclusive language. Since congregations are made up of cultural norms, churches can have either a conservative bent or lean more toward being progressive (liberal). Clergy are typically addressed as reverend or pastor (e.g., Rev. Lucy or Pastor Lucy). The New Revised Standard Version (NRSV) is the Bible translation suggested by the denomination, but readings from other versions may be read. The Book of Worship for various worship services and hymns and songs from The New Century Hymnal and Sing! Prayer and Praise are mostly used. The lectionary is often followed.
* Information for this and more worship information can be found at www.ucc.org and many UCC hymns are located at http://nethymnal.org/.

The Baptist Worship Service

There are many forms of Baptist churches in the U.S.; however, the Southern Baptist Convention and the American Baptist Church are the two largest bodies, with the Southern Baptist Convention being the more conservative. As indicated by its name, the primary Baptist distinctive is the practice of believer's baptism rather than infant baptism. Many Baptist congregations are evangelical in doctrine, yet Baptist beliefs are not framed by ritual but rather more by congregational tradition that can vary due to the congregation's autonomy and geography. Similar to Presbyterians, Scripture and preaching are fundamental to the Baptist service. Respecting tradition, many Baptist congregations read Scripture from The King James Bible (KJV) or The New King James Bible (NKJV), along with congregants bringing personal Bibles to worship. While singing and prayers are important, sacramental rituals called ordinances are less frequent yet still revered. There has been tension among some Baptist congregations for introducing contemporary music (some call it "rock gospel music") since it breaks tradition. In addition, worship can be a traditional, blended, or contemporary type service depending on the congregation's taste or ethnic makeup. Furthermore, Baptist congregations can be more lively or reserved in their enthusiasm, which might be influenced further by the church's heritage. Whereas other denominations offer occasional altar calls (coming forward to accept a relationship with God), this practice is seen more often in a Baptist service. Clergy are addressed as reverend or as pastor (e.g., Rev. John or Pastor John).

* Information for this and more worship information can be found at http://allaboutbaptists.com/worship.html and a limited selection of music at www.sbc.net.

The Catholic Worship Service

The Catholic service may vary upon the geography and size of the congregation, and whether it is high church (more formal) or low church (less formal); however, Mass is the centrality of worship. Simply put, Mass is a celebration – worship and an attitude of adoration expressed through liturgy (order of service); moreover, the traditional service is typically low-key, while the contemporary services are more upbeat. When clergy begin or conclude the service by procession, parishioners typically stand out of respect. The Eucharist is the pivotal part of the worship experience (the Mass), while reverence of the Scripture reading (e.g., Old Testament, Psalm, New Testament, and the Gospel) is still fundamental to the service, which is partly expressed through kneeling when read. The worship service includes litanies (reading responses) that are prayers and confessions, as well as hymns that are sung by parishioners. Prayers for denominational leadership are also found to be common. Beginning with carrying in the cross and the Mass book, the first part of Mass focuses on the Word (Scripture and homily/preaching) and the second part gives focus to the Eucharist, both of which use rites (liturgical traditions). Priests and deacons are commonly addressed as reverend or father (e.g., Rev. Marcus or Fr. Marcus). The altar area is typically off-limits to those who are not ordained, and only Catholics are permitted to partake in the Eucharist. The lectionary is mostly followed. Helpful for newer interpreters working in the Catholic setting, <u>Signing the Scriptures</u> (a 3 book series), by Joan Blake, offers suggestions for interpreting Scripture passages.
* Information for this and more worship information

can be found at www.aboutcatholics.com and a limited selection of hymns at http://midihymns.homestead.com/midiindex.html.

The Pentecostal Worship Service

Some Pentecostal congregations do not have a denominational affiliation, but share a worship style and a belief in congregational autonomy. For those congregations that have an association with a denomination, these churches might belong to the Assemblies of God. Pentecostals have one central belief that affects all of their interactions, their worship practices, and their other beliefs: that God is still present and active within the world. Because of this, there should be some evidence of God's presence as well as an attempt to connect through the Holy Spirit. Pentecostal services are lively, and worshipers typically lift their voices in praise and raise their hands in honor and respect, both expressing joy and gratitude. It is not uncommon for a person (or persons) to dance and/or clap or even speak in tongues when deeply moved or inspired. In some ways, worship attempts to recapture Pentecostal revivals. Pentecostal services do not follow rituals, but do include singing of traditional hymns and contemporary songs or both, Scripture readings, prayers, and preaching (this is stressed), all of which engages the parishioners and can be based on the tradition of the congregation. Clergy are addressed as reverend or pastor (e.g., Rev. Mike or Pastor Mike). The King James Bible might be used, but the Bible version is dependent on the congregation, and more congregations are using more recent versions such as the New International Version. Altar calls occur often as well. * Information for this and more worship information can be found at

http://home.messiah.edu/~mb1386/Pentecostal.html.
From the Assemblies of God website, information
about music can be located at
http://music.ag.org/worship_music_resources.aspx.

Cross-Cultural Venues

More and more professional degree curricula
across different industries now require a class or
seminar in cross-cultural awareness. Whether professionals work in mental health services, legal services, or
interpreting services, they will need to work with all
populations, backgrounds, cultures, and communication
needs. Interpreters must be able to interact with others
and recognize differences in order to make accommodations. The willingness to accept different kinds of
people--to get to know them, respect them, and like
them--enables interpreters to bridge communication
and cultural needs more effectively.

A one-size-fits-all approach will not accommodate
the needs of all people. Cross-cultural awareness goes
beyond respect for differences. Consider the following
when working in cross-cultural settings:

❑ Do not assume that there is one right way
(yours!) to communicate. Constantly question
your assumptions about the "right way" to
communicate. For example, think about your
body language; postures that indicate receptivity
in one culture might indicate aggression in another.

❑ Do not assume that breakdowns in communication occur because other people are on the

wrong track. Search for ways to make communications work rather than searching for who should receive the blame for the breakdown.

❑ Listen actively and empathetically. Try to put yourself in the other person's shoes. Especially when another person's perceptions or ideas are very different from your own, you might need to operate at the edge of your own comfort zone.

❑ Suspend judgment, and try to look at the situation as an outsider.

❑ Remember that cultural norms may not apply to the behavior of any particular individual. We are all shaped by many, many factors –our ethnic background, our family, our education, and our personalities—and are more complicated than any cultural norm could suggest. Check your interpretations if you are uncertain what was meant.[xviii]

The successful interpreter begins with self-knowledge, and uses that as a springboard to embrace other cultures with an open mind. Two useful resources are Cross-cultural Servanthood: Serving the World in Christlike Humility by Duane Elmer (2006) and Building a Healthy Multi-ethnic Church: Mandate, Commitments and Practices of a Diverse Congregation by Mark DeYmaz (2010).

Tensions within Churches

Many people look to the church when they search for guidance and healing. In the book, <u>PASTORS AT GREATER RISK</u>, authors H.B. London, Jr. and Neil B. Wiseman (2003), describe tensions, referred to as "hazards," that effect congregations.[xix] A few issues that influence congregations are members' personal problems, the consumer mentality, unrealistic expectations, and financial strains (lack of tithing). Congregational growth may well have hit a plateau or declined since past decades, which can cause a deterioration of social conditions within the church.

Adam Hamilton[36], a United Methodist minister, wrote a book about six tensions that spill out of society into sanctuaries. Because of diversifying biblical beliefs, these tough issues covered by Hamilton are:

❑ Separation of Church and State

❑ Creation and Evolution in the Public Schools

❑ The Death Penalty

❑ Euthanasia

❑ Prayer in Public Schools

❑ Abortion

---

[36] <u>Confronting the Controversies</u> by Adam Hamilton (2005) exposes controversial issues that many churches face.

❑ Homosexuality[xx]

Tension-filled congregations may potentially affect the interpreter. Good coping skills will help the interpreter to maintain equilibrium and not let tensions in the congregation affect the work. Remaining neutral and refraining from sharing one's thoughts on such topics is the general rule of thumb for interpreters, in part, so the interpreter does not mistakenly influence others and/or unnecessarily cause a personal conflict.

Summary

Interpreters must consider dynamics when interpreting in church settings. Culture, level of awareness, doctrine, context, history, and types of worship services all influence the interpreting conditions for interpreters. Interpreters should be aware of social diversity within congregations when deciding whether or not to accept or decline religious interpreting assignments for the first time. With further experience and additional education (formal or informal), interpreters will become adept at working in various settings in churches. The dynamics of the church setting can also include worship service (the most common), music, counseling, weddings, funerals, social services, education, and meetings.

How Accessible Is Your Church?
Determining The Needs & Resources For Ministry & Mission With Hard-of-hearing & Late-Deafened People

PART ONE of this audit focuses on the needs of hard-of-hearing people who can use Assistive Listening Devices.

PART TWO focuses on the needs of late-deafened people who *must* have information communicated visually. The following audit checklist was developed by the United Methodist Congress of the Deaf and comes from the publication, *Breaking the Sound Barrier in Your Church*.

I. Which Of The Following Sound Adaptations Has Your Church Made To Encourage Participation By Hard-of-hearing People?

❑ ❑ Amplification for the whole congregation? NOTE: This does not substitute for an assistive listening system for hard-of-hearing people or those using cochlear implants.

❑ ❑ Microphone positioned away from speaker's lips, to accommodate people who are speech reading (also known as lip reading)?

❑ ❑ Lavaliere (lapel) microphone worn by liturgists and/or preacher(s) not using a stationary microphone?

❑ ❑ Wireless microphone for use in the nave for sharing of joys and concerns or additional announcements?

❑ ❑ Strategically placed microphone(s) so that persons using assistive listening devices may hear organ/piano, soloists and choir?

❑ ❑ Assistive Listening System (FM, infrared, audio loop)?

❑ ❑ Receivers with jacks and neck loops for the assistive listening system (needed by people with cochlear implants or hearing aids with T-switches)?

❑ ❑ Person assigned to ensure that receiver batteries are charged (or replaced as the case may be) weekly?

❑ ❑ Assistive listening receivers set out on table in or close to sanctuary, making for easier access by hard-of-hearing people or those with cochlear implants?

❑ ❑ An attendant on hand to assist in selection of proper unit and explain its operation?

❑ ❑ Are posters placed at entry points telling of the availability of assistive listening devices, and where to find them?

❑ ❑ Lighting in front of liturgists, preachers, choir members, to facilitate easier speech reading?

Yes No In The Sanctuary:

❑ ❑ Using the church's Yellow Page, website, and newspaper advertisements to tell of its audio and visual enhancements for hard-of-hearing and late-deafened people?

❑ ❑ When remodeling or building new sanctuary, architect requested to research latest acoustical technology?

Yes No In Meeting Rooms:

❑ ❑ Meetings held in rooms with good acoustics (carpets, drapes)?

❑ ❑ Good lighting on speaker's face? (Should not have the light source behind the speaker.)

❑ ❑ Amplification used most of the time?

❑ ❑ Microphone positioned away from speaker's mouth?

❑ ❑ Microphone used by all speakers, including those in audience during feedback or discussion time?

❑ ❑ All presentations be done from the front (to facilitate hearing and speech reading)?

❑ ❑ Comments/questions from audience repeated by speaker (if microphone is not available to the audience)?

❑ ❑ Semicircular seating arrangement used for discussions to facilitate speech reading?

❑ ❑ FM or audio loop assistive listening system available?

❑ ❑ Receivers with jacks and neck loops available for assistive listening system?

❑ ❑ Videos selected for and presented in closed-captioned version?

❑ ❑ TV sets and VCR units equipped with closed-caption circuitry, remote control available, and instructions or attendant on hand to operate the system?

2. Does Your Church Supplement Sound with Sight for People Who Are Late-Deafened In The Following Ways? NOTE: These methods also benefit hard-of-hearing people *AND* the congregation at large!*

Yes No In Meetings

❏ ❏ Written agenda, even for "small" meetings.

❏ ❏ Graphic recording throughout meetings, even small ones

❏ ❏ Overhead projection, especially of action proposals

❏ ❏ Computer Assisted Note-taking or similar system, in "real time," and visible to all

Yes No During Worship:

Are the following visible to all worshipers? (Note that most hymnals and pew Bibles are in small print)

❏ ❏ Words of hymns?

❏ ❏ Words of anthem or solo?

❏ ❏ Litanies, prayers, scripture?

❏ ❏ Words of the liturgies?

❏ ❏ Children's moments?

❏ ❏ Sermon?

❏ ❏ Joys and concerns?

❏ ❏ Announcements?

Methods used to make the words of worship and other church events seen as well as heard:

❏ ❏ Handouts?

❏ ❏ Copies of the sermon available in advance?

❏ ❏ Overhead projection to large screen in sanctuary?

❏ ❏ Computer assisted note-taking (CAN or a similar system) projected onto large screen or a TV monitor?

3. Are Your Church Staff & Office *Hearing Accessible*?

Yes No

❏ ❏ Do you have at least one telephone with volume control/amplification?

❏ ❏ Do you have a TTY (telecommunication device for the deaf, also known as a TDD) or a video phone (VP)?
❏ ❏ Do you have a personal listening device available for counseling sessions and home/hospital visits? (e.g., FM transmitter/receiver, Williams Pocketalker, Sound Wizard)

*Compiled by:*The United Methodist Congress of the Deaf Standing Committee on Church Accessibility Promotion: Hard-of-hearing and Late-Deafened People. To read obtain the expanded booklet go to www.umcd.org/Publications.htm and download the PDF document. A printed booklet can be obtained by contacting president@umcd.org.

ENDNOTES

[x] "Assistive Listening Devices". Hearing Loss America of Association. Retrieved 11 Aug. 2006. www.hearingloss.org/learn/assistivetech.asp#link1.

[xi] "Assistive Listening Devices". Hearing Loss America of Association. Retrieved 11 Aug. 2006. www.hearingloss.org/learn/assistivetech.asp#link1.

[xii] "Interpreting and working with Deafblind People." The Interpreter's Friend. Retrieved 21 Sep 2006. www.theinterpretersfriend.com/db/Ig4db.html#(2).

[xiii] "Usher Syndrome." National Institute on Deafness and Other Communication Disorders. Retrieved 21 Sep 2006. www.nidcd.nih.gov/health/hearing/usher.htm.

[xiv] Justo Gonzalez. THE STORY OF CHRISTIANITY Volume 1. San Francisco: Harper, 1984. 265.

[xv] Justo Gonzalez. CHURCH HISTORY: An Essential Guide. Nashville: Abingdon Press, 1996. 72.

[xvi] "Types of Christianity". Wikepedia. Retrieved 11 Aug 2006. http://simple.wikipedia.org/wiki/Christianity#Types_of_Christianity.

[xvii] Mellowes, M. (1998). *The Black Church*. PBS. Retrieved from www.pbs.org/godinamerica/black-church.

[xviii] "Working on Common Cross-Cultural Communication Challenges". AMPU. Retrieved 25 Aug 2006. www.wwcd.org/action/ampu/crosscult.html.

[xix] H.B. London, Jr. and Neil B. Wiseman. PASTORS AT GREATER RISK. Ventura: Regal Books, 2003.

[xx] Adam Hamilton. Confronting the Controversies: Biblical Perspectives on Tough Issues. Nashville: Abingdon Press, 2005.

Chapter 4 – Accepting the Interpreting Request

The process of interpretation in a church setting actually begins before arrival at the sanctuary. The interpreter has the responsibility to consider the ethical dimensions of an assignment prior to accepting it and must be able to think objectively, which can be ethically challenging. Often, interpreters wish to interpret in the church setting for personal reasons. Faith-driven motivation can be a good reason to interpret in such a setting; however, the new interpreter must be professionally competent and capable of stepping into the role of interpreter.

If your faith setting needs to recruit an interpreter, going to the RID website is the best place to begin the search.[37] The website offers an interpreter database, which you can search by state. Also, RID lists interpreting agencies (referral agencies) by state, similar to the individual interpreter search. Going through an interpreting agency is more costly, but for some people it is easier to do this than calling or emailing individual interpreters. Sometimes, student interpreters needing practice hours might be capable of provide interpreting services, especially if they have a background in this type of setting. Contacting an interpreter education

---

[37] RID has a registry of interpreters, interpreting agencies, and interpreting education programs by state. The website is www.rid.org.

program in your state is a good place to start (see the footnote below).

Standard Practice Paper

RID's Standard Practice Paper: Interpreting in Religious Settings is not only informative, it delineates the skills, factors, and logistical concerns interpreters will want to think about in this work. It, and other practice papers, can be located at RID's website. Experienced interpreters from various religious backgrounds met as a committee to collaborate and draft a document that provides approaches and issues the profession and those with interpreting needs will want to consider when they work in a religious setting. New interpreters with a Christian faith who want to work in church settings will find the Standard Practice Paper to be useful because of the guidance, considerations, and resources that it includes. Other Standard Practice Papers are referenced throughout the document; these are worth reading for better insight and clarity about the role of an interpreter. Such papers are:

* Standard Practice Paper: Professional Sign Language Interpreting

* Standard Practice Paper: Business Practices: Billing Considerations

* Standard Practice Paper: Multiple Roles in Interpreting (see Appendix D)

* Standard Practice Paper: Team Interpreting

* Standard Practice Paper: Self-Care

Interpreting in Religious Settings

STANDARD PRACTICE PAPER

The Registry of Interpreters for the Deaf, Inc., (RID) Standard Practice Paper (SPP) provides a framework of basic, respectable standards for RID members' professional work and conduct with consumers. This paper also provides specific information about the practice setting. This document is intended to raise awareness, educate, guide and encourage sound basic methods of professional practice. The SPP should be considered by members in arriving at an appropriate course of action with respect to their practice and professional conduct.

It is hoped that the standards will promote commitment to the pursuit of excellence in the practice of interpreting and be used for public distribution and advocacy.

About Interpreting in Religious Settings

Religious interpreting occurs in settings which are spiritual in nature. These settings can include worship services, religious education, workshops, conferences, retreats, confession, scripture study, youth activities, counseling, tours and pilgrimages, weddings, funerals and other special ceremonies. Religious interpreting poses unique challenges and requires specific skills and knowledge to address those needs. Special consideration should also be given to the interpreting environment and to interpreter compensation.

Specialized Skills

Professionals interpreting in a religious context should have fluency in a signed language (e.g. American Sign Language or Signed English) and a spoken language (e.g. English or Spanish). In addition, knowledge of a source language of an original text found in scripture such as Arabic, Hebrew, Latin or others would enhance the overall interpretation. It is ideal for the interpreter to have familiarity with the sacred text; however, the interpreter may need to work with an English translation.

Some interpreters enter the field by working in a religious venue. For some persons, interpreting in a religious setting is a spiritual calling. Interpreters are strongly encouraged to enhance their skills by working with a religious mentor who is a seasoned and/or certified interpreter before working independently. For additional information about mentoring, read RID's SPP titled, *Mentoring*.

333 Commerce Street ■ Alexandria, VA 22314
PH: 703.838.0030 ■ FAX: 703.838.0454 ■ TTY: 703.838.0459
www.rid.org

STANDARD PRACTICE PAPER

Specialized Knowledge

Interpreters will want to be aware of the consumer's cultural expectations and preferences that are specific to the environment. Interpreters in religious settings should also have access to and familiarize themselves with:

- Specialized vocabulary both signed and spoken that relate to the specific setting
- Texts specific to the setting (e.g. Koran, Torah, Bible)
- Materials used (e.g. sermon notes, homilies, multimedia presentations)
- Belief system(s), doctrine(s), creed(s) and ceremonial prayer(s)

Interpreters should be aware of how their own beliefs may potentially conflict with the beliefs of a different faith. Interpreters will want to accept assignments in a religious setting where they can faithfully and impartially interpret the message. Whether an interpreter needs to be a practicing member of a certain faith or follower of its precepts is a decision made by those requesting interpreting services. These issues should always be discussed with the interpreter and consumers prior to delivery of interpreting services.

In addition, interpreters who are members of RID must adhere to the NAD-RID Code of Professional Conduct regarding confidentiality. The interpreter should keep all interpreted information confidential, such as confessions, counseling and private meetings.

Working Environment

The religious interpreting environment requires advance preparation and cooperation on several fronts. Prior communication with a specific on-site contact along with access to the person(s) in charge of the presentations and presenters themselves is critical. The members affiliated with the particular setting should also be made aware of the interpreting services to be rendered, and all parties should understand the role of the interpreter.

The contact person should ensure the interpreter is provided with the necessary materials needed for the interpreter to appropriately prepare and assist in the logistics, placement and smooth integration of the interpreter's services into the religious activity. These arrangements should be made in advance of the date of the service or event.

STANDARD PRACTICE PAPER

Preparation

Each interpreter's access to all the materials, along with the order of each event/ceremony, with sufficient time to prepare appropriately, is central to the interpreting function.

Specific musical arrangements, lyrics and the meaning behind poetic language require analysis and rehearsal. This level of preparation by the interpreter is necessary in order to render a piece of music or poetic expression that is accurate, artistic, culturally modified and as visually inspiring and insightful as the audio portion. In this specialized setting, preparation by the interpreter requires commitment to ensure quality interpreting, such as matching the music flow, using the correct sign modality, providing an accurate rendition of the frozen text, displaying the appropriate emotions and actions, etc.

Long or complex events may require a team of two or more interpreters. Additionally, a musical or dramatic program may require weeks of preparation that may necessitate involvement of the interpreter (s) in the rehearsals. Preparation would also include information and detailed attention as to what is or is not acceptable, permissible to (or not to) interpret and appropriate attire.

Materials

Materials include but are not limited to music, sacred text or readings, along with the translations.

These materials can be provided in a printed and/or recorded format. Subsequently, the contact person will want to ensure the interpreter(s) are provided with lists of names that may be read, the agenda, announcements, copies of sermons, speeches, poetry, scripts of any artistic performances, songs and the like in advance.

Placement of Interpreter:

While the interpreter's placement may vary, it is important for the interpreter to consider acoustics, sight line, lighting, background, location and availability of equipment, but special consideration should be given to a religion's accepted protocol in a religious service. For the benefit of the participants, the interpreter should be sensitive to the following:

STANDARD PRACTICE PAPER

- Space for a music stand to place materials
- Hierarchy
- Gender roles
- Areas deemed sacred
- Multimedia
- Videotaping
- Physical movement inherent to the service

Compensation

If a professional interpreter views religious interpreting as service/ministry to the organization or a charitable contribution, she/he may expect payment. In situations when interpreters do not charge for their services, interpreters may want to consider educating their religious communities about potential expenses of services to develop awareness. Some interpreters accept payment but may donate it back to the religious establishment. For additional information about billing practices, read RID SPP titled, *Business Practices: Hiring an Interpreter/Billing Considerations*

ADDITIONAL RESOURCES

El Paso CC National Multicultural National Interpreting Project
Mary L. Mooney, Project Director
El Paso Community College
P.O. Box 20500
El Paso, TX 79998
(915) 831-2432 V/TTY
(915) 831-2095 FAX
E-mail: marym@epcc.edu
www.epcc.edu/Community/NMIP/Welcome.html

Jewish Deaf Congress (Formerly Congress of Jewish Deaf)
President: Martin Florsheim
(718) 740-0470 TTY
(718) 740-4994 FAX
E-mail: DCCNEWS@aol.com
www.jirs.org/jirs/jirs0005ys.htm

Episcopal Conference for the Deaf
E-mail: JLCroft@juno.com
www.ecdeaf.com

National Catholic Office for the Deaf
7202 Buchanan Street
Landover Hills, MD 20784-2236
(301) 577-1684 V/Fax
(301) 577-4184 TTY/Video Phone
E-mail: info@ncod.org
www.ncod.org

International Catholic Deaf Association
United States Section
7202 Buchanan Street
Landover Hills, MD 20784
(301) 429-0697 TTY
(301) 429-0698 FAX
Email: homeoffice@icda-us.org
www.icda-us.org

TEXT RESOURCES

Blake, Joan *SIGNING THE SCRIPTURES: A Starting Point for Interpreting the Sunday Readings for the Deaf (Year A)*. Liturgy Training Publications, 2004.

Blake, Joan *SIGNING THE SCRIPTURES: A Starting Point for Interpreting the Sunday Readings for the Deaf (Year B)*. Liturgy Training Publications, 2005.

Blake, Joan *SIGNING THE SCRIPTURES: A Starting Point for Interpreting the Sunday Readings for the Deaf (Year C)*. Liturgy Training Publications, 2003.

Yates, Jr., Leo *INTERPRETING AT CHURCH: A Paradigm for Sign Language Interpreters.* BookSurge, LLC, 2007.

Interpreter Interview

Some churches establish a Deaf ministry committee or taskforce, which may include a subcommittee whose task it is to hire an interpreter.[38] An informal interview with the interpreter may be done over the phone, through e-mail, or in person. Interpreters may expect the following interview questions:

1. Do you hold professional certification? If not, what experience do you have? (Although it is not always necessary to have, licensure or certification is an indication of the interpreter's professional abilities.)

2. Can you explain the role of an interpreter so that we can understand it? (Include information about your responsibilities.)

3. Do you have a degree or certificate from an Interpreter Education Program? (Attending an Interpreter Education Program is not absolutely necessary for hiring interpreters, but does provide a better understanding of the interpreter's background.)

4. How does the level of your education compare to the education level in the church? (This is important, because the interpreter must be able to comprehend and match the language appropriately when interpreting.)

---

[38] An interpreter may be on the committee or have a role in the interpreter search and interview. Also, Deaf people should be on the Deaf ministry committee.

5. Do you speak in a professional manner? Do you exhibit a paternalistic attitude or condescending behaviors toward Deaf persons? (This is a red flag.)

6. Can you work at most worship services?

7. Are you a member of any professional organizations?

8. Do you have experience working in this type of setting?

9. Have you been active in a state organization or an RID affiliate chapter? (This shows a commitment to the interpreting field and a desire for professional development.)

10. Do you know the Code of Professional Conduct (code of ethics)?

There are additional questions that a hiring committee could ask; moreover, they are likely to ask questions specific to the church's needs. For example, if there is a need, will you interpret at mid-week activities?

Considerations Before Accepting

Most assignments in the church setting are for provision of interpreting during worship services. Before accepting the assignment, the interpreter should consider a few ethical questions such as the following:

1. Do I have the ability to accurately and efficiently interpret the service?

2. Is this denomination different, or is it similar to what I am used to interpreting?

3. If this church's doctrine and theology is different than my own, will my biases interfere with the integrity of the message?

4. Are there any potential conflicts or boundary issues with the consumers (deaf and hearing individuals are considered consumers)?

5. Will I have adequate preparation time before the day of the worship service?

Only assignments with which the interpreter feels comfortable and competent should be accepted.

Accepting the Assignment

To get information that will enable the interpreter to better prepare for the upcoming service, he or she will need to ask some initial questions when services are requested by the church or parish.

1. What is the time and date of the event?

2. How long will the service run? (Consider using a co-interpreter if it is beyond 1½ to 2 hours long.)

3. How do people typically dress for the service, formal or casual?

4. Where is the church located? Can directions be given?

5. Who is the contact person upon arrival at the church? What is the contact person's cell phone number?

6. Will any rehearsals or earlier services be held that the interpreter may attend and view? Will materials be given (e.g., sermon, music, etc.)?

7. When can the interpreter obtain the bulletin, any special music, scripts, and the sermon?

8. Does the consumer have any special needs (e.g., low vision)?

9. What is the consumer's name?

10. What is the fee to be paid to the interpreter? Will it include travel reimbursement?

It is crucial to receive bulletins, music, and sermons in advance. The interpreter may need to be persistent in order to get these materials, but they will help with overall job performance. Also, keeping track of hours worked and request types (e.g., meeting or worship), like through an excel spreadsheet, may help the treasurer or committee with budget planning.

Many interpreters organize their preparation materials (bulletin, music sheets, etc.) in a three-ring notebook. This helps to ensure that sheets of paper do not fly off the music stand while interpreting. The interpreter can see the material more easily if it is enlarged to a 16-point or 20-point font and will be less likely to lose the place on the page. Different colored one-inch sticky notes placed on the materials can differentiate between music, prayers, creeds (e.g.,

Apostle's Creed), Scripture, and the sermon and make the materials more visible as the interpreter flips to the needed page. In addition, with these materials anchored in a notebook, the interpreter can be a little more at ease, knowing the materials are safeguarded from breezes.

Music Stand

The interpreter should request a music stand on which to place the bulletin, any notes (e.g. the 3-ring notebook), hymnal, or music sheets. The height of the stand may need to be adjusted so the interpreter can easily read these materials, yet not so high that it interferes with the interpreter's signing space. Some interpreters actually store a portable music stand in the trunk, just in case the church cannot provide one.

Worship Space

Architecture for sanctuaries varies greatly from one building to another. Where there is a commonality to some sanctuary layouts, some worship services are now being held in such locations as schools, store fronts, and movie theaters. Upon arrival, the interpreter must determine the best location to stand or sit in order for consumers to best utilize the interpreting services. If the church has experience with interpreters, then there will be a pre-determined location for the interpreter. Visual barriers that could prevent the consumer from seeing the interpreter (e.g. flags or banners) should be moved before the service begins. Some sanctuaries have one pulpit for both the laity and the clergy to share, while other sanctuaries have a lectern (for laity) and a pulpit (for clergy). The following is one common layout, where the Communion table is in front of the pulpit; however, it can either be in front of the pulpit or behind it.

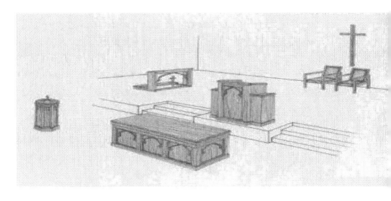

The following is another traditional sanctuary floor plan.

CHURCH FLOOR PLAN
EXAMPLE

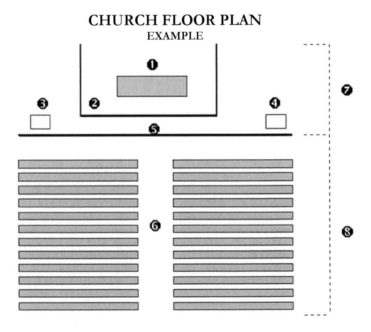

1. Communion table, most often called the altar.
2. Communion railing, also called the chancel railing, with provisions for kneeling.
3. Pulpit, used by clergy for gospel readings and sermons.
4. Lectern with Bible, used by lay readers for scripture readings.
5. Boundary between nave and sanctuary; usually the floor of the chancel is three steps higher than the floor of the nave. In Orthodox churches, the boundary may be in a slightly different location and may consist of a screen covered with icons.
6. Congregation. Western churches have pews, but in most Orthodox churches the congregation still stands.
7. The sanctuary or chancel.
8. The nave, where the congregation sits.

An interpreter might be placed in front of the pulpit (3) or the lectern (4), after first consulting with consumers.

More and more churches have websites. This is a great resource, with pictures of the worship space that will enable the practitioner to assess the space ahead of time. Upon arrival on the premises, there may be certain spaces in the sanctuary that are considered sacred, and clergy may be the only individuals to enter them. Interpreters must respect these sacred spaces. There may be occasions when negotiation with church officials becomes necessary so that clear message delivery can occur.

Is the interpreter supposed to stand or sit? Interpreters that were surveyed have given both answers. It is easier for the interpreter to more fully make use of the interpreting space, dance in place while interpreting a song, or take small steps to accentuate the message while standing. Deaf congregants sitting in the third row or further back will be able to better see the interpreter who is standing. Consumers should be consulted regarding their preferences; however, either is acceptable.

Choice of Language

Before the assignment begins, it is advantageous for the interpreter to meet the consumer and assess the consumer's choice of language. Like hearing people, Deaf people's use of language varies due to influences of education and background. Language preference is predicated by several factors including age, ethnicity, region, education, gender, and context. Observation of the consumer's communication style enables the interpreter to better gauge where choice of language is on the language continuum.

During this language assessment, there are indicators the interpreter can observe in order to determine whether interpreting or transliterating is warranted. If the interpreter arrives to the assignment and finds consumers with various language styles (e.g. Signed English, Contact Sign, and ASL), the rule of thumb is to sign ASL. It is best to have one linguistic choice (e.g. ASL) and not try to code-switch (move back and forth between Signed English and ASL); this prevents the consumers from becoming confused. Some language and cultural indicators to look for are the following:

❑ The consumer's choice of syntax (English grammar or ASL grammar)

❑ Use of initialized signs continuously throughout the conversation (indicating Signed English)

❑ Has a sign name (indicates an ASL user)

❑ Use of a cochlear implant (may indicate Signed English)

❑ Mention of attendance at a Deaf residential school or having been mainstreamed in a public school

After the conclusion of the language assessment, consultation with the consumer can validate the interpreter's observation. An assertive consumer may even sign his or her language preference to the interpreter without being asked.

Meeting the Speaker

Interpreters will want to meet the speaker(s) who participate in the worship service. Interpreters usually interpret for liturgists, choir directors/music coordinators, and clergy. Participants not accustomed to having an interpreter might feel awkward at first or feel the need to speak more slowly for the interpreter. If this is the case, the interpreter may want to reassure the speaker that he or she is experienced with interpreting at a normal pace. Furthermore, the interpreter can ask if there are any changes in the liturgy, as well as where the speaker will stand when speaking[39]. Meeting the participants will enable the interpreter to be aware of the dynamics in the worship service.

---

[39] Some speakers remain at the lectern or pulpit, while some walk around. If the speaker does walk around while speaking, a gentle reminder not to walk in front of the sightline may be needed.

In essence, the interpreter is part of the worship team. The interpreter's role is as important as that of others who preside over the worship service. Consultation with the other speakers displays the interpreter's professionalism and models a commitment to the interpreting role in the service. Each member of the worship team has a critical role.

Conclusion of the Service

It is not uncommon for those who do not know sign language to come up and thank the interpreter. After all, sign language is a visual language that captivates many first-time onlookers. In contrast, if the assignment did not go well for some reason, saying farewell is still a dignified professional behavior that the interpreter should exhibit.

Interpreters should not be surprised if feedback is given by the consumer; in fact, a new interpreter might want to ask for feedback. Feedback may include additional signs to add to the lexicon, encouragement to continue as an interpreter, and/or helpful resources (e.g., newsletter or church directory) to educate the interpreter with the congregation's psychodynamics. It is best for the interpreter to accept the feedback gracefully in the hope it will be of some benefit.

Reflection is a helpful process that enables the interpreter to monitor professional growth. The interpreter may want to keep a journal, which can help pinpoint ambiguous concepts, difficulties during the service (e.g., not being able to hear), and unfamiliar words or signs. Study and reflection can help the interpreter to reduce future errors and mistakes. Writing in a journal assists the interpreter to better understand the work and helps to monitor professional development. In addition, consultation with colleagues is another reflection technique that some interpreters engage in within their community. Internet message boards are helpful, too (e.g. Yahoo groups). All interpreters will benefit from reflection.

Summary

An assessment of the intricate tasks of an interpreting assignment is the ethical responsibility of the interpreter. Preparation for the assignment includes communication, organization, and coordination with others involved in the service. Faith-based reasons for accepting the interpreting assignment ought to be secondary, with professional competency to do the job effectively the primary consideration. Interpreting in church settings is usually fulfilling for the interpreter, who helps to fill a communications void and enables spiritual growth for those who benefit from professional interpreting services. Often, interpreters feel interpreting is a ministry, which it is, and an important contribution to the church.

Chapter 5 - Intricacies of Interpreting

This chapter is an introduction to the background information about interpreting that is important for practitioners to know. Here we will begin to lay the foundation for the knowledge portion of religious interpreting in addition to offering pointers for skill development.

Gaining Knowledge & Mastering Language Skills

In order for the message to be understood, analyzed, and delivered to consumers, working inter-preters must have language fluency in ASL and English. Language in itself is only part of the framework for interpreters. Furthermore, interpreting involves an intrinsic process that incorporates cognitive abilities and dexterity. The ability to combine skills and knowledge, along with being bilingual and bicultural, is a must for a successful interpreter.

Effective interpreters must have an extensive English vocabulary and repertoire of signs. Just imagine driving a car on two wheels; eventually the car will flip over and crash because vehicles must drive on four wheels. Likewise, interpreters must be fluent in both languages, or they risk "crashing."

Professionals in all industries rely on informational resources, and this is particularly true for sign language interpreters. A few helpful resources for interpreters working in religious settings are as follows:

1. American Sign Language Dictionary: Unabridged Edition (1998) by Martin Sternberg.

2. 601 Words You Need to Know to Pass Your Exam (2005) by Murray Bromberg and Julius Liebb.

3. Westminster Dictionary of Theological Terms, 2nd Ed (2014) by Donald McKim.

4. Holman Illustrated Bible Dictionary (2003) by editors: Butler, Brand, Draper, and England.

5. Interpretation SKILLS: English to American Sign Language (1993) by Marty M. Taylor, Ph.D.

6. SO YOU WANT TO BE AN INTERPRETER? 4th ed. (2007) by Janice H. Humphrey and Bob Alcorn.

7. Deaf Ministry: Ministry Models for Expanding the Kingdom of God (2015) by Leo Yates, Jr.

These resources, though not exhaustive, will benefit new and seasoned interpreters alike. Online resources such as ASLPro.com might be helpful as well. Having extra-linguistic knowledge is imperative for interpreters who work in specialized fields like religion.

Sign Language

ASL is a visual-gestural language composed of handshapes and hand movements. Each sign has five general *parameters* (characteristics):

1. Handshape
2. Orientation (palm)
3. Location
4. Movement
5. Facial expressions

A common sentence structure in ASL is *topicalization*. This is used when the object of the sentence is at the beginning.

ASL: ALL SIN, GOD FORGIVES.
English: God forgives all sins.

Another frequently used sentence structure is *rhetorical questions*; these are similar to questions, yet are statements.

ASL: JEREMIAH FRUSTRATED, WHY? HE
    FEEL OVERWHELMED.
English: Jeremiah is frustrated because he is
    overwhelmed.

When a subject precedes a verb and ends with where, what, why, or who, it is a *Wh-question*.

ASL: ISRAELITES TRAVELED, WHERE?
English: Where did the Israelites travel?

If a reference to time is part of the sentence, then the *time marker* is signed at the beginning. This is a TIME + SUBJECT + VERB sentence structure.

ASL: 33AD, JESUS CRUCIFIED, DIED & BURIED.
English: Jesus was crucified, died, and buried in 33AD.

These are only a few of many sentence structure examples in ASL.

When users of ASL communicate, they typically leave out articles (the, a, an) and the verb "to be" (is, are). Grammatical rules for ASL leave out these two linguistic features. When one does sign an article or a "to be" it is for purposes of specificity.

Non-manual signs (certain facial expressions) and classifiers (specific handshapes) are part of ASL. Classifiers and non-manual signs are used as adjectives and adverbs (descriptors), which provide clarity to the concept or idea being signed.

EXAMPLES OF ASL CLASSIFIERS

Language users can borrow words from another language; this typically occurs because there is no equivalent sign or word in the user's native language. An example of no equivalent sign is the word BANK. There is no common sign in ASL for BANK, so most users will fingerspell the word. According to the rules of fingerspelling, it is acceptable to borrow from written English for communication purposes. ASL users not only borrow from written forms of language, but also borrow signs from other sign languages. Examples of loan signs from other sign languages are the newer signs for JAPAN, ITALY, and RUSSIA.[xxi]

Enthusiasts have the option to learn ASL online at a website such as ASL University at www.lifeprint.com. One insightful and informative book on linguistics is <u>LINGUISTICS of American Sign Language: An Introduction, 4th Ed</u> (2005) by Clayton Valli and Ceil Lucas. Learning the linguistics of ASL is highly recommended for interpreters who wish to become certified. An easy-to-read book for students who want to learn ASL is by authors, Barbara Bernstein Fant, Betty Miller, and Lou Fant titled, <u>The American Sign Language Phrase Book</u>[xxii] However, the best way to learn ASL is still conversing with Deaf and ASL users or in a formal educational setting and immersing oneself in the culture.

Signed English is a model of the English language, not intended to represent the mechanics of the language, but to produce sign words and markers of what is spoken. Generally, Signed English follows the rules of English grammar. Users of Signed English may have attended an oral school, were mainstreamed (attended a public school), or perhaps learned it after a progression of hearing loss. ASL and Signed English share many of the same lexicons of signs, but are distinguished mostly by syntax and culture. In addition, Signed English includes the heavy use of initialized signs, whereas ASL relies on these much less frequently. English is the native language for many Signed English users.

Contact signing, traditionally known as Pidgin Signed English (PSE), is another language-based system that uses features from both ASL and English. A variety of people, Deaf and hearing, use contact signing as a mode of communication. Contact signing features signing in an English word order, English words uttered on the mouth, fingerspelling, the use of non-manual signs, and body shifting. The system borrows lexical items from ASL and Signed English.[xxiii]

General Knowledge

Beyond reading books or journals, many professionals enroll in college classes in order to further their education. Students explore various subjects when they enroll in general studies classes (e.g. English, psychology, political science, humanities, etc.) at a community college or university. This higher education enables interpreters to work more effectively in numerous settings. Those who have not been in school for many years can start out as special students and take only one class just to get their feet wet.

Enrollment in classes such as public speaking, English, or a class in one's discipline (i.e. your religion) will improve the interpreter's language – this is imperative for working interpreters. Professionals across the board now enroll in online college classes to take classes from home or at work to make education a little more convenient. It cannot be overstated; higher education is imperative for professionals in this industry.[40]

---

[40] Earning a higher education has helped me immensely as an interpreter. The general knowledge that I learned from my college classes and graduate level classes enables me to think critically, and, thus, to better analyze the discourse to be interpreted. When I first went back to college, I went with trepidation. I felt I did not have an adequate high school education and knowledge to enter college level classes. After all, it had been a number of years since I graduated from high school. To my surprise, the whole process was not as bad as I anticipated. There is a support system in place at most colleges, which includes advising, testing, tutoring, and counseling.

Interpreters also attend interpreting related workshops/seminars and conferences in order to improve upon their knowledge and skills (and meet CEU requirements). These interpreting workshops, seminars, and conferences provide opportunities to network and consult with other colleagues in the field. RID approved workshops, seminars, and conferences are listed on RID's website.[41] All interpreters need improvement in some area(s) of their work, and continued education is an essential approach to improvement.

It is also helpful for the interpreter to keep up with current events. Familiarity with the latest news and trends prepares the interpreter for moments when they are mentioned during a sermon, Sunday school class, or in casual conversations. People keep up with daily news by reading the newspaper in print or online, by watching the news, by reading magazines such as *Time* or *Newsweek*, and by listening to National Public Radio (NPR) while driving. Knowledge of what is going on in the world keeps the interpreter one step ahead.

Interpreting Models

The profession has adopted *interpreting models,* also known as *interpreting philosophies,* for interpretation. The interpreter's responsibility is to accommodate the psychodynamics of the congregation. The interpreter is supposed to use each model according to conditions surrounding the assignment. After choosing the model,

---

[41] RID approved workshops are located at www.rid.org.

the interpreter is able to draw upon the model and apply it to the work.

Interpreters, in whatever setting, are ethically obligated to be prudent as they determine which model[xxiv] is to be applied. Each model is briefly described here:

❑ The *Helper model* of interpreting involves concepts of pity, dependency, and paternalism. It can foster dependency, inhibit identity development, and alienate Deaf and hard of hearing participants from communicating directly with their hearing peers. [Use of this model has a tendency to disempower the Deaf person. One might possibly use this model with a Deaf person who has developmental disabilities.]

❑ In the *Conduit/Machine model* of interpreting, an interpreter conveys information from one language to another without any personal or cultural context. [With this model, the deaf consumer has already been acculturated into hearing culture and generally needs no cultural mediation.]

❑ In a *Bilingual-Bicultural model* (bi bi) of interpreting, cognitive processing between both English and ASL is required by the interpreter for semantic equivalency. [For example, if the Deaf person describes light flashing when the phone rang, the interpreter will either filter that by saying, "When the phone rang, I answered it." or add in, "When the strobe light signal flashed— that's a notification device—I answered the TTY."]

❑ In the *Ally model* of interpreting for adults, decisions about interpreting are made within the social and political culture surrounding Deaf and hard of hearing adults. The interpreter needs to make a conscious effort to be aware of power imbalances in the religious setting. [For instance, the interpreter will point it out to the hearing consumer if the Deaf person is being marginalized and not treated equally.]

Typically, interpreters use the conduit and the bilingual/bicultural (bi bi) more frequently than other models. If the helper model is used, caution and additional consideration are needed.[42] New interpreters should become familiar not only with these four models, but with other available interpreting models as well. Exposures to what other professionals do will help diversify the interpreter's possible choices even more.

The four models are from the Education Interpreting Performance Assessment ® (EIPA).[43] EIPA established these guidelines for educational interpreters; however, religious interpreters may wish to consider adoption of these philosophies as well.

---

[42] Interpreters that plan to take the computerized test (knowledge section) for the NIC ought to be familiar with four models: helper, conduit (machine), communication facilitator, and bilingual and bicultural (bi bi).
[43] EIPA Diagnostic Center at Boys Town Research Hospital in Omaha, Nebraska, developed the EIPA for interpreters in educational settings in the early 1990s. Permission by Brenda Schick is granted for this citation.

Before the establishment of RID, the helper model was the philosophy that most volunteers and amateurs used. Pioneers who established RID believed the helper model oppressed and subsequently influenced the exclusion of Deaf people from the dominant culture. The helper model is less commonly used; however, none of the models are to be discarded because each model serves a purpose. The interpreter determines which is the most suitable for any given situation.[44]

Interpreting Process

Outside the United States, a number of countries view interpreters as professionals. Great Britain considers British Sign Language (BSL) interpreting a legitimate profession that meets the communications need of Deaf and hearing parties. One British city government recognizes the intensive work by interpreters. An online article posted by the Bradford city government in the U.K. briefly summarizes the interpreting process.

The Interpreting Process
Sign language interpreters may look very active with their hands, but in actual fact most of the hard work is going on in their heads. They have to listen carefully, watch for the

---

[44] Some religious interpreters I have met (certainly not all) seem to follow the helper philosophy. The helper model includes a paternalistic attitude that wrongfully stigmatizes the deaf population. From my observation, the majority of the deaf community do not see themselves as having a disability; instead, they view communication to be the barrier, not their hearing loss.

message, extract the meaning and then find an appropriate way to express this in the second language.

As with any other interpreted language, every English word doesn't necessarily have a corresponding sign in BSL and each language has its own grammatical structure. The interpreting process involves expressing the same meaning using a different vocabulary and grammatical structure. This means

❑ Only ONE message can be interpreted at a time. [This condition is a challenge for practitioners when interpreting music that has two different lyrics sung simultaneously.]

❑ Interpreting requires intense concentration and can be very tiring. At top speed interpreters may be processing up to 20,000 words per hour. The recommended time for interpreting is 20 minutes. Interpreters can work longer than this, but over long periods the quality of the interpretation will suffer. [Some worship services and church programs extend beyond two hours. Interpreters should strongly consider working with a team in these situations.]

❑ For meetings and events longer than 2 hours at least two interpreters are necessary. [Ninety minutes is becoming the norm to have a team.]

❑ The mental processing takes time, and there will be a delay as the message passes from one language to another.[xxv]

As stated in the online article, the interpreter's mental faculties begin to deteriorate from peak performance after twenty minutes. Interpreters must have mental agility in order for the interpreting process to be optimal. In addition, RID encourages interpreters to work as a team when the length of a worship service goes beyond one and a half to two hours.

Simultaneous and Consecutive Interpreting

Most interpreters perform simultaneous interpreting, also known as real-time interpreting, for consumers. When simultaneous interpreting occurs, the interpreter begins to produce the message in the target language a few seconds, generally three to eight, after the speaker begins. This *lag time* is needed for the interpreter to comprehend, analyze, and then produce the communicated message. If the interpreter does not allow sufficient time to elapse after the speaker begins, the interpreter may need to make corrections to the delivered message because insufficient information was not first accumulated. In contrast, when music is to be sung or signed by the congregation, the lag time for simultaneous interpreting is usually shorter.

Consecutive interpreting involves a pause or a break between language conversions. First the interpreter listens to the source language, usually a phrase or passage, and then the speaker pauses, so the practitioner can interpret the message into the target language. It is not surprising that some interpreters may feel pressure or anxiety when performing consecutive interpreting. This is because the speaker's long and possibly detailed message may result in accidental deletions by the interpreter. An accidental deletion may occur when the interpreter reaches process capacity in his or her short-term memory.[xxvi]

Even though some spoken language interpreters might do consecutive interpreting more often, there are occasions that sign language interpreters do it as well.

An example might be when foreign missionaries share testimonies with congregations; or if the church has a ministry for immigrants, the interpreter may be asked to interpret a meeting with a Deaf immigrant, a translator, or a member of a ministry team.

Language Register

An interpreter needs to recognize the *language register* from the source language in order to produce the correct register for the target language. *Register* is the variation of a language, signed or spoken, that is normally used for a specific purpose or a social setting. For instance, when preaching a sermon, the preacher will normally use a formal register. This is recognized by grammatically correct choices, use of a higher vocabulary, and one-way participation (where the minister is the only person communicating).

There are five general classifications that language is assigned to, and each classification has a low degree and a high degree. Language registers most commonly used are: xxvi

❑ **Frozen:** Printed unchanging language such as bible quotations. [Examples: Scripture, creeds, and hymns]

❑ **Formal:** One-way participation, no interruption. Technical vocabulary; exact definitions are important. Includes introductions between strangers. [Examples: Sermons, pastoral prayers, and some teaching]

❑ **Consultative:** Two-way participation. Background information is provided — prior knowledge is not assumed. [Examples: Litanies, announcements, Bible study, and pastoral counseling]

❑ **Casual:** In-group friends and acquaintances. No background information is provided. [Examples: Study groups, fellowship, and prayer groups]

❑ **Intimate:** Non-public. Intonation is more important than wording or grammar. Private vocabulary. [Example: Prayer partner]

Distinguishing the appropriate register enables the interpreter to produce an equivalent and coherent message. Language registers usually vary according to context. Using an example of a worship service, a minister will greet the congregation using a formal register.

Formal	**Casual**
Good morning	Wuz up

Again, within the context of worship, here is an example of a register that is consultative.

Consultative (this example is of a litany)
Leader: We are here to praise the Lord.
People: We praise the Lord.
Leader: It is right to give thanks.
People: We give thanks to the Lord.

The interpreter's competency is expanded when he or she is able to maneuver among registers.

Linguistic Expansion

Whatever *modality* of language is being interpreted (signed, spoken, or written), the interpreter will eventually face the circumstance of not having an equivalent word or sign (gloss) for the target language. This occurrence is common in all languages (i.e. translating from written Hebrew to written English). When there is no equivalent sign or word in the target language, the concept can be expressed by *using a phrase of words or signs.* Normally, this will not be a problem if the interpreter is not glossing or shadowing the source language (interpreting word for word).[xxvii]

It is acceptable to establish a temporary sign (create a new symbol) when a sign is not available, but it must be agreed upon between two or more language users. When a term or a name is repeated throughout a discourse, ASL users usually set up a sign for it. *Iconic* signs (a sign resembling the word) are typically formed more often than *arbitrary* signs (a sign *not* having any resemblance to the word). For example, there is no standardized sign for Jesus' earthly father, Joseph. The temporary sign MARY HUSBAND might be established to denote Joseph throughout a discourse.

Morphological rules (a subfield of linguistics) state when two signs are combined to make a *compound sign*, a new meaning will emerge.[xxviii] For instance, the sign PURPLE combined with the sign SPOT creates the sign BRUISE. When the interpreter processes the source language, and realizes there is no equivalent meaning in the target language, he or she might be able to express the idea through use of a compound sign. One theological term that this technique can be applied to is *repentance.* In its simplest form, *repentance* means to be sorry and to change one's ways. If the sign for SORRY and the sign for CHANGE are combined, the sign REPENT is created. In a sense, the interpreter is expanding his or her repertoire of signs.

Another linguistic rule that assists interpreters is *lexical borrowing*. This rule implies that a word can be borrowed from another language. Frequently, this is seen when the user fingerspells or signs a word from another language because there is not a gloss rendition in ASL.

ASL incorporates the use of *acronyms*. Acronyms are abbreviated letters of a full word. In both English and ASL, acronyms are used quite often. When a hearing person writes the name of a state onto an envelope, such as 'CA' (for California), an abbreviation is used. Some acronyms in ASL have been naturally inherited over decades. 'SS' (social security) and 'TH' for townhouse are common acronyms, and they are generally context specific. When the interpreter sets up an acronym for the first time, the full word is to be fingerspelled (i.e. Book of Revelation = REV), followed by the acronym.

New interpreters are encouraged to consult with ASL users beforehand in order to include these features (sign choices). In some cases, there may already be signs established by the consumer.

Expansion Techniques

Professor Shelly Lawrence[45] presented seven expansion techniques during a Conference of Interpreters' Trainers (CIT) conference. [46] These techniques enable interpreters and users of ASL to elaborate (unpack) subjects and concepts, and subsequently to give the message a deeper meaning. This is accomplished by using ASL features of location, space, height, and depth.[xxix]

1. **Contrasting**: This feature highlights an idea by juxtaposing two <u>opposite</u> ideas in order to emphasize one of them. For example, in English we might say, *"The Israelites worship the One True God."* Using the contrast feature in ASL can produce, *"Pagans worship various gods, and the Israelites worship the One True God."* With the addition of this contrasting idea, the original premise is emphasized. Sometimes this is done by stating the positive, then the negative (i.e., what something *is*, followed by what it *isn't*). Other times, the reverse occurs (i.e., a negative is followed by a positive).

2. **Faceting**: Faceting describes a feature whereby several different signs are given sequentially to express one idea more clearly. Although sever-

---

[45] The expansion system is borrowed by permission from Shelly Lawrence's 1996 and 2003 papers.
[46] Readers are recommended to read the full version in its entirety. It can be acquired by purchasing the CIT 1994 Proceedings journal through CIT's website. The URL is www.cit-asl.org.

al signs are used, this feature actually narrows a concept to a more exact or specific image. The use of faceting often seems to cluster around the use of adjectives or adverbs. The multiple signs used in faceting, however, all serve to guide the viewer in a particular direction. The idea of *redemption*, for example, can be produced in ASL by signing: FORGIVE, LOVE, REC-ONCILE.

3. **Reiteration**: Reiteration refers to signs that are repeated in a text exactly the same way as they were initially stated. That is, a sign or signs are used again, reiterated, within a passage. It appears that reiteration implies emphasis: that something is important to the storyline, has cultural significance, or has high emotional impact to the signer. For the purpose of emphasis, it seems that adjectives and adverbs are used and repeated. For instance, in English: *The Israelites traveled in the desert.* In ASL: WALK, JEWISH PEOPLE WALK DESERT.

4. **Utilizing 3-D Space:** Space is utilized to set up nouns that later get replaced with pronouns (referential space); space is also used to describe proximal relationships (topographical space). Moreover, because Deaf people view the world primarily through their eyes, visual description and detail is an important component of ASL discourse. Classifiers are one way visual information is conveyed. When looking at a whole utterance, space is used meaningfully to create cohesion in the text (spatial mapping). For instance, during a Scripture reading, cities are sometimes mentioned. Utilizing 3-D space can establish markers when cities are mentioned.

5. **Explaining by examples:** Another feature of ASL is to explain by the use of an example. If a term needs to be defined or a concept needs to be clarified, it is done by using many examples. In English, if a term needs to be explained, the initial approach would be to define the word; to say it in other words. In ASL however, a list of examples would follow the idea that requires explanation. In ASL, forming signs: PRAY, READ SCRIPTURE, SING will indicate the English word for *worship*.

6. **Couching or scaffolding**: "Couching" or "scaffolding" occurs by virtue of the differences between the two languages. One way ASL can expand vocabulary is to explain an item or give foundation or support to a concept. This can be done in a variety of ways that may include 3D space, explaining by example, contrasting, or by simply explaining the concept. An example of this is *Jeremiah is a prophet. A prophet, called by God, speaks to the king and the people. Sometimes, a prophet predicts future events.*

7. **Describe, then Do**: The "Describe, then Do" feature can be observed when the signer shifts from a narrative style of discourse to direct style of discourse or from narrator to character. This occurs when an action or situation is described, then "acted out" with the use of a perspective shift. In English: *I left for church.* In ASL: I LOCK HOUSE - DOOR. I IN CAR AND DRIVE. I GO CHURCH.

Initially, new interpreters will have to visualize, experiment, and practice these features. Some techniques may be used more than others; however, each method will help the interpreter to produce a clearer and crisper message. Also, the opposite can be done by applying *compression techniques* by filtering a part of the message.

Errors and Omissions

Novice interpreters, as well as experienced interpreters, will have moments when an omission occurs. An omission is when part of the message (sentence, phrase, or concept) cannot be interpreted because it was not heard, understood, or retained. This frequently happens to new interpreters because of inexperience, distraction (emotional or environmental), and/or lack of concentration. The interpreter may feel a sense of panic but must keep his or her composure. Loss of composure may cause the consumer to lose confidence in the interpreter's ability.

Interpreters, first and foremost, are human. Interpreters cannot interpret one hundred percent of everything that is signed or spoken. There will be times when the interpreter misunderstands the speaker and interprets the wrong information. When the interpreter realizes there was a misinterpreted message, the most responsible (and ethical) thing to do is to repair the mistake. Consumers depend on the interpreter to produce the message accurately, and it is the interpreter's duty to recover the message.

One example is a situation that happened during a Christmas Eve service. The interpreter thought she heard the preacher say that Jesus ordered all the male babies two and under to be killed, and that is what she interpreted. Moments later, she realized she had corrupted the information. She corrected it with the right information (King Herod ordered the massacre, not Jesus). For her to leave uncorrected the first message that Jesus gave the order would have been detrimental to the entire sermon, as well as possibly damaging to the consumers' spiritual faith. No doubt, the interpreter made the right choice when she corrected the message.

Monitoring

Part of the process of interpreting includes self-monitoring by the interpreter. This important aspect of the process enables the interpreter to recognize potential problems and identify contributing factors that affect one's work. Once the interpreter is aware of hindrances, then adjustments can be made to lessen or eliminate them. Below is a short list of what to monitor when interpreting from English to ASL.

❑ Ensure the consumer's sightline is clear so the interpreter can be seen.

❑ The interpreter must be able to hear the speaker so there are no misunderstandings.

❑ Continue to match the speaker's register, and adjust the interpretation if needed.

❑ Look for acknowledgments, either a head nod or smile, to be sure that what the interpreter produces is being understood by the consumer. [During a natural break or pause, if no indication is seen, it is appropriate to consult with the consumer.]

❑ Articulate the message clearly.

❑ The interpreter must be aware of his or her own feelings so the delivered message is not accidentally contaminated.

❏ Form signs and movements so that they flow naturally and consistently.

❏ Watch for possible environmental intrusions, such as lights being turned down or a procession in the middle of the sightline.

This partial list is a good start. In addition, if the interpreter is working with a co-interpreter, both interpreters can work together to monitor the work.

When interpreting from ASL to English, part of the same list will be included as part of the self-monitoring process.

❏ Project your voice for the audience to hear.

❏ Speak clearly and naturally, so the Deaf person's affect is being matched by the interpreter.

❏ Omit filler words such as, "um." [i.e. "Um, today's Scripture, um, is from, um, Psalm 23. Um…"]

❏ Recover or repair the interpretation when needed.

For additional guidance, the interpreter can read over the certification rating scales on RID's website.[47] Even if the interpreter does not feel ready to take the certifi-

---

[47] The rating scales are located at www.rid.org. This outline helps the interpreter know what to prepare for when taking the NIC test.

cation exam, the rating scale is a helpful guide for understanding what is expected from interpreters in the profession.

Mentoring

Practical experience is one of the best tools for learning how to interpret. A mentor can provide invaluable insight and guidance for the new interpreter. Techniques, additional vocabulary, and feedback are just a few of the benefits that are gained from a mentor. Along with this, mentors can assist in fostering self-discovery and awareness so the mentee can realize why he/she makes certain linguistic choices. Many professions require some type of apprenticeship for new professionals who enter the field, and the interpreting profession is no exception to this standard.[48]

For some novice interpreters, mentors may be hard to come by because of geographical and/or time constraints. Some professional interpreters are unwilling to step into the world of religious interpreting for fear they will be stereotyped[49], or they lack expertise (background knowledge), or they are inexperienced in this type of setting.

Some affiliated chapters of RID keep a list of interpreters who mentor new interpreters. Today's

---

[48] The Standard Practice Paper: Mentoring is worth reading. It is at www.rid.org.

[49] Some interpreters (emphasizing only *some*) look down on religious interpreters for what they perceive to be lack of skill and competency, failure to follow the same professional standards (CPC), and accepting work before one is qualified.

technology allows for professional mentoring to occur from remote locations and even across different time zones. With web conferencing, for example, you can upload short video streams of your work and get feedback through email, phone and/or instantly through a video conversation through Skype or Face-time. One-on-one human contact and working as a team is the primary approach for mentors and mentees, because of the role modelling, immediate feedback from work, and the safety net that mentees have when working with a mentor. As stated in chapter two (Skill Development), Signs of Development offers virtual mentoring. The website is www.signs-of-development.org/website/paceM.html .

The National Consortiusm of Interpreter Education Centers (NCEIC) offers **The Mentorship Toolkit** on its website. The Mentorship Toolkit includes activities, articles, videos, rubrics for evaluating performances, and other resources – a wealth of helpful information. There is no reason why a mentor and a mentee cannot establish a relationship over the phone and the Internet. The Mentorship Toolkit is located at www.interpretereducation.org/aspiring-interpreter/mentorship/mentoring-toolkit/.

Goals and Objectives

Every interpreter is different, and needs vary according to strengths and weaknesses. In chapter 1, the QAS list of competencies are listed, which can be areas to work on. Along with these competencies, several goals to consider working on are:

Signing:

- ❏ ASL/Sign vocabulary
- ❏ Structuring space
- ❏ Grammar
- ❏ Fluency and affect
- ❏ Clarity of signs

English:

- ❏ English vocabulary
- ❏ Eloquence of speech
- ❏ Fluency and affect
- ❏ Clarity

Message:

- ❏ Message content (is it equivalent)
- ❏ Message matches speaker's register
- ❏ Interpreting process
- ❏ Appropriate body composure

When working on goals, one or two (no more than three) can be worked on at one time. Self-assessment by the mentee, which can be guided by the mentor, is highly encouraged.

Work done with a mentor can help the new interpreter considerably. The mentor's experiences, specific[50] and effective[51] feedback, and a reasonable

---

[50] *Specific feedback* is what new interpreters need to be proficient. An example is, "Your fingerspelling was not produced correctly. When you produce the letter 'e' it is to look like this."

amount of encouragement are what the mentee should expect from a mentor. Obviously, the new interpreter needs a mentor with professional experience. The mentee will also want someone who can analyze work in an honest and objective manner. Humility on the part of the mentee is necessary when hearing feedback. Some mentors prefer to charge a fee when they share their expertise, while others will not charge the new interpreter/IEP student because they see it as a professional obligation. Mentoring is crucial because it will help form a foundation for the budding interpreter.[52] Being mentored at the beginning of an interpreting career is the most responsible approach.

Team Interpreting

One or more interpreters can share the responsibility of a worship service, Sunday school/Bible study session, and other church-related activities. When the context and content of the interpreting assignment are complex, or when the assignment is over sixty or ninety minutes, working as a team[53] is highly recommended. Teamwork helps to lessen the risk of developing

---

[51] *Effective feedback* integrates specific information for improvement, along with acknowledgment of what is signed or interpreted correctly. Generally, there should be balance in the discussion between the interpreter's strengths and weaknesses. It is also beneficial if the mentor guides the mentee to assess his or her own work.

[52] My own mentoring experience has evolved. There was a sense of intimidation I used to feel when meeting or working with my mentors; however, most of my mentors had a way of making me feel at ease. The expanded learning I received from mentoring is priceless.

[53] RID provides a Standard Practice Paper that is a helpful guide for team interpreters. It is at www.rid.org.

cumulative motion injury, which is common for interpreters who work alone for long periods of time.[54]

During a worship service, team interpreters can switch off every fifteen to thirty minutes, or they can divide parts of the service between themselves. While one interpreter is interpreting, the other will support, monitor, and provide (*feed*) missed information. The working relationship between the two interpreters should include communication, trust, mutual respect, flexibility, and support. Essentially, both interpreters will work in some fashion the entire time.

One instrument for communication for team interpreters is a writing journal. Used as a professional log, a journal is helpful for discussion purposes after the service; what worked well and suggestions for next time can be written down. Interpreters can feel support through written dialogue; moreover, it underscores teamwork between professionals. Another instrument is the cell phone, in which team interpreters text one another feedback.

---

[54] Interpreters are encouraged to maintain healthy working standards. For more information, RID publishes a Standard Practice Paper on cumulative motion injury. It is located at www.rid.org.

EXAMPLE OF TEAM COMMUNICATION

11am – 11:15am I'm glad you started. I felt I am not able to keep up with the announcements.

11:15am – 11:30am Ron has repeated 'it is well with your soul' four times. Instead of fingerspelling 'soul' lets set up a sign for it. By the way, I loved your version of the Lord's Prayer.

11:30am – 11:45am Thanks for feeding me the name, Jeremiah. I couldn't make out what he was saying. Glad you signed the song. I learned something from ya.

11:45am – 12pm He is using the term 'prophet' as messenger. Instead of signing prophet as foretelling the future, lets set up the sign 'messenger.'

When a service or event goes longer than two hours, some consumers wish not to pay for two interpreters. If the event is four hours, some unscrupulous requestors will hire one interpreter for the first two hours and hire the second interpreter for the last two hours. Obviously, if this occurs, it is not considered teaming. The attempt to cut costs actually undermines everyone involved. After an hour or so the interpreting process is already breaking down, which means more mistakes will come about, and the consumer may not receive the correct message. In addition, the second interpreter, who comes into the assignment unable to consult and prepare as professionals do, will be at a loss.

Unfortunately, some people also have misperceptions about Christian interpreters. Some Christians—sometimes the interpreters themselves—expect them to be martyrs and continue to interpret for hours on end with no relief.[55]

To promote a team approach, the interpreter must not only educate consumers and other participants that the integrity of the message will remain more intact (particularly when a service goes beyond an hour), but also must influence those in charge (usually a coordinator or the one who pays for the service) that Deaf ministry is a significant part of the overall mission of the church. Furthermore, a certain amount of flexibility and humility by the interpreters is needed, in part to build cohesion. Incorporation of an interpreting team can crack open a door of understanding for consumers. A team will help the congregation to understand that a cooperative approach is viable and necessary; it can help redefine standards of interpreting within religious settings. A professional service is being provided. Teamwork can help to establish an inclusive environ-

---

[55] I was once contracted to provide services at a revival that was hosted by a televangelist, and the requestor only scheduled two hours for my services. After two and half hours, the televangelist began the sermon; I informed the deaf consumers that I was unable to continue because of mental and physical exhaustion. While one consumer understood, the other abruptly responded by saying, "That's why I asked for Christian interpreters." Apparently, a Christian interpreter must have interpreted much longer than what is recommended, thus establishing a precedent for unhealthy and inappropriate professional standards. Interpreters, and those who follow some faith tradition, are not expected to work in abusive situations, and they should not – ever.

ment for all parties involved.[56]

Professional Development

As stated before, many interpreters learn the trade through an apprenticeship like program in their church. For those seeking further interpreting training, there are a few colleges and schools that offer more in-depth training. A few are

❑ Church Interpreter Training Institute (CITI) through Concordia Theological Seminary. The CITI program offers a summer course that covers a range of topics related to religious interpreting. Their website is www.ctsfw.edu.

❑ The organization, Deaf Missions, hosts Christian interpreters conference. Along with interpreting training, Deaf Missions offers other training through their Deaf Missions training center (Deaf ministry related). Their website is www.deafminissions.org.

❑ The Professional Christian Church Interpreters conference is held annually through the God's Hands Agency, Inc. in Orlando, FL. Their website is www.godshandsagency.com.

❑ RID, through their search function, lists workshops, as well as RID chapters (by state) where

---

[56] For additional reading about team interpreting, RID published an excellent resource titled, <u>Team Interpreting as Collaboration and Interdependence</u> by Jack Hoza (2010).

they too offer workshops and conferences. The website is www.rid.org.

Considering Humility

Interpreters often find themselves humbled in their work, perhaps due to the presence of other more experienced interpreters in the congregation, working with interpreters who are better skilled, or receiving feedback or criticism from consumers. In this work it is helpful to have some humility, in part because it helps to foster respect with consumers, the interpreting team, and other church staff. At times, the role of the interpreter can be misunderstood or undervalued; however, when the interpreter shows humility the potential for conflict can sometimes be avoided and negotiation and/or education (i.e., sharing of best practices) can take place.

Pride in our work does have a positive effect since it promotes self-confidence; the flip side to this notion is that when the interpreter has too much pride it can be a causal factor for interpersonal conflicts between the practitioner and his or her consumers, interpreting team, and/or church staff. Psychologically, a certain amount of ego is healthy, and balancing it with humility takes discipline. My advice: it is always better to take the road of humility.

Summary

Chapter five gives the interpreter a view of terms, processes, and approaches for work in church settings. Those who contemplate becoming interpreters ought to delve deeper into the art and science of interpreting.

There are still other facets of interpreting to be explored that are not covered in this book. Whether one studies independently by reading journals and textbooks or studies in a formalized venue, it is possible to learn the idiosyncrasies of language and interpreting.

ENDNOTES

xxi National Consortium of Interpreter Education Centers. (n.d.). *The Mentorship Toolkit*. Retrieved from www.interpretereducation.org/aspiring-interpreter/mentorship/mentoring-toolkit/.

Chapter 6 - Analysis & Application

Understanding content is a necessity for interpreters. Interpreters who do not understand content are not able to interpret effectively. In simple terms, interpreters cannot interpret what they do not understand. Chapter six addresses analysis techniques, which can be added to the interpreting tool belt; it is laid out according to the author's personal and professional approach for interpreting frozen text. Bear in mind that this interpretation is only one of several ways to approach frozen text.

Several parts of a worship service will incorporate frozen text, thus, the practitioner gains the advantage of preparation beforehand. A few schemes of frozen text are Scripture, music, prayers, creeds, and litanies (interactive text). Some frozen texts are a challenge for beginning interpreters. With the insight presented herein, however, the interpreter may be able to draw a roadmap to apply to the work.

To look deeper and study the semantics, the interpreter must carefully examine threads in a paragraph or words in a stanza. Often the practitioner must rely on a combination of textual resources and experience in order to produce a message equivalency in the target language.

Lectionary

The Revised Common Lectionary is a set of prescribed scriptural readings that are recommended for churches to read and/or preach upon. Within a three-year period, churches that use the lectionary will expose their congregations to the greater part of the Bible. Four biblical readings coinciding with the Liturgical Calendar[57] are recommended each week, including passages from the Old Testament, Gospel, and New Testament. At the conclusion of year C, the cycle returns to year A; thus, the scripture passages are repeated every three years. Interpreters who have a church that follow the lectionary are fortunate because they can prepare in advance. There are different lectionaries for different denominations, though, so practitioners will want to be sure to obtain the right one. The lectionary is optional; not all churches use it.

Commentaries

Most preachers, as they write their sermons, will read commentaries from biblical scholars. Commentaries provide background information, somewhat like footnote references; moreover, commentaries are the result of an exegesis (an in-depth study of a scriptural passage). Understanding sociopolitical conditions in biblical times offers readers an inside look into the

---

[57] The Liturgical Calendar consists of seasons that many churches subscribe to which, when followed, will begin with the season of Advent. The seasons are Advent, Christmas, ordinary time, Lent, Easter, Pentecost, and ordinary time. Feasts and/or festivals, such as Epiphany, All Saints Day, and Ascension Sunday, are celebrated during the particular church seasons.

circumstances surrounding the text that are not easily grasped from simply reading the passage.

Commentaries are published in a few different ways. One commentary may include in one volume a series of biblical books (i.e. Genesis, Exodus, Leviticus, Numbers, and Deuteronomy); another commentary may include all sixty-six books from the Bible; or in still another, only one biblical book. For sign language interpreting purposes, the interpreter can use commentaries as a resource to obtain additional information about the context of a passage or story.

Online commentaries are available, almost all of which offer much older information and do not include more recent discoveries (e.g. Dead Sea Scrolls) or insights gained within the last twenty years. One such website is www.bible.crosswalk.com. Crosswalk has access to concordances, various Bible translations, parallel Bibles, commentaries, and other useful features. The Matthew Henry Commentaries on the Whole Bible is a decent and somewhat in-depth resource that is available for free. Also, The Text This Week (www.textweek.com/scripture.htm) offers commentaries that are available through a Scripture search.

Some interpreters receive requests to provide services for Bible studies. Bible study goes much more in depth than what is read and preached during a worship service, and one should use all available resources prior to the Bible study. This is when a commentary would be useful as a primary resource, along with the use of secondary resources (e.g., parallel Bible, study Bibles, etc.).

Scripture

Each religion has its own terminology and phrase-ology. Understanding religious language usually takes a number of years; most new interpreters do not have that long. Near the end of this book is a short glossary, which includes some theological terms to assist new interpreters as they analyze biblical texts. Interpreters do not have to be at a loss when resources are available.

The practitioner needs to study the text to discern the main idea. The process of interpreting Scripture - that is, pulling back the layers to see the heart of the text's meaning - is called *exegesis*. Exegesis is primarily concerned with intentionality: What did the author intend his original readers to understand? What did the biblical author mean? Following are some areas of exegesis to keep in mind:

1. Survey the historical context in general.

2. Consider the broader biblical and theological contexts.

3. Consult secondary literature.

4. Become thoroughly acquainted with your para-graph or pericope (a selection from a text).

5. Analyze sentence structures and syntactical rela-tionships.

6. Analyze significant words.

7. Research the historical-cultural background.

Relationships, present or historical, are a significant point to remember about Scripture. Much of Scripture comes back to this point; whether it speaks of Yahweh (God) as He provides manna to the Hebrews in the desert, protects Daniel in the lion's den, or sends the Apostle Paul on missionary journeys, the text relates to the idea of relationships. When in doubt about the scriptural meaning, ask the minister or priest.

Parallel Bible

Whether one uses an online Bible or a book one can actually hold, one will need a method for seeing the surface level of the text. One helpful technique is to use a parallel Bible. Generally, four translations in one volume are preferred. The Bible translation to use typically depends on the church's preference. For example, in the United Methodist denomination, the New Revised Standard Version (NRSV) is commonly used throughout. A more fundamentalist church may prefer to use the King James Version (KJV) or New King James Version (NKJV).

Seeing the nuances in the translations[58] that biblical interpreters used for *specific words or ideas* can provide the interpreter a useful gloss equivalency, and better insight to the meaning of the text.

---

[58] These four translations are cited by permission by Zonderan Publishing. They come from the Today's Parallel Bible (2000).

Helpful Resources

Good resources to have when interpreting at church.

1. Parallel Bible – shows two or more translations, which can help clarify what the passage means, as well as provide alternative English words that can give possible sign glosses.

2. NIV Study Bible – footnotes can explain words, phrases, and themes.

3. Life Application Study Bible – can give personal application from the Scripture, which might be mentioned in a sermon.

4. Bible Commentary – will expound on the Scriptures, more than what Study Bible footnotes might provide.

5. Deaf Ministry – educates the interpreter to this specialized setting.

6. Bible Dictionary – helpful in explaining biblical, theological, ecclesiastical, and doctrinal words.

KJV	NIV	NLT	NASB
1 Kings 2:1-4	1 Kings 2:1-4	1 Kings 2:1-4	1 Kings 2:1-4
David's last words and death	*David's Charge to Solomon*	*David's Final Instructions to Solomon*	*David's Charge to Solomon*
2 Now the days of David drew nigh that he should die; and he charged Solomon his son, saying, 2I go the way of all the earth: be thou strong therefore, and shew thyself a man; 3And keep the charge of the LORD thy God, to walk in his ways, to keep his statutes, and his commandments, and his judgments, and his testimonies, as it is written in the law of Moses, that thou mayest prosper in all that thou doest, and whithersoever thou turnest thyself: 4That the LORD may continue his word which he spake concerning me, saying, If thy children take heed to their way, to walk before me in truth with all their heart and with all their soul, there shall not fail thee (said he) a man on the throne of Israel. * King James Version	**2** When the time drew near for David to die, he gave a charge to Solomon his son. 2 "I am about to go the way of all the earth," he said. "So be strong, show yourself a man, 3 and observe what the LORD your God requires: Walk in his ways, and keep his decrees and commands, his laws and requirements, as written in the Law of Moses, so that you may prosper in all you do and wherever you go, 4 and that the LORD may keep his promise to me: 'If your descendants watch how they live, and if they walk faithfully before me with all their heart and soul, you will never fail to have a man on the throne of Israel.' * New International Version	**2** As the time of King David's death approached, he gave his charge to his son Solomon: 2"I am going where everyone on earth must someday go. Take courage and be a man. 3Observe the requirements of the LORD your God and follow all his ways. Keep each of the laws, commands, regulations, and stipulations written in the law of Moses so that you will be successful in all you do and wherever you go. 4If you do this, then the LORD will keep the promise he made to me: `If your descendants live as they should and follow me faithfully with all their heart and soul, one of them will always sit on the throne of Israel.' * New Living Translation	**2** As David's time to die drew near, he charged Solomon his son, saying, 2"I am going the way of all the earth Be strong, therefore, and show yourself a man. 3"Keep the charge of the LORD your God, to walk in His ways, to keep His statutes, His commandments, His ordinances, and His testimonies, according to what is written in the Law of Moses, that you may succeed in all that you do and wherever you turn, 4so that the LORD may carry out His promise which He spoke concerning me, saying, 'If your sons are careful of their way, to walk before Me in truth with all their heart and with all their soul, you shall not lack a man on the throne of Israel.' * New American Standard Bible

As the interpreter compares the translations, it is important to begin with the subtitle and continue to the end of the scripture passage.

Chapter Title

At first glance, after the chapter title, one sees three distinct, yet similar titles. From this, one can infer that David is on his deathbed (KJV). It would be useful to read the chapter before, or even the introductory pages to the book, to gain a little background to better understand the content in chapter two. If one looks only at chapter two, it is uncertain if David was dying from old age, whether he was hurt in battle, or was terminally ill. It is only certain that David is at death's doorstep.

The title gives a glimpse of the content. At the time, it is likely that people were grieved at the thought of David dying. People were probably coming to see him so they could gain closure and say their good-byes. Everyone probably sensed the sad mood, especially David himself and his son, Solomon.

Even though the mood was distressed, it must have been a very important occasion for David and his family. David's son was receiving instructions (NLT) in order to continue his dynasty. Two of the titles state, "*David's Charge to Solomon.*" This indicates David transferred some type of responsibility to Solomon.

Verse 1

Beginning with verse one, the NLT informs readers that David is a king. This is significant. Again, the charge/instructions to be given from David's deathbed indicate he wants Solomon to continue the dynasty. No doubt, this scene is important because Solomon is to continue his royal responsibility for his father and for Israel.

Verse 2

What is interesting about verse two is how each translation uses the same word: "earth." The NLT clues us in a bit more to what David means. David is dying and will then return to "where everyone on earth must someday go." This resonates the common burial liturgy spoken at burial ceremonies, "…ashes to ashes, dust to dust…" We come from dust (remember Adam in Genesis), and we return to dust. David is referring to his impending death.

Verse 3

The list of various mandates (statutes, command-ments, ordinances, and testimonies) in the Law of Moses (NASB) strongly warns Solomon not to waiver in his faith and to stick close to God for instructions and guidance. Why? Because his faith will ensure that he (and Israel) are open to the Lord for direction. David's emphasis to the Law of Moses refers to Israel's covenant with God.

Verse 4

In all four translations, it is clear that David reminds Solomon of *God's promise* to keep the royal line in David's family. The NIV translation states that David instructs Solomon to be 100% faithful. The phrase, "…if they walk faithfully before me with all their heart and soul…" indicates every part of Solomon's life, as well as every part of his future descendants' lives, is to be dedicated to the Lord. It is clear that nothing less is acceptable.

Parallel Bible Conclusion

Talk about pressure! The family, present and future, and the country are riding on Solomon's shoulders. There is no way he can do it alone. To be able to carry such responsibility, Solomon will have to keep his faith at the forefront of his life.

The parallel Bible provides expanded awareness of what the text is stating. Each translation is important in its own right, yet when combined with the others, will magnify the meaning of the text. This tool gives insight to the scripture passage, which provides interpreters with a better understanding to aid in the work of interpreting.

Study Bible

A study Bible[59] is another asset. Footnotes, maps, charts, cross-references, and concordances are all in one volume, as if readers have a mini-library at their fingertips. Footnotes and cross-references are the primary source of information, while maps and charts provide secondary information. Do not disregard the maps; it is helpful when interpreting to have a mental image of where to sign placement markers of the city or cities mentioned in a scripture passage. A study Bible is a *must-have resource* for interpreters to analyze and understand the background to the scripture passage.

In the same passage (1 Kings 2:1-4), note how the footnotes enhance understanding of the passage:

---

[59] The *NIV Study Bible* (2002) is a good resource; I use this often.

2:1 *he gave a charge.* Moses (Dt 31:1-8), Joshua (Jos 23:1-16) and Samuel (1Sa 12:1-25), as representatives of the Lord's rule, had all given final instructions and admonitions shortly before their deaths.

2:2 *the way of all the earth.* To the grave (see Jos 23:14). *be strong.* See Dt 31:7, 23; Jos 1:6-7, 9, 18.

2:3 *observe what the Lord your God requires.* See Ge 26:5; Lev 18:30; Dt 11:1. *Walk in his ways.* A characteristic expression of Deuteronomy for obedience to covenant obligations (Dt 5:33; 8:6; 10:12; 11:22; 19:9; 26:17; 28:9; 30:16). *his decrees and commands, his laws and requirements.* Four generally synonymous terms for covenant obligations (see 6:12; 8:58; 2 Ki 17:37; Dt 8:11; 11:1; 26:17; 28:15,45; 30:10,16). *that you may prosper.* See Dt 29:9.

2:4 *that the Lord may keep his promise to me.* David here alludes to the covenanted promise of an everlasting dynasty given to him by God through Nathan the prophet (see notes on 2Sa 7:11-16). Although the covenant promise to David was uncondi-tional, individual participation in its blessing on the part of David's royal descendants was condi-tioned on obedience to the obligations of the Sinaitic covenant (see 2Ch 7:17022). *with all their heart and soul.* See Dt 4:29; 6:5; 10:12; 30:6. *you will never fail to have a man on the throne of Israel.* Both Solomon and his descend-ants fell short of their covenant obligations. This led to the division of the kingdom and eventually to the exile of both the northern and southern kingdoms. It was only in the coming of Christ that the fallen tent of David would be restored (see notes on Am 9:11-15; Ac 15:16) and the promise of David's eternal dynasty ultimately fulfilled. When the nation and its king turned away from the requirements of the Sinai covenant, they experienced the covenant curses rather than blessings; but in all this God remained faithful to his covenant promises to Abraham and to David (see Lev 26:42-45; Isa 9:6-7; 11:1-16; 16:5; 55:3; Jer 23:5-6; 30:9; 33:17, 20-22,25-26; Eze 34:23-24; 37:24-28).

The footnotes above shed light on the scripture passage to be examined. These references penetrate beyond the surface meaning presented in the parallel Bible.

Verse 1

At first glance, the chapter title is the premise in verse one. Read the footnote once more.

[**2:1** *he gave a charge.* Moses, Joshua and Samuel, as representatives of the Lord's rule, had given final instructions and admonitions shortly before their deaths.]

This reference places David with the great rulers over Israel. Furthermore, the reference states that Moses, Joshua, Samuel, and DAVID were representative of the Lord's rule. This emphasizes the authenticity of David's authority. Do not overlook the word *admonitions.* Admonition means warning – it is a key word here. One can gather from this and other references that David's message is genuine, and Solomon must adhere to it.

Verse 2

The same reference is seen in the parallel Bible. Read the reference once more: [*the way of all the earth.* To the grave.] As in the parallel Bible, the study Bible's footnote references imminent death. After reading the passage in Deuteronomy 31:7, one will read that when Moses was on his deathbed, he too exhorted Joshua (as he appointed him to be the next leader) to be strong and courageous.

Verse 3

The first footnote reference is transparent: to adhere to the Lord's command. The second reference:

[*Walk in his ways.* A characteristic expression of Deuteronomy for obedience to covenant obligations].

As in the parallel Bible notation, this indicates Israel's covenant with God. Read the following footnote reference:

[*his decrees and commands, his laws and requirements.* Four generally synonymous terms for covenant obligations.]

One can infer that the *covenant* is a significant point. The reference to Deuteronomy 29:9 for [*that you may prosper.*], also emphasizes that Israel will prosper; it will receive God's favor by keeping the covenant.

Verse 4

Reading the footnotes for verse four, God's promise to David that his family will remain on the throne is dependent upon his descendants" observance. The reference foretells that David's descendants will fall short and thus lead to Israel's division into two kingdoms. The inevitable failure by David's descendants should not be revealed in the interpreted message, however, because there is no hint of it in the scripture passage. Rather it can be extra-linguistic knowledge.

One Version

After studying the scriptural passage, the interpreter now has an idea where the discourse is headed. Key concepts from the passage are as follows:

❑ David's death is imminent

❑ Solomon will become the new king (an inference)

❑ David instructs and cautions Solomon

❑ God promises that David's lineage will remain in power as long as his descendants keep God's covenant

With these in mind, the following is a demonstration of role-shifting to distinguish a narrator and the role of David. The interpreter imagines being in the shoes of the biblical character. When David's lines are delivered, the affect (facial expression) should display a look of sadness.

Role shift – Left (emphasizes narrator is speaking) PAST. SAD. SHORT BEFORE DAVID (finger-spell David) DIE. HE EXPLAIN SON SOLOMON (fingerspell) HIS NEW IM-PORTANT RESPONSIBILITY.

 Role shift – Right (emphasizes David is speaking) ME DIE SOON. YOU CONTINUE COUR-AGE. YOU NOW RULE. OBEY GOD, MUST YOU. YOUR ROLE MODEL, WHO? GOD. YOU NOT VIOLATE HIS ORDER, HIS REQUIREMENT, HIS RULES. WHY? MOSES LAW REQUIRE ALL JEWS FOLLOW. YOU FOLLOW, THEN FAMILY AND ISRAEL WILL SUCCESS. LORD PROMISE ME IF FUTURE CHILDREN FOLLOW SAME AND HAVE FULL FAITH INCLUDE HEART AND SOUL, MEANING NOT OPPRESS PEOPLE, NOT MARGINALIZE BUT ENCOURAGE PEOPLE CARE FOR OTHER PEOPLE, AND WORSHIP OUR ONLY GOD, THEN OUR FAMILY AL-WAYS RULE AND LEAD ISRAEL.

It should be easy to recognize the places where features from the expansion system are incorporated. In addition, the extra-linguistic knowledge gleaned from the footnotes was added. Drawing from personal knowledge, [...MEANING NOT OPPRESS PEOPLE, NOT MARGINALIZE BUT ENCOURAGE PEOPLE, CARE FOR OTHER PEOPLE, AND WORSHIP OUR ONLY GOD...], the interpreter includes the actions and behaviors God ultimately wants from the people of Israel.

The novice interpreter who is unable to follow the speaker/reader can read and sign the passage from notes. Extra-large font size will make it visibly easier.

Practice. Practice. Practice. One recommendation is to verbally record a reading of the text, and play it back and attempt to interpret it. If video equipment is available, the practitioner can record a video of the practice session and then observe the interpreting performance. Students in interpreting education programs often do this.

Music

Music is not as difficult as one might initially think. In order to interpret music artistically, it is necessary to prepare in advance. [60] Attendance at many music-interpreting workshops reveals a common observance: All of the workshop leaders emphasize rehearsing beforehand. With that said, the interpreter must insist on getting the hymns, songs, or sheet music before the

---

[60] A great resource for interpreting music is located at www.theinterpretersfriend.com/songs/toc.html#christian. Christian hymns are posted on the site with how to interpret or transliterate the songs.

day of the service. A number of churches have Deaf parishioners lead songs; they are prompted/fed by interpreters. Deaf congregants usually copy sign the Deaf parishioner that leads the song.

It is not always possible to hear the precise words sung by a congregation. Because the interpreter wants to keep up with the rest of the congregation, this can be an interpreter's worst nightmare. Having the lyrics in front of the interpreter may lessen the anxiety. It will then only be necessary to return to and read the lyrics in order to complete the song.

It is useful for the interpreter to have a personal copy of the hymnal in which to write glosses (signs) above the English words. There is a website on the Internet (www.cyberhymnal.org) with lyrics and an organ rendition of many common hymns. For praise songs, the Internet is useful once again. Suppose the song, "Shout to the Lord" is to be sung during the worship service. Going to the Google website and typing in, *lyrics for "Shout to the Lord"* will provide many sites that include these lyrics. Of course, it could be necessary to sift through several websites to find what exactly is wanted.

Observation of role models like Mark Mitchum[61] can help an interpreter to visualize how to perform a song. Often during interviews, an actor or actress will reveal that a particular classical actor/actress was the inspiration for a role. Interpreters can borrow this

---

[61] Mark Mitchum is a deaf performer who specializes in signing music. Some of his videos can be purchased through www.markmitchumweb.com.

method for signing music. The beginner will want to learn how to integrate rhythm, melody and tempo. This allows consumers to distinguish between discourse and songs. Creativity may come easier to some than to others. Need some pointers? Purchase or borrow some music videos with deaf or hearing performers as a start and use them for practice. Attend theatrical shows and concerts that provide interpreting services. A wonderful resource by Raymont L. Anderson, <u>Visual Music: Interpreting Songs in American Sign Language</u>. It's a helpful guide for both novice and experienced interpreters.

Deaf Missions has a library of videos (biblical and music) that consumers may borrow, as well as deaf ministry tools. Interested readers can go to the website at www.deafmissions.org. Most people need help in the beginning and these ideas may get the creative juices to flow.

For additional help, the Liturgical Interpreting group on Facebook can provide some assistance. There are many seasoned interpreters, who belong to the group, share their experience and insight.

Analyzing and Signing Music

Just like Scripture, the first part of the process is to read and analyze the lyrics. Whether interpreting or transliterating the music, one must strive to sign the music in a conceptually correct manner. When transliterating the music, choose conceptually representational signs and put them in the order of the lyrics. When needed, concepts can be rearranged in the interpretation if it helps to represent the music more eloquently. What is important is that the message stays intact. Steer

clear of these words: *a, an, the, be, being, been, was, were*.
These do not need to be included in the interpretation.
Using signs *before* and *past* can replace the words *was* and
were when something historic is emphasized.

A popular hymn that is sung and signed during
worship services and some funeral services is "Amazing
Grace." Read the first stanza.

> *Amazing grace! How sweet the sound that saved a wretch
> like me! I once was lost, but now am found; was blind, but
> now I see.*

One would not sign the word "sound." Instead, sign
the word "message." Most Deaf people cannot hear
sounds, so reframe it to be culturally compatible. Write
the gloss above the word being replaced in the hymnal,
or print out a new version (with the gloss) of the music.

There are numerous ways to sign "Amazing
Grace," and using different versions from time to time
will keep things interesting. Below is one version of it.

WONDERFUL GRACE! YOUR MESSAGE SWEET
BECAUSE YOU SAVE SINNER LIKE (sign 'same')
ME. BEFORE I RESIST, BUT NOW I ACCEPT,
PAST I REVOLT YOU, BUT NOW UNDER-
STAND.

The main concept of this entire song is God's grace.
Grace is freely given, not earned, in order to reconcile
everyone back to the Creator. With this in mind, other
versions are waiting to be created. Be innovative, and
try to come up with a preferred version. Try a thesau-
rus to find a gloss.

It is helpful to know a little bit about music. If the interpreter knows when a sung word is prolonged (the note held), this will allow the interpreter to exagger-ate/prolong the sign. A music note, as well as a word that has a hyphen "-" in or after the word, is an indica-tor.

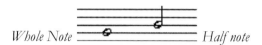

Whole Note   *Half note*

The exaggerated sign can begin from the interpreter's dominant hand (or the other hand) and continue slowly to the other side of the body until the next sign begins. See the following illustrations.

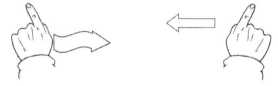

Another technique is to shift the body diagonally to the right or to the left, like with role shifting. The interpret-er has space to alternate the signing direction: the (diagonal) left, the center, and the (diagonal) right. This too helps distinguish music from discourse. See the following.

<u>ALTERNATE SIGNING DIRECTION</u>

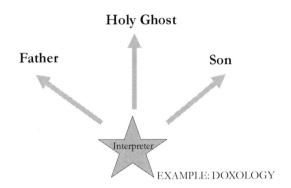

Still, another method is to repeat a sign which can give it (or the concept) emphasis. By signing a word in a left diagonal direction and then shifting to the right and repeating the sign, this can give an artistic flare.

The following is the hymn, "Amazing Grace." See which words require an exaggerated sign.

To create visual pictures and describe meaningful concepts that produce imagery is a goal for new interpreters. This takes practice to achieve.

Sermons

A sermon, a message, and a homily are common titles for the discourse in a speech of exhortation. The message that a minister or priest preaches can be as short as five minutes or may go on for over an hour. A copy of the manuscript or outline is beneficial, because it helps the interpreter know what the main concepts are as well as in what direction the speaker is headed. Cooperative preachers can make a big difference in the interpreter's performance. Some preachers do not like to share their manuscript or outline with anyone, perhaps because of insecurity; whatever the reason, the new interpreter will need to be politely insistent. Get *something*, even if it is verbal (e.g., "The points to my sermon are…"). For some, sharing the Standard

Practice Paper by RID may help the preacher to understand and be forthcoming with his or her sermon ahead of time.

New and seasoned interpreters alike should feel apprehensive if a manuscript or an outline cannot be studied beforehand. The consumer deserves to receive the same inspirational message as the rest of the congregation. The interpreter's delivered message may lack inspiration because of insufficient preparation (i.e., being able to decide ahead how to best sign or voice the point or illustration in the target language).

The following are several types of sermons that are commonly preached. These may be helpful to those who don't understand where the preacher is going. To identify one of these sermon structures may help.

❑ **Ladder** – The ladder outline builds one point on another. Each rung (step) of the ladder carries the listener higher and higher toward a truth or teaching. Usually it is one point built upon another.

❑ **Diamond** – The diamond outline takes a great truth and polishes the different facets of that truth in much the same way as a jeweler might polish a precious diamond. You arrive at the truth through scriptural exegesis. The points of the sermon can be done in any order.

❑ **Cable** – The cable sermon is a stream of consciousness preaching. The preacher moves from point to point. Some preachers will wander from the point.

❑ **Label** – A label sermon classifies people or things into easily remembered categories. The point to be emphasized the most will be last. Jesus used this often.

❑ **Rebuttal** – In a rebuttal sermon, the preacher speaks about a point of view that he or she disagrees with and dismantles it by criticism.

❑ **Synthesis** – This type of sermon will present two contradictory ideas and join them to form a new truth.

❑ **Diagnosis/Remedy** – This outline is based on a medical model. First, a problem will be diagnosed, and then a remedy offered. The word of God comes as a part of the remedy.

❑ **Narrative** – Preachers will retell a Bible story in their own creative words.

❑ **Topical** – Some ministers or priests will speak on a specific topic. It may be because it is something the congregation needs to hear, or because the minister or priest wishes to convince the congregation of a certain point of view.

Sermons are meant to have some scriptural application. Look for this when listening and analyzing the message. Furthermore, be sure to match the preacher's affect.

Prayers

Prayers read from a book pose difficulty because when text is read, the speaker may read at a faster pace.

Like the other parts of the service, a copy of the prayer in hand ahead of time will enable the interpreter to practice signing it. Some congregations read prayers from a prayer book, or selected prayers from a hymnal. When a speedy reader makes it difficult for the practitioner to interpret concurrently, then the practitioner will probably want to return and read from the notes. One approach is to interpret only key words, such as subjects and verbs, and leave out prepositional phrases, adjectives, and adverbs. This allows the practitioner to interpret the main ideas in the prayer. Granted, this may be a watered-down interpretation, but the significant points of the message will be present.

Extemporaneous prayers are common for many congregations. Whether someone is reading the names of those who are ill, or individual parishioners in the congregation are speaking in turn, interpreting this portion can be a challenge. If the names are spoken at a reasonable pace, then fingerspelling both the first and last name is possible. On the other hand, if a speedy reader reads the names from a list, then fingerspelling only the last name may be the better option. Some congregations list prayer requests in their bulletins. This list of names will aid the interpreter with fingerspelling the names correctly. Almost without exception, someone will speak too softly for the interpreter to hear, and most likely, others in the congregation will miss the name as well. If it seems inappropriate to ask for clarification, simply interpret what you thought you heard (add, "I think I heard..."), or be forthcoming and state, "Interpreter could not hear."

The Lord's Prayer

Congregations, whether weekly or during a special occasion, will pray in unison the Lord's Prayer, the prayer that Jesus taught his disciples. Like hymns and Scripture, it can be signed in various ways, and still retain the main concept of each phrase of the prayer. Below is a transliterated version of the Lord's Prayer. Begin with your eyes looking to the ceiling, and ask the consumer to pray with you/copy you.

> *Our Father, who art in heaven, hallowed be thy name. Thy kingdom come. thy will be done, on earth, as it is in heaven. Give us this day, our daily bread. And forgive us our trespasses, as we forgive those who trespass against us. And lead us not into temptation, but deliver us from evil. For thine is the kingdom, and the power, and the glory forever and ever. Amen.*

OUR FATHER, WHO LIVE HEAVEN, HOLY YOUR NAME. YOUR KINGDOM COME HERE. YOUR WANT, WE FOLLOW HERE SAME HEAVEN. GIVE US TODAY OUR DAILY BREAD. FORGIVE OUR SIN, AS (same) WE FORGIVE THOSE WHO SIN AGAINST US. LEAD US NOT TEMPTATION, BUT SAVE US FROM EVIL. YOUR KINGDOM, POWER, AND GLORY FOREVER. AMEN.

Generally, the Lord's Prayer might be prayed when the Eucharist or a Holy Baptism is performed. Because deaf consumers will copy the interpreter, the practitioner will more than likely need to interpret at a slower pace. If the prayer has not been memorized, it will be helpful to sign from notes.

Creeds

The purpose of the creed is to establish conformity of belief among Christians, and this is commonly said as a public profession of faith. Because of differing and heretical beliefs, the Church felt one common belief was needed. A council paved the way and wrote the creed.

The Nicene Creed

The original Nicene Creed was first adopted in 325 at the First Council of Nicaea, which was the Ecumenical Council. At that time, the text ended after the words, "We believe in the Holy Spirit." The second Ecumenical Council in 381 added the remainder of the text except for the words "and the Son" (for how the Holy Spirit originated); this is the version still used by Eastern Orthodox and Greek Catholic churches today. This second version is one of the reasons that the Eastern Church and the Western Church are no longer together.[62] The third Ecumenical Council reaffirmed

---

[62] The Roman Catholic Church added the words *"and the Son"* (the filioque clause) to the description of the Holy Spirit, in what many have argued is a violation of the Canons of the Third Ecumenical Council. The original phrase was "And the Holy Spirit…who proceeds from the Father." The words "And in the Holy Spirit…who proceeds from the Father *and the Son.*" were not included by the Council of Nicaea nor of Constantinople, and most Eastern Orthodox theologians consider their inclusion to be a heresy.

the 381 version, and stated that no further changes could be made to it, nor could other creeds be adopted.xxx One approach to interpreting the Nicene Creed is to have the minister explain to the consumer the theological meaning before the service and then gloss the creed when it is time to interpret it. Further information about The Nicene Creed can be read at www.creeds.net.

Apostle's Creed

Another popular creed, the Apostle's Creed, was written sometime between the second and fourth centuries. There are slight variations among denominations, but the essential elements still remain in the creed. Similar to the Nicene Creed, it too was written to establish clear beliefs because a number of clergy deviated from common beliefs. One or both creeds are incorporated into confirmation (becoming members) curricula. Below is a transliterated version of the Apostle's Creed.

> *I believe in God, the Father almighty, creator of heaven and earth. I believe in Jesus Christ, his only Son, our Lord, who was conceived by the Holy Spirit, born of the Virgin Mary, suffered under Pontius Pilate, was crucified died, and was buried; On the third day he rose again; he ascended into heaven, he is seated at the right hand of the Father, and he will come to judge the living and the dead. I believe in the Holy Spirit, the holy catholic Church, the communion of saints, the forgiveness of sins, the resurrection of the body, and the life everlasting Amen.*

I BELIEVE GOD, OUR ALMIGHTY FA-THER, HE CREATE HEAVEN AND

EARTH. I BELIEVE JESUS CHRIST, FA-
THER ONLY SON. HE OUR LORD. VIR-
GIN MARY PREGNANT FROM HOLY
SPIRIT, THEN BORN JESUS. JESUS SUF-
FERED. WHEN? DURING PP (fingerspell P
P) RULE JERUSALEM AND OTHER AREA.
HOW JESUS SUFFER? JESUS CRUCIFIED,
DIED, BURIED; THREE DAYS LATER
JESUS ALIVE AGAIN. HE ASCEND
HEAVEN. JESUS SIT NEXT HIS FATHER
AND RULE. JESUS WILL COME AGAIN
FOR JUDGE BOTH LIVING AND PEOPLE
FINISH DIE. I BELIEVE HOLY SPIRIT,
HOLY CHRISTIAN CHURCH, GROUP
PAST BELIEVERS, GOD FORGIVE ALL
SINS, PAST AND PRESENT BELIEVER
WILL JOIN JESUS AND LIVE WITH GOD
FOREVER. AMEN.

The term 'catholic' when spelled with a lower cap
means universal, not the Roman Catholic Church.
When congregations say these in unison, the interpreter
will want to interpret/sign at a slower pace.

Summary

This introduction to analysis techniques orients the
interpreter to parts of the worship service, as well as
schemes of frozen text. It is in the practitioner's best
interest to prepare for an assignment by examining and
developing an interpreted version of frozen text that
best meets the consumer's language needs. For longer
texts, written notes will be beneficial. Because each text
(prayer, song, etc.) will need to be decoded by the
interpreter, knowing what resources are available will

produce a better message that is more equivalent to the source language.

_____

ENDNOTES

xxi Clayton Valli & Ceil Lucas. LINGUISTICS of American Sign Language: An Introduction. Washington, DC: Clerc Books, 2002, 69.

xxii Barbara Bernstein Fant, Betty Miller, & Lou Fant. The American Sign Language Phrase Book, 3rd ed. New York: McGraw-Hill, 2008.

xxiii Clayton Valli & Ceil Lucas. LINGUISTICS of American Sign Language: An Introduction. Washington, DC: Clerc Books, 2002. 188.

xxiv "Classroom Interpreting: EIPA Written Test and Knowledge Standards". Boys Town National Research Hospital. Retrieved 19 Aug 2006. www.classroominterpreting.org/EIPA/standards/interpreting.asp.

xxv "Using a British Sign Language Interpreter or Communicator". City of Bradford Metropolitan District Council. Retrieved 18 Aug 2006. www.bradford.gov.uk/health_wellbeing_and_care/disability/using_a_ british_sign_language_interpreter_or_communicator.

xxvi "The Role of Consecutive in Interpreting Training: A Cognitive View". AIIC. Retrieved 18 Aug 2006. www.aiic.net/ViewPage.cfm/article262.
xxvi M. Joos. The Five Clocks. New York: Harcourt, Brace and World, 1961.

xxvii Danica Seleskovitch and Marianne Lederer. A SYSTEMATIC APPROACH TO TEACHING INTERPRETATION. Translated by Jacolyn Harmer. Paris: Office of the European Communities, 1989, 124.

xxviii Scott K. Liddell. Grammar, Gesture and Meaning in American Sign Language. New York: Cambridge University Press, 2003, 15.

xxix Shelly Lawrence. Interpreter Discourse: English to ASL Expansion. Oct. 1994. Interpreter Discourse: English to ASL Expansion. Revised ed. Jan. 2003.

Chapter 7 - Weddings & Funerals

Two ceremonies that interpreters may be requested to provide services for are funerals and weddings. In a Christian context, funerals and weddings are, in fact, a worship service. The funeral and wedding ceremony need special attention because of the ambiance surrounding the ceremony. Both services can be emotionally taxing, yet personally fulfilling, when everyone is included in the communication.

The Dying Process

Before the funeral, interpreters may be asked to provide interpreting services for the transition from life to death. In a hospital setting, when a patient reaches the onset of death, a chaplain is usually called to be present with the family. Most hospitals have chaplains on-call for occasions such as these. When Deaf family members are among those saying good-bye, some chaplains or nurses will check what resources are available for the Deaf person(s) as well.

The dying moments are holy and sacred for everyone present. Certainly, there is a sense of loss and feelings of grief, but there is possibly anger as well. These feelings are normal, and people go through stages when they grieve. Moments at the end of life may feel surreal for the interpreter when he or she does not know the family.

Interpreters requested to be present at the end of someone's life might not know what to do or might feel

a sense of helplessness. This is quite common. Interpreters are not necessarily there to interpret for the
chaplain. In all actuality, a grieving Deaf family member
may be comforted by having an interpreter there,
because of the accessibility for open communication
with hearing family members.

Because of the sacredness of the last moments of
life, if a chaplain steps out of the room, the interpreter
will want to ask the family if he or she should step out
as well. Those going through bereavement may wish to
do so in private, and this is to be respected by the
interpreter. However, if family members wish for the
interpreter to remain, then he or she should stay.
Family members, aware that the interpreter specializes
in religious interpreting, may derive solace from the
interpreter's presence.

Compassion and sensitivity will be part of the
interpreter's role. During these moments, if a family
member needs a drink of water, a tissue, or a nurse to
be called, it is appropriate for the interpreter to be
accommodating. Granted, interpreters do not usually
step outside of the interpreting role, but in this particular setting one ought to be flexible.

Family members may share special memories, vent
their feelings, or start up a conversation (a common
coping mechanism) with the interpreter. All of this
should be interpreted. Overall, when the interpreter is
present in the room, it is better to be reserved and give
family members space.

Most Protestant chaplains will offer prayers for
everyone present; prayers for strength, hope, and
comfort are usually requested. If the chaplain is a priest,

he may give last rites[63], especially if the patient is Catholic. Part of last rites is the Sacrament of Healing, and the interpreter can expect the patient to be anointed by the priest. Confession may be included for those who wish for spiritual healing; the interpreter may wish to reiterate to those present that *everything is confidential.*

Interpreters can benefit from a better understanding of the liturgy. Extra-linguistic knowledge will be useful in these circumstances. Online articles about last rites can be read at http://catholicism.about.com/od/thesacraments/g/Last_Rites.htm.

Funerals

Funeral planning usually begins shortly after a death occurs. The person who requested the interpreter may be a family member of the deceased, a funeral director, or a minister. Emotions may run high when

---

[63] **Catholic Law: Canon #844** states, "Catholic ministers may lawfully administer the sacraments only to Catholic members of Christ's faithful, who equally may lawfully receive them only from Catholic members.
Canon #844, 4, specifically legislates, "If there is danger of death or if, in the judgment of the diocesan bishop or of the bishops' conference, there is some other grave and pressing need, Catholic ministers may lawfully administer these same sacraments to other Christians not in full communion with the Catholic Church who cannot approach a minister of their own community and who spontaneously ask for them, provided that they demonstrate the Catholic faith in respect of these sacraments and are properly disposed."

the interpreter has a relationship with the deceased or with the family members. Interpreters may have to interpret the entire funeral process[64] or only the funeral service.

If the interpreter is somehow associated with the departed, he or she has every right to mourn and experience grief like everyone else. In this case, it may be better to request an interpreter who is not associated with the family to do the service. Most certainly, it is the decision of the interpreter, but he or she will need to ensure it is possible to continue to function in the interpreting role in the midst of grief.

The interpreter may need to work through the emotional impact of a death or funeral. It is advisable to talk with a colleague about the experience. An interpreting discussion group can offer a good way to talk about it with other professionals who may have had similar experiences. In addition, some interpreters write about the experience in a journal. The process of writing can bring out the feelings associated with the death. Processing one's feelings is what is needed, as death is difficult for people. Working through it helps interpreters remain emotionally and spiritually healthy.

Fees

Practitioners who interpret funeral services are entitled to be compensated. Some interpreters who

---

[64] The funeral process is accompanying families to the funeral home, interpreting the funeral arrangements, and pastoral care before and after the funeral. As a word of caution, the interpreter should not help the family make financial decisions.

know the deceased may not want to charge a fee, so their services will be *pro bono*. Interpreting a funeral service is comparable to interpreting a standard worship service. A two-hour minimum is what some interpreters feel is fair to charge. Attendance at the wake before the funeral may be considered part of the preparation because it allows the interpreter to meet family members and those who might participate in the service. In some cases, the funeral home pays the interpreter directly, as they do the organist and minister who perform the service. The interpreting fee is generally added to the total cost of the funeral. It may seem crass to charge a fee; however, professionals are providing a much-needed service.

Preparation

The interpreter should be informed of the cause of death, as some aspects of the service may refer to it. The minister's approach to the funeral service is usually based on the cause of death. A funeral for a patient who died from terminal cancer will be somewhat different than that of a suicide victim or a child who died a senseless death. The minister's objective may be to cause lament for a victim who died from a drive-by shooting, or may saturate the service with hope and reassurance because of the passing of a beloved grandfather.

Preparation for a funeral service is much like that for weekly church services.[65] Materials to be requested for preparation are prayers, obituary, eulogy or sermon,

---

[65] A good online resource about funerals is located at www.lectionarystudies.com/funerals.html.

poems, scriptural passages, family names, and songs.
The interpreter should not be surprised, however, if
some or all of these are given minutes before the
service. In addition, the interpreter will want to know
vital information about the deceased beforehand, such
as a nickname, background information, and surviving
family members' names.[66] Because of lack of preparation time and emotional intensity, novice interpreters
should avoid interpreting funeral services.

There is a wide range of Scripture that can be read,
just about for any occasion surrounding the circumstance of death. Some passages of Scripture are chosen
to provide reassurance for those attending the service
and other passages substantiate doctrine or beliefs that
are shared with those gathered. For many, passages of
Scripture that are read are slanted toward the faith
tradition of the deceased's family or that of the clergy
preaching. It will make a difference in the interpreter's
work if he or she can receive ahead of time what
Scripture passages will be read. Chapter six includes
analysis techniques that the interpreter can use in order
to prepare for the texts that will be read. The following
are a few common passages that are sometimes read.

---

[66] Background information can be written notes that the
interpreter can place on the music stand. This is so the interpreter can sign names or other pertinent information (e.g.,
where the deceased was born, schooling, life achievements, etc.)
correctly.

Old Testament Readings
2 Samuel 12:16-23
Job 19:23-27
Isaiah 40:1-11

Psalm Readings
Psalm 23
Psalm 27
Psalm 121

New Testament Readings
Romans 8:31-39
1 Corinthians 13
1 Thessalonians 4:13-18

Gospel Readings
John 14:1-7
Luke 18:15-17
Matthew 11:25-30

One common scriptural passage that is read at funeral services is Psalm 23. This is a comfort for many people who are grieving. It is not uncommon to use the King James Version. Here is Psalm 23, and one version of how to interpret it.

Psalm 23 *(*KJV*)*

1The LORD is my shepherd; I shall not want. 2He maketh me to lie down in green pastures: he leadeth me beside the still waters. 3He restoreth my soul: he leadeth me in the paths of righteousness for his name's sake. 4Yea, though I walk through the valley of the shadow of death, I will fear no evil: for thou art with me; thy rod and thy staff they comfort me. 5Thou preparest a table before me in the presence of mine enemies: thou anointest my head with oil; my cup runneth over. 6Surely goodness and mercy shall follow me all the days of my life: and I will dwell in the house of the LORD forever.

LORD MY SHEEP-SUPERVISOR. EVERY-THING, HE GIVE. WHEN I REST HE WATCH PROTECT ME: HE LEAD ME CLOSE QUIET WATER-FLOW. HE INSPIRE ME. HE POSI-TIVE INFLUENCE ME. WHY? HONOR HIS

NAME. IF I EXPERIENCE DANGER, ME
NOT AFRAID. WHY? BECAUSE HE WITH
ME; HIS SHEEP-POLE GIVE ME COMFORT.
HE PREPARE TABLE FOR ME, SAME-TIME
MY ENEMY WATCH. HE ANOINT MY
HEAD; HE BLESS ME AGAIN-AGAIN. YES,
ALL MY LIFE MY LORD ALWAYS GIVE ME
GOOD AND MERCY: AFTER I DIE, I WILL
GO LIVE HEAVEN FOREVER.

Readers are encouraged to produce their own version
of Psalm 23, or seek other versions as well. The
footnotes in the NIV Study Bible will be helpful to
understand some of the metaphors in Psalm 23.

Funeral services may take place in a chapel at the
funeral home, at a nearby church, or at the burial site.
With the cost of funerals or because of the deceased's
wishes, some services do not include the presence of
the body, but only an urn (cremation) and a picture.
Wherever the service is located, the interpreter will need
to assess and make logistical decisions accordingly.

Interpreter Placement

Poster boards on easels and PowerPoint presentations are now more common at funeral services and
should be included when working out the logistics[67] of
where the interpreter will be located. If the coffin is
present, the interpreter will stand at one end of the
coffin or by the speaker. The interpreter may need to
stand on a raised platform in order to be seen by
attendees toward the back.

---

[67] Logistical considerations about placement are covered in
chapter 3.

Stand either to the right or left of the coffin, not blocking people's view.

There are some similarities among funeral services such as singing hymns and reading scriptural passages; however, each service is unique because of the dynamics of the service. If the service includes a time of sharing, where attendees either stand at their seat or come to a podium, then it is possible that there will be a need to interpret interactively (sign to voice, and voice to sign). The interpreter may need to prompt the minister to ask people who wish to share to come up front.

Funeral Liturgy

The following is one common outline for a funeral service. Some aspects of it may not be included. Usually, the minister follows the wishes of the family when preparing the service.

Welcome and/or Gathering
(Sometimes Scripture may be read, such as John 11:25, 26.)

Song or Hymn

Introduction and/or Opening
(The faith tradition is usually emphasized during this point in the service. For example, "We gather in the

name of Jesus Christ…" and the purpose for the
gathering is said.)

Meditation/Prayer
(A meditation may be a passage read from a book, such
as *Chicken Soup for the Soul.*)

Scripture Readings

Eulogy or Sermon
(A eulogy is usually a message about the deceased's life.
Sometimes the obituary is read. The eulogy is typically
spoken by a lay person (non-clergy). A sermon is
commonly preached by a clergy person and is based on
Scripture that highlights the deceased's life and/or
provides reassurance to loved ones.)

Personal Words
(Personal words are usually spoken by family and
friends.)

Poem
(Poetry is sometimes read during the eulogy or sermon
in order to accentuate the message.)

Prayer/Meditation
(Sometimes The Lord's Prayer is prayed.)

Reflection
(Perhaps a hymn is sung.)

The Benediction
(The final blessing or exhortation before people leave.)

The Committal
(Taken place at the cemetery.)

The committal service, at the cemetery, usually has less attendance by funeral guests. A funeral director typically gives instructions at the end of the funeral service about the committal service. To read up on the parts (and their meaning) of a funeral service, <u>IN TIMES OF CRISIS AND SORROW: A Minister's Manual Resource Guide</u> by Carol Marie Noren (2001) is a helpful resource.

There is a trend among committal services[68]. Often, a recitation of the Lord's Prayer ensues, as well as the burial liturgy: "We commit his body to the ground; earth to earth, ashes to ashes, dust to dust." This poignant and meaningful sentence is a challenge to interpret. It is probable that most people do not know what it means, but for the interpreter it is advantageous to know. In essence, it refers to Genesis 3:19.[69] Since the sentence does not give a clear meaning, the interpreter can provide the direct meaning as an interpretation. Time permitting, it is appropriate to sign the English translation, and then sign the meaning.

---

[68] Interpreting funeral services is a ministry in itself. Those interpreters who wish for more information about different aspects of the funeral service are encouraged to read the book, <u>Creating Meaningful Funeral Ceremonies: A Guide for Caregivers</u>, by Dr. Alan D. Wolfelt (2011).

[69] This reference is to Genesis 3:19, the consequence of the fall from grace of Adam and Eve as a result of sin. They and everyone will experience death and return to dust from where Adam (man) was first made.

Funeral Terms

For interpreters unfamiliar with funeral terms, the following, adapted from <u>In Times of Crisis and Sorrow</u>, may be helpful.[xxxi]

Casket/Coffin: Is an upholstered oblong box in which a person is buried. Coffin is often said in place of casket.

Committal: Words spoken at the graveside, commending the deceased into God's hands and reminding those attending of their hope in God.

Cortege: A funeral procession.

Cremains: Ashes of the cremated remains.

Embalming: Preserving a dead body by replacing the blood and organs with a dyed perfume solution.

Eulogy: A commendatory formal statement about the deceased either incorporated into the sermon or meditation or said separately.

Funeral director: A person licensed to arrange the legal disposition of deceased bodies, who may also conduct or arrange rites (services) for the bereaved.

Homegoing: A term used in the traditional Black church for the funeral service.

Memorial Service: A worship service, similar to the funeral service, at which the body of the deceased is not present.

Mortician: A person who prepares deceased bodies for burial or cremation and offers a variety of goods and services to the bereaved.

Pall: A heavy cloth draped over the coffin.

Pallbearer: A person who carries, or accompanies, the deceased's casket at a funeral.

Repast: Term used in the traditional black church for the

meal or gathering following a funeral or memorial service.

Vault: A concrete or metal box that holds the casket in the ground.

Viewing: Synonym for wake and visitation.

Visitation: Set hours at a private home, funeral home, or church where people may come and pay their respects to the bereaved. The casket may be open or closed during visitation.

Wake: Traditionally, a watch held over the body of a dead person prior to burial. The term visitation has mostly replaced wake.

Weddings

Interpreters may be a primary or secondary need by the wedding party. If the bride and/or groom have the need for an interpreter, the practitioner is usually requested early in the planning process and will be considered essential to the service. On the other hand, if someone other than the couple needs interpreting services, then it will be a secondary need. A primary need often involves additional work for the interpreter because of pre-marital counseling sessions with clergy, final planning sessions with hearing family members and vendors, rehearsal (and dinner), pictures, and the actual ceremony—all of which may require the interpreter's presence. A secondary need may only require initial consultation, rehearsal, and the ceremony. Most of the time, the interpreter will be requested to come to the reception, not so much to enjoy the festivities, but to interpret post-ceremonial activities.

Most wedding ceremonies are meticulously planned. Like worship service preparation (see chapter six), the interpreter will need to acquire the liturgy, lyrics for songs, poetry, and the wedding vows. Some of these can be acquired early in the process, but it can be expected that some pieces will be given or changed at the last minute.

Interpreter Placement

Consideration of placement will need to be completed before the actual ceremony, and this is typically done during the rehearsal. The interpreter will need to consult with decision-makers and provide input for where the interpreter can be best viewed. It is better to use a team of interpreters when the couple is Deaf so both the Deaf party and the audience can have communication access.

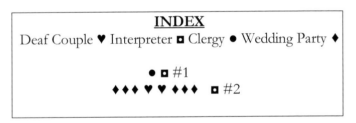

For this arrangement, one interpreter will be for the wedding party and the second interpreter for the audience. The sightline is uninhibited and can be seen by the Deaf couple and wedding party. If an interpreting team is unavailable, then the #1 interpreter can possibly stand on a raised platform; if the interpreter does not use a raised platform, then the wedding party blocks the sightline from the audience. Interpreters will want to keep in mind that the clergy performing the wedding will be holding an open Bible or book of worship, and the interpreter's arms and hands may need to be further extended past the book.

When only the audience needs an interpreter, the interpreter will want to be diametrically to the right or to the left of the wedding party and face the audience. Normally, the interpreter is located close to the speakers, but in this context, audience members will not want the interpreter to block their view of the couple. It is not uncommon to place the interpreter within the wedding party. When this occurs, the interpreter usually dresses the same as the rest of the wedding party. On occasion, an interpreter may sit in the congregation with his or her back to the couple while facing the person(s). Flexibility is needed to accommodate everyone involved.

Family members or close friends of the couple may participate in the ceremony by saying a prayer, singing/signing a song, or reading a scriptural passage. During the rehearsal, the interpreter will want to find out if a Deaf person is a participant. If so, then the interpreter will want to have a script of his/her own. Normally, the interpreter will sit in the front row in order to interpret from ASL to English. A clear sightline and a script (and a microphone if available) are needed. An alternative approach is to stand next to the Deaf person at the podium, but audience members may conclude that the interpreter is doing the reading instead of the Deaf person. The first approach is generally preferred.

More times than not, consumers in the audience will not be consulted as to where the interpreter is to be placed. The interpreter, as the communication specialist, will need to look at the overall logistics (e.g., the environment, liturgy, rituals, consumer needs, etc.) and decide on the location. The interpreter will usually suggest (or inquire to drop a hint) to the wedding coordinator that pews or seats be reserved for those who must utilize the interpreter. This will reiterate accessibility needs.

Negotiation

Wedding planners and the wedding party members usually feel stressed and anxious before the wedding, and these feelings can be transferred to the interpreter. Wedding planners generally have high expectations about how the ceremony will come out, and the interpreter needs to work within this framework of desire.

Wedding ceremonies may be as short as fifteen minutes or run as long as two hours depending on whether the wedding planners wish to have a short and quaint ceremony or a long extravaganza. The length of the service is typically driven by spiritual beliefs, ethnic or cultural conditions, and socioeconomic influences. When there is only one interpreter and the ceremony is expected to extend past an hour and a half, the interpreter may need to negotiate what is not going to be interpreted. You may opt to forgo the music before the service to give full attention to the ceremony itself. Interpreters need to keep in mind there is a usually a reception afterwards, and their work may not be done at the end of the ceremony.

Fees

Whether the interpreter charges for his or her interpreting services typically depends on the relationship between the interpreter and the couple. Indeed, weddings are much more complicated because of preparation and rehearsal. There is no industry-wide set fee for interpreting weddings. However, from the writer's observations, a number of interpreters charge per hour. They include preparation time, rehearsal time, the ceremony, and the reception. The interpreter will want to consider any attire that must either be rented or purchased, as well as travel expenses. Some interpreters will charge a flat fee such as $100 or $150 (or more), which includes preparation, rehearsal, ceremony, reception, and additional expenses. Others do not charge anything because the interpreting service is to be a wedding gift.

Legal Component

Earlier it was stated that the wedding ceremony is a worship service[70]. Even though it is a worship service, there is a legal component to the ceremony because the state will recognize the union between the couple. Most people, except for the minister, overlook this part of the ceremony.

The seriousness of the wedding ceremony mandates that interpreters be qualified. There can be little room for error on the part of the interpreter due to legalities. If an inexperienced interpreter has a pre-established relationship with the wedding party, and for sentimental reasons the interpreter is to be used, then it would be wise to consult with a certified or highly experienced interpreter, perhaps with both interpreters working in a mentoring capacity, and interpreting the wedding together.

---

[70] A good resource for wedding preparation is the book, The Knot Guide to Wedding Vows and Traditions: Readings, Rituals, Music, Dances, and Toasts by Carley Roney (2003).

Wedding Liturgy

Like funerals, there are a plethora of choices for Scripture passages that can be read during a wedding service. The following are a few Scripture passages that are sometimes read.

Old Testament Readings
Genesis 1:27, 28a, 31a
Ruth 1:16
Song of Solomon 2:10-14, 16a

Psalm Readings
Psalm 127
Psalm 128
Psalm 150

New Testament Readings
1 Corinthians 13:4-7
Ephesians 3:14-19
Colossians 3:12-15

Gospel Readings
Matthew 5:1-10
Mark 10:6-9
John 2:1-12

The clergy person (sometimes called the *presider* or *officiator*), wedding planner, and the couple usually decide upon the prescribed format of the service.[71] Below is an example of a wedding ceremony. Some parts can be arranged to occur earlier or later in the service.

INTRODUCTION

The Welcome
(Sometimes a verse of Scripture may be read and the purpose for the gathering is said.)

Preface
(The faith tradition is usually emphasized during this

---

[71] A good online resource about a Christian wedding service is at www.lectionarystudies.com/weddings.html.

part of the service and describes the purpose of marriage according to Scriptural beliefs.)

The Declarations or The Consent
(The presider addresses the couple and asks them to declare their intent in front of the congregation. For example, "Will you take *N* to be your wife? To have and to hold from this day forward...")

The Collect or Prayer
(This prayer usually requests a blessing for the marriage.)

Readings
(Typical readings are passages of Scripture.)

Sermon
(Most sermons are short Scriptural based messages giving marriage advice to the couple.)

THE MARRIAGE

The Vows
(The couple face one another and pledge their vows. A common vow is, "I, *N*, take you, *N*, to be my husband, to have and to hold from this day forward; for better, for worse, for richer, for poorer, in sickness and in health...")

The Giving of Rings
(Depending on the preference from the couple, a unity candle may be lit at this point of the service.)

The Proclamation
(The presider pronounces the couple husband & wife.)

The Blessing of the Marriage
(A prayer and/or blessing is said by the presider.)

Prayers

The Dismissal or Benediction
(The final blessing or exhortation before people leave.)

For more in depth explanations for each part of the wedding service, <u>Words for Your Wedding: The Wedding Service Book</u> by David Glusker (1999) is an excellent resource. Appendix F has a sample wedding liturgy as well.

Wedding Phrases

The following, adapted from the *Words for Your Wedding*, may be useful for interpreters who are less familiar with the parts of a wedding ceremony or service.[xxxii]

Gathering Words: Typically at the beginning of the service, words are said to call the congregation to order. Opening words state the purpose of the gathering.

Opening Prayers: A synonym for *Invocation.* Commonly said early in the service, it reminds those present this worship assumes the presence of God.

Charge to the Couple: A statement of emphasis to the couple and others present that the wedding commitment is among the most serious of all decisions. The couple is asked to declare before God and the congregation that they recognize the importance of their pledge.

Declaration of Consent: An agreement to marry. Generally, this occurs prior to the exchange of vows.

"_____, will you have _____ (or woman/man) to be your wedded spouse (or wife/husband), to live together in holy matrimony? Will you love her/him, comfort her/him, honor and keep her/him in sickness and in health, and forsaking all others, be faithful to her/him as long as you both shall live…?"

Answer: "I will."

Exchange of Vows: An agreement of a couple in the presence of official witnesses to take one another as spouses. These words of commitment are often considered the most significant in the ceremony. "I_____, take thee,_____, to be my husband/wife/spouse, to have and to hold, from this day forward, for better, for worse, for richer, for poorer, in sickness and in health, to love an cherish, till death us do part. This is my solemn vow."

Pronouncement or Declaration: This is the moment when the officiator states the marriage between the couple, usually a climax in the wedding service. "Forasmuch as you, _____ and _____, have consented together in this sacred covenant, and have declared the same before God and this company, I pronounce you husband and wife, in the name of God. Amen."

Benediction and Blessings: The words or prayer concluding the wedding service and sending out the people into the world reminding all that God goes with us.

Summary

It can be stressful to interpret for weddings and funerals. The consumers' emotions may affect the interpreter. Consultation and preparation are sometimes increased due to these services being considered special services or events. Also, additional experience is typically needed to interpret these services, in part due to high stress, the demand for professionalism, and the need for familiarity. In addition, because funerals and weddings are not ordinary events for people, interpreters may need to show additional sensitivity and patience. The liturgy for both services varies according to a number of factors, including culture, denomination, special requests by the family, and faith tradition. Most likely, interpreters in these settings will always be remembered for their part in these intimate and vulnerable moments.

ENDNOTES

xxxi Noren, C.M. (2001). *In Times of Crisis*. San Francisco: Jossey-Bass Publishing.

xxxii Glusker, D. & Misner, P. (1999). *Words for Your Wedding: A Guide to Planning Your Ceremony*. HarperOne Publishing.

Conclusion

A church setting is a special opportunity for new interpreters. Since it is an opportunity, newcomers will soon realize the importance of maintaining good relationships with those who utilize their services. In addition, an interpreter's fine reputation adds value to the work. When relationships and reputation are valued, interpreters will most likely have positive experiences. Neither a relationship nor a reputation is acquired in a week; yet, they are obtainable, and at the very least, should be worked toward.

New interpreters are highly encouraged to continue developing their knowledge and skills, even their interpersonal skills. It takes time to become proficient. Though knowledge and skills are only two components of what makes an interpreter a professional, they are essential in formal settings like in the church or parish. Several references are provided in the appendix that newcomers can study further in order to progress in this area. RID's online store has a number of materials that aspiring interpreters can purchase.

Aspiring interpreters who work one-on-one or in informal settings can use their experiences to become more proficient. As a new interpreter practices, those who use the interpreter will need to be made aware. Perhaps they can give feedback if they are used to working with interpreters. New interpreters engaged in a mentoring relationship will have more opportunities to enhance their skills. Highly qualified or certified interpreters can consult or work with novice interpreters, which will likely improve the novice's skills more than if the novice worked without a mentor.

Over the past few decades, there has been an increase in awareness of the professional services that interpreters provide to organizations, institutions, and communities. Compared to decades before, professional interpreting services are more readily available to secular and faith communities. This is due to the influx of interpreters entering the profession since the passing of the ADA and FCC regulations. Increasing demand for interpreters to work in video relay centers, as well as in the community, continues to challenge the profession. In addition, the profession is experiencing difficulty in meeting the present demand for qualified interpreters. With the development and recognition of the profession, higher standards are required of professionals by the communities in which they work. This puts the obligation on IEPs and interpreters to work with those who wish to enter the profession.

Sometimes having additional humility is necessary when negotiating or making reasonable requests. Interpreters are a part of a team that collaborates with other ministry professionals. Whether they are clergy, music directors, or educators, interpreters engage in the overall functionality of the worship service. It is a privilege for interpreters to take part in the communication process that connects two languages and two communities. Through the interpreting services, participants are able to grow spiritually and take part in the faith community. This awesome responsibility requires that interpreters produce quality work that fulfills the needs of those who use their services.

There is no doubt in my mind that some interpreters in church settings are called by God. God uses interpreters with varying skills, including those new to the vocation. Some interpreters only work in a religious venue, while they hold full-time employment elsewhere. These religious interpreters contribute to the church and sometimes without recognition. Interpreters are vastly important, because of their gifts, their calling, and their willingness to be a bridge between two languages and cultural communities; with that said, their work needs to be done responsibly and professionally. New and seasoned religious interpreters who lack an association with RID are encouraged to become associate members; they too have a place under the umbrella of RID.

There are many churches who are inclusive of Deaf, hard-of-hearing, late-deafened, and Deaf-blind individuals and their families. Often, it is the interpreter or the team of interpreters who lead the church's efforts to start and build a Deaf ministry. An interpreted ministry is a form of Deaf ministry, and this is a great way for churches to be welcoming of those from the Deaf community. Besides providing interpreting services during worship, an interpreted ministry often includes educating leadership and the faith community about Deaf culture and accessibility needs, advocacy, teaching sign language classes, promotes the Deaf ministry, hosts Deaf awareness events (i.e. Deaf awareness Sunday or a disability awareness Sunday), represent the church at Deaf-related events, encourage Deaf leadership in the life of the church (i.e. to be worship liturgists and serve on church boards and committees), and/or assist with the church's outreach ministry programs (i.e. visiting shut-ins or home-bound people and Deaf prison ministry).

Many interpreters working in a religious context find this type of work fulfilling. For the writer of this book, interpreting in a church setting literally changed my life. When I began, I did it "to help out" my Deaf parents. Before I knew it, I was working in another church that did not have an interpreter. As I listened to the liturgy and heard the sermon week after week, I was transformed. The purpose for my life became clearer, and I soon realized that I had a responsibility to God, the church, the interpreting profession, the consumers, and to myself to continue my professional development. With that said, I eventually felt called to write this book. Though the book does not cover every nuance of interpreting in a church setting, it can be a paradigm for those interested in pursuing it.

References

Religious Signing by Elaine Costello (2009) is essential for expanding additional signs and becoming familiar with some English based signs. This book should be on every interpreter's bookshelf. ISBN 0553342444 Soft cover, 10.7 x 7.7 x 0.8 pages 250 $20.00

Boundaries by Dr. Henry Cloud and Dr. John Townsend (2002) contains information about emotional boundaries. This is insightful for interpreters. ISBN 0310247454 Soft cover, 8.4 x 5.6 x 0.8 pages 304 $14.99

Pastors at Greater Risk by H.B. London and Neil B. Wiseman (2003) offers an inside look at what clergy commonly face in ministry. ISBN 0830732373 Soft cover, 8.5 x 5.6 x 0.7 pages 334 $14.99

SO YOU WANT TO BE AN INTERPRETER? 4ᵗʰ ed. by Janice H. Humphrey & Bob J. Alcorn (2007) is a comprehensive book for prospective learners. It touches on many aspects of the interpreting profession. ISBN 0964036770 Soft cover, 1.2 x 6.2 x 9.2 inches pages 493 $75.00

Encounters With Reality: 1001 Interpreter Scenarios by Brenda Cartwright (1999) delves into realistic ethical dilemmas faced by professionals in various settings. ISBN 0916883280 Soft cover, 0.8 x 6.0 x 9.0 pages 206 $45.00 (used through Amazon.com)

Building a Healthy Multi-ethnic Church: Mandate, Commitments and Practices of a Diverse Congregation (2010) by Mark DeYmaz provide readers with insight and examples for congregations to become a multicultural church. ISBN 0787995517 Hard cover, 6.3 x .08 x 9.3 pages 240 $20.98

Confronting the Controversies by Adam Hamilton (2005) connects readers with tough issues that many churches face. ISBN 0687045673 Soft cover, 8.7 x 5.6 x 0.4 pages 144 $9.00

LINGUISTICS of American Sign Language: An Introduction, 4th ed. by Clayton Valli, Ceil Lucas, and Kristin J. Mulrooney (2005) is the most recent book offered by these authors. This is a must have for learning grammatical rules in ASL. ISBN 1563682834 Hard cover, 10.3 x 7.2 x 1.3 pages 560 $75.00

Communicating in Sign: Creative Ways to Learn American Sign Language by Diane P. Chambers (1998) is a simple to read book for those who want to learn about ASL. ISBN 0684835207 Soft cover, 9.2 x 7.4 x 0.5 pages 176 $13.00

American Sign Language Dictionary Unabridged (1998) by Martin L. Sternberg is a crucial resource for ASL users who want to expand the lexicon. ISBN 0062716085 Hard cover, 9.6 x 7.8 x 2.2 pages 1008 $60.00

601 Words You Need to Know to Pass Your Exam (2005) by Murray Bromberg & Julius Liebb is a wonderful resource for expanding an interpreter's vocabulary in many subject areas. ISBN 0764128167 Soft cover, 10.8 x 7.8 x 0.6 pages 256 $12.99

Westminster Dictionary of Theological Terms (1996) by Donald McKim is a resourceful guide for deeper knowledge of everyday and academic theological terms. ISBN 0664255116 Soft cover, 8.9 x 6.0 x 0.8 pages 8.9 x 6.0 x 0.8 pages 310 $24.95

Holman Illustrated Bible Dictionary (2003) by Editors: Butler, Brand, Draper, and

Interpreting: An Introduction (Revised 1990 ed.) by Nancy Frishberg introduces

England bridges a reader's everyday language with religious concepts and language. ISBN 0805428364 Hard cover, 9.6 x 6.6 x 2.3 pages 1704 $29.97

readers to many facets of the interpreting profession. A little bit of the material is outdated; however, it is still a good resource for interpreting students. ISBN 0916883078 Soft cover, 0.8 x 6.2 x 9.2 pages 244 $22.50

Today's Parallel Bible (2000) by Zondervan Publishing is essential to understanding Scripture (frozen text) so it can be interpreted appropriately. ISBN 0310918367 Hard cover, 9.4 x 6.9 x 2.2 pages 2880 $49.95

NIV Study Bible (2002) by Kenneth L. Barker is one of the most important reference books on the bookshelf. It helps readers to understand contextual information about Scripture. ISBN 0310923077 Soft cover, 8.3 x 5.5 x 1.6 pages 2240 $24.99

The Knot Guide to Wedding Vows and Traditions: Readings, Rituals, Music, Dances, and Toasts (2003) by Carley Roney guides readers through a wide range of wedding ceremonies. Definitely a helpful resource. ISBN 0767902483 Soft cover, 9.2 x 7.5 x 0.6 pages 224 $16.00

Creating Meaningful Funeral Ceremonies: A Guide for Families (1999) by Dr. Alan D. Wolfelt leads readers and interpreters through the funeral process. A good resource for those who wish to interpret funerals often. ISBN 1879651203 Soft cover, 8.5 x 8.5 x 0.2 pages 80 $12.95

HANDBOOK OF DENOM-INATIONS IN THE UNITED STATES 13th edition (2010) by Craig D. Atwood is a resource that gives a description of thousands of denominations, their

Celebrating Judaism in the Home: A Manual for Deaf Jewish Families (1996) by Rabbi Miriam Biatch includes insight to Judaism, holidays, and a dictionary. Soft cover, 127 pages.

histories, doctrinal beliefs, and membership statistics. ISBN 0687057841 Hard cover, 8.9 x 5.6 x 1.5 pages 400 $24.00

Special order: Temple Beth Solomon of the Deaf, 13580 Osborne Street, Arleta, CA 91331. 818/896-6721 TTY

The Story of Christianity: Volume One: The Early Church to the Reformation (2010) by Justo Gonzalez is a helpful resource for background into the history of the Church. ISBN 0060633158 Soft cover, 9.3 x 6.1 x 1.2 pages 528 $25.95

The Story of Christianity: Volume Two: The Reformation to the Present (2010) by Justo Gonzalez is the second book in the series. ISBN 0060633166 Soft cover, 9.4 x 6.2 x 1.1 pages 560 $25.95

How to Be a Perfect Stranger: A Guide to Etiquette in Other People's Religious Ceremonies (1999) by Arthur J. Magida is very informative for interpreters working outside their own tradition. ISBN 1893361012 Soft cover, 9.0 x 6.8 x 1.2 pages 435 $19.95

Professionalism is for Everyone: Five Keys to Being a True Professional (2012) by James R. Ball shows readers how to be a professional. Great insight. ISBN 1887570055 Soft cover, 7.2 x 5.0 x 0.3 pages 72 $9.95

5 Steps to Professional Presence: How to Project Confidence, Competence, and Credibility at Work (2000) by Lisa Scherrer Dugan explicates behavior and mannerisms for the working professional. ISBN 1580624421 Soft cover, 9.2 x 7.4 x 0.8 pages 256 $14.95

The Mask of Benevolence: Disabling the Deaf Community (1999) by Harlan L. Lane defines circumstances of how the Deaf community has been oppressed from society. Very insightful. ISBN 1581210094 Soft cover, 8.2 x 5.2 x 1.0 pages 334 $11.95

The Church and Deaf People: A Study of Identity, Communication and Relationships with Special

IN TIMES OF CRISIS AND SORROW: A Minister's Manual Resource

Reference to the Ecclesiology of Jürgen Moltmann (2004) by Roger Hitching engages readers with historical and present struggles of Deaf people within the church. Very insightful literature. ISBN 1842272225 Soft Cover, 0.8 x 6.0 x 8.8 pages 235 $27.99

Words for Your Wedding: The Wedding Service Book (1986) by David Glusker describes the parts of the wedding service and includes different services by denominations. ISBN 0060631317 Soft Cover, 7.9 x 5.3 x 0.5 pages 176 $14.95

Team Interpreting as Collaboration and Interdependence (2010) by Jack Hoza provides an exhaustive look at teaming. ISBN 0916883523 Soft Cover, 6 x 9 pages 214 $59.95

Guide (2001) by Carol Marie Noren engages readers by providing various parts of the funeral service, by depicting various services and it includes a glossary. ISBN 0787954209 Hard Cover, 9.3 x 7.2 x 1.2 pages 352 $24.95

VISUAL MUSIC: INTERPRETING SONGS IN AMERICAN SIGN LANGAUGE (2009) by Raymont L. Anderson immerses readers in the artistry of signing and interpreting music. ISBN 1434372529 Soft Cover, 8.9 x 6 x 0.8 pages 248 $14.49

Interpretation SKILLS: English to American Sign Language (1993) by Marty Taylor provides a standardized format for discussing English to ASL interpretation. ISBN 0969779208 Soft Cover, 8.4 x 5.4 x 0.3 pages 93 $27.08

Appendix A – Organizations

The following are Deaf and/or interpreting related organizations.

National Catholic Office for the Deaf
7202 Buchanan Street
Landover Hills, MD 20784-2236
Voice - 301- 577- 1684
TTY - 301 - 577 – 4184
www.ncod.org
(has links to many dioceses)

The United Methodist Committee on
Deaf and Hard of Hearing Ministries
www.umcd.org

Deaf Missions
21199 Greenview Rd.
Council Bluffs, IA 51503
Phone: (712) 322-5493 (Voice/TTY)
www.deafmissions.com

Deaf Video Communications
25 W 560 Geneva Road, Suite 10
Carol Stream, IL 60188-2231
(630) 221-0909
www.deafvideo.com

National Alliance of Black Interpreters (NAOBI)
DC Chapter
PO Box 90532
Washington, DC 20090
www.naobidc.org

Registry of Interpreters for the Deaf, Inc.
(RID)
333 Commerce Street
Alexandria, VA 22314
(703) 838-0030 Voice
(703) 838-0459 TTY
(703) 838-0454 Fax
www.rid.org

National Association of the Deaf (NAD)
814 Thayer Ave
Silver Spring, MD 20910
(301) 587-1788
www.nad.org

American Sign Language Teachers Association
(ASLTA)
P.O. Box 92445
Rochester, New York 14692-9998
www.aslta.org

Conference of Interpreter Trainers (CIT)
P.O. Box 254623
Sacramento, California 95865-4623
Phone: 619-594-7417
www.cit-asl.org

Central Piedmont Community College
Interpreting Education Department
PO Box 35009
Charlotte, NC 28235
(704) 330-2722
www.cpcc.edu/interpreter_education/
(Offers online classes)

American Consortium of Certified Interpreters
(ACCI)
PO Box 7451
Stockton, CA 95267-0451
(209) 475-4837 Voice / TTY
www.acci-iap.org

Jewish Deaf Community Center
507 Bethany Road
Burbank, CA 91504
www.jdcc.org

American Association of the Deaf-Blind
(AADB)
8630 Fenton Street, Suite 121
Silver Spring, Maryland 20910-3803
(301) 495-4402 TTY
(301) 495-4403 Voice
(301) 495-4404 Fax
www.aadb.org

Northeastern University Quality Assurance Screening
Regional Interpreter Education Center
American Sign Language Program
405 Meserve Hall
Boston, MA 02115
617-373-2463 Voice
617-373-3067 TTY
www.asl.neu.edu/riec

LCMS Deaf Missions, Lutheran Church - Missouri
Synod
1333 S. Kirkwood Road
St. Louis, Missouri 63122-7295
888-899-5031 TTY
800-433-3954 ext. 1321 Voice
www.lcmsdeaf.org

Concordia Theological Seminary
Church Interpreter Training Institute (CITI)
6600 N Clinton Street
Fort Wayne, IN 46825-4996
260-452-2100 voice
http://www.ctsfw.edu/Page.aspx?pid=727

The Association of Visual Language Interpreters of
Canada
PO Box 29005 Lendrum
Edmonton, Alberta, Canada T6H 5Z6
780-430-9442 Voice / TTY
780-988-2660 Fax
www.avlic.ca

Gallaudet University
800 Florida Avenue, N.E.
Washington, D.C. 20002
202-651-5050 (visitor's center) Voice / TTY
www.gallaudet.edu

CODA International, Inc.
P.O. Box 30715
Santa Barbara, CA 93130-0715
www.coda-international.org
(Children of Deaf Adults)

Appendix B - Church Internet Sites

Resources listed can be used to research doctrines, history, and other useful information.

African Methodist Episcopal Church (AME)
1134 11th Street, N.W.
Washington, DC 20001
www.ame-church.com

African Methodist Episcopal Zion Church
P.O. Box 32843
Charlotte, NC 28323
www.amez.org

American Association of Lutheran Churches
801 West 106th St., #203
Minneapolis, MN 55420
www.taalc.org

American Baptist Association
4605 N. State Line Avenue
Texarkana, TX 75503
www.abaptist.org

Assemblies of God International
1445 Boonville Avenue
Springfield, MO 65802
www.ag.org

Baptist General Conference
2002 South Arlington Heights Road
Arlington Heights, IL 60005
www.bgcworld.org

Church of God (Seventh Day)
330 West 152nd Ave.
P.O. Box 33677
Denver, CO 80233
www.cog7.org

Church of the Nazarene
6401 The Paseo
Kansas City, MO 64131
www.nazarene.org

Church of the Untied Brethren in Christ
3002 Lake Street
Huntington, IN 46750
www.ub.org

Episcopal Church
815 Second Avenue
New York, NY 10017
www.ecusa.anglican.org

Jehovah's Witnesses
25 Columbia Heights
Brooklyn, NY 11201-2483
www.watchtower.org

Lutheran Church - Missouri Synod
1333 South Kirkwood Road
St. Louis, MO 63122-7295
www.lcms.org

Mennonite Church USA
421 South Second Street, Suite 600
Elkhart, IN 46516
www.mennonites.org

Orthodox Church in America
P.O. Box 675
Sysosset, NY 11791-0675
www.oca.org

Pentecostal Assemblies of the Word, Inc.
3939 Meadows Drive
Indianapolis, IN 46205
www.pawinc.org

Pentecostal Church of God
4901 Pennsylvania
P.O. Box 850
Joplin, MO 64802
www.pcg.org

Presbyterian Church (USA)
100 Witherspoon Street
Louisville, KY 40202
www.pcusa.org

Presbyterian Church in America
1852 Century Place
Atlanta, GA 30345-4305
www.pcanet.org

Roman Catholic Church Council
3211 Fourth Street
Washington, DC 20017
www.vatican.va

Seventh-day Adventist Church
12501 Old Columbia Pike
Silver Spring, MD 20904-6600
www.adventist.org

Southern Baptist Convention
901 Commerce Street, Suite 750
Nashville, TN 37203
www.sbc.net

United Church of Christ
700 Prospect Ave
Cleveland, OH 02108
www.ucc.org

United Methodist Church
PO Box 340007
1009 19th Avenue S.
Nashville, TN 37203-0007
www.umc.org

Appendix C – Suggestions for New Interpreters

The following suggestions are from certified &/or qualified religious interpreters.

1. Preparation is a must. Get hold of the preparation materials (sermon, scripture passages, music, and announcements) ahead of time.

2. Study the church's/denomination's doctrine.

3. When signing music, sign the meaning of the song instead of glossing the stanzas.

4. If a new term is used, sign or speak the meaning of it as well.

5. Be familiar with the customs of the church.

6. Reflection after interpreting is important; it is a good method for learning. Learn the definition of new terms, more than likely they will be repeated.

7. Keep up to date on current events.

8. Study Scripture because faith is based on it.

9. Be open to feedback and suggestions.

10. The work of religious interpreters is to be taken seriously. Interpreters are the vessel to directly influence the spiritual lives of others.

11. "Never lose the wonder of the miracle that you participate in."

12. Have a book on theological terms.

13. Be mentored before working by yourself.

14. Be prepared to work with a population with varying language needs.

15. Establish a relationship with the church, not just with the pastor, but with the music ministry, youth minister, education director, and other ministry leaders.

16. Continue with professional development. It is crucial!

17. Do not ignore your own spiritual growth.

18. The Spirit will be there to help and guide you.

19. Spend time with native ASL users.

20. Know the congregation's history.

21. Learn the Deaf participants' preferred signs for religious terms.

22. Have access to a resource library.

23. Find out who the pillars of the church are (longest attending members), and memorize their names.

24. Meet with the minister/speaker to understand the message (and its points) being preached.

25. It is easier to interpret in your own faith tradition.

26. Continue professional behavior before and after the service (e.g., not using profanity).

27. Follow the social norms and language preference of the congregation.

28. Become the best interpreter you can be!

29. Know the ins and outs of the service. Will there be Communion? Will people come forward for prayer?

30. Gain language fluency.

31. Some people have the heart, but not the skill. Both are necessary.

32. Be flexible.

33. Do not assume Deaf people know religious vocabulary.

34. "Religious interpreting is at best, a Holy Spirit driven thing."

35. Know the signs for countries and major cities around the globe.

36. Have a good rapport with worship team leaders.

37. Have other colleagues to discuss things with, perhaps begin a peer discussion group.

38. Represent the profession well.

39. Think about getting business cards made.

40. Maintain integrity in your work. Arrive before the service begins, and keep your word.
41. It is okay to be friends with the Deaf people, just do not become their pastor.

42. If you are not able to make it the worship service, work out communication methods (e.g., email, fax, or phone) beforehand. This will help prevent deeper frustration in those who wonder where the interpreter is.

43. Do not speak for the Deaf people (don't make decisions for them).

44. Turn your cell phone off before the service begins. You will be embarrassed if it is your phone that disrupts the service.

45. Find other interpreters who will work at the church as well. Two or three interpreters who can rotate Sundays will reduce full reliance on one interpreter.

46. Locate religious interpreting workshops to attend, even if they are out-of-state. Be sure the instructors are certified or qualified. Other types of interpreting workshops are helpful, too.

47. Consider joining RID as an associate member. This will help you keep up with news in the profession.

48. Study the book, <u>So You Want to be an Interpreter,</u> <u>4th Ed</u>.

49. After interpreting for a few years, consider mentoring novice interpreters who work in Christian settings.

50. Some parishioners want to learn how to sign. Encourage one of the Deaf parishioners to teach a sign language class, assist him or her, or co-teach it.

51. See if the Deaf parishioners wish to sign in the choir or lead songs.

52. Interact with Deaf people outside of church, see how they live, see how they enjoy (or not) church and why. Adapt what you learn to the service.

53. If possible, go to a Deaf church and see how they sign certain concepts, and how they artistically sign songs.

54. Some congregations offer an earlier worship service. Take advantage of this opportunity and sit in on the service. This will help to prepare for the interpreted service.

55. Include the Deaf parishioners in the service, have them sign songs, read Scripture, or sign litanies.

56. Provide suggestions to church leaders regarding how they can reach out to the Deaf community.

57. Finally, make sure it is God who wants you there. Everyone else may want you interpreting, but it's most important to know what God wants. Pray for His guidance before and during the service, and remember to do it for God's glory.

58. Online sign dictionary websites (videos) are available and the following websites are, for the most part, pretty accurate. Keep in mind; however, a few signs might be considered regional signs (only known to certain areas) or just might be conceptually inaccurate altogether. Use professional discretion.
www.deafmd.org (medical signs)
 www.signingsavvy.com (general signs)
www.aslpro.com (general sign dictionary and a religious sign dictionary)

59. Be sure to read the book, *Deaf Ministry: Ministry Models for Expanding the Kingdom of God*, since an interpreted ministry is one aspect of deaf ministry.

I wish to extend a special appreciation to the following interpreters for their wisdom, suggestions, and their support for this section of the book.

Karl Kosiorek
Bishop Peggy Johnson
Sarah Yates
Cari Mitchell
Jennifer Bell
Carol Tipton
Linda Brown
Margaret Stanton
Cheryl Wilcox
Tina Burke
Eileen Colarusso
Barbara Tolker
Diane Rehling
PJ Carberg
Gail Goggin
Torri Diaz

Appendix D – Standard Practice Paper: Multiple Roles in Interpreting

Multiple Roles in Interpreting

The Registry of Interpreters for the Deaf, Inc., (RID) Standard Practice Paper (SPP) provides a framework of basic, respectable standards for RID members' professional work and conduct with consumers. This paper also provides specific information about the practice setting. This document is intended to raise awareness, educate, guide and encourage sound basic methods of professional practice. The SPP should be considered by members in arriving at an appropriate course of action with respect to their practice and professional conduct. It is hoped that the standards will promote commitment to the pursuit of excellence in the practice of interpreting and be used for public distribution and advocacy.

About Multiple Roles in Interpreting

Interpreters work in a variety of settings and situations; some are employees of institutions, agencies and companies, and some are self-employed. Interpreters who are self-employed are less likely to encounter situations in which non-interpreting duties are expected of them. Interpreters who are employed full-time by businesses, school districts, universities, government agencies, hospitals or mental health-care providers, for example, might perform other duties when not interpreting. These types of jobs may be referred to as multiple role jobs.

Examples of multiple role positions include but are not limited to:

* Nurse/Interpreter
* K-12 Educational Interpreter/Track Coach
* Job Coach/Interpreter
* Certified Deaf Interpreter/Interpreter Trainer
* University Student Advisor/Interpreter
* Interpreter Supervisor/Interpreter
* Company Interpreter/Sales Representative

Different job models are used depending on which duties are primary and which duties are secondary. Clearly outlining an employee's job duties is significant in terms of resolving potential role conflicts. One approach is to determine a percentage for each portion of the job; for example, 70 percent interpreting and 30 percent coaching.

In multiple role positions, conflicts can arise between the interpreting role and other job requirements. In general, the NAD-RID Code of Professional Conduct (CPC) guides interpreters to avoid role conflicts, as exemplified by CPC tenet 3.3.: "Avoid performing dual or conflicting roles in multidisciplinary (e.g. educational or mental health teams) or other settings." The best time to deal with potential role conflicts is before they occur. When developing a job description for a multiple role position, consideration should be given to the interpreting responsibilities as well as any other employment requirements.

STANDARD PRACTICE

Developing multiple role positions

When developing and implementing a multiple role position with interpreting responsibilities, best practices include:

* requiring interpreter certification and appropriate education and training
* providing professional development opportunities
* developing a pay formula that considers the multiple roles and compensates the employee for having dual skills
* defining confidentiality boundaries for both the interpreting role and other required roles, in a variety of situations
* recognizing the interpreter's need to limit the number of hours spent physically interpreting, especially if the interpreter works alone
* specifying the amount of time expected for interpreting versus other job duties, noting whether interpreting is a primary or secondary duty
* determining a process to use when role conflicts do arise, so they can be resolved effectively
* considering hiring outside interpreters to cover sensitive meetings, such as, personnel reviews, reprimands or grievance procedures, that might be a conflict-of-interest for staff interpreters

When functioning in a multiple role job with interpreting named as the primary role, interpreters generally do not:

* reveal, report or use confidential information obtained while interpreting
* perform the interpreter role and another role simultaneously
* interpret beyond their competency level
* routinely perform tasks that might exacerbate physical problems sometimes associated with interpreting
* interpret for long periods of time without relief
* perform other duties when needed for interpreting

When interpreting is not named as a primary role, conflicts can still occur. To respect consumers' rights and confidentiality, great care must be taken to inform all parties:

* of the role in which the person is functioning
* of the possible future use of the information gained in that situation
* that there may be legal mandates that override the NAD-RID Code of Professional Conduct

Interpreter credentials

Employers of interpreters can verify interpreter competency. An appropriate indicator of an interpreter's level of competence is the interpreter's credentials. The most reliable credentials in the United States are those established by the National Association of the Deaf (NAD) and the Registry of Interpreters for the Deaf, Inc. (RID).

STANDARD PRACTICE PAPER

NAD-RID Code of Professional Conduct

The NAD-RID Code of Professional Conduct is the foundation of the interpreting profession. Every employer of interpreters should become familiar with this document as it will have significant influence in the development of multiple role positions.

RID believes that through multiple role positions, interpreters can be placed in many settings in which the hiring of a full-time interpreter would not otherwise be feasible or justifiable. By developing a multiple role position, the hiring entity benefits by having an employee with dual skills. RID believes that knowing the potential issues regarding multiple roles and having a plan in place to resolve conflicts is crucial to the success of such positions. Planning for possible challenges avoids compromising accessibility for all involved parties.

STANDARD PRACTICE PAPER

3   Multiple Roles in Interpreting

Appendix E – Advocacy

The work of advocacy will periodically be a part of the interpreter's work. It can be in a moment of educating someone, a full writing campaign to legislatures, and works in between. Not surprising, the church is known for doing social justice and will often include advocacy in this focus of ministry. This appendix orients readers about advocacy and includes the nuts and bolts for the interpreter. The following is from the Registry of Interpreters for the Deaf and can be adopted for your personal use.[72]

What is advocacy?

The American Heritage Dictionary defines advocacy as "the act of pleading or arguing in favor of something, such as a cause, idea, or policy; active support." That's true, but it can be even simpler. Advocacy allows people and groups to share their opinion with policymakers. These policy makers are usually your elected officials and they vote on many important issues that affect you and people like you. But policymakers can't represent you and your views

---

[72] Registry of Interpreters of the Deaf. (2015). "Advocacy 101." Retrieved from http://www.rid.org/advocacy-overview/ advocacy-toolkit/advocacy-101/.

effectively if you don't communicate with them. Advocacy is a powerful tool to help promote the goals and interests of the profession and the Deaf community.

When to Advocate

You should advocate anytime there is a policy proposed that will affect you. But you don't have to wait for someone to propose a change to get involved. Be proactive! If you have an idea for a new law or policy, contact your elected officials. They have the ability to propose legislation that their constituents request. So if you have an idea, share it – that idea might become a law.

Where to Advocate?

Advocacy can happen at all levels of government and in many different ways. Whether you decide to focus on local, state, or federal issues will depend on you and your interests. Some issues are more appropriately addressed at the state and local level. Still others are better addressed through federal legislation and/or regulation. For example, policies related to Vide Relay Service (VRS) are promulgated through the Federal Communications Commission (FCC), a federal agency. Conversely, many states have enacted legislation regulating interpreters practicing within their borders.

Why Advocate?

Many advocates start because they witness or experience what they perceive as an injustice. Perhaps you are a certified interpreter losing opportunities to uncertified interpreters because your state doesn't have a licensure requirement. Or perhaps you are having a hard time convincing organizations and businesses that you are a professional who should be compensated for your time and work. Each advocate has a different reason for becoming more involved, however, most get involved because they encountered a situation that made them say, "Something has to be done!" This situation defines your core issue or cause and will become the basis of your advocacy efforts.

How to Advocate

Everyone approaches advocacy differently, but some principles hold true no matter your approach. First and foremost, be honest. Your credibility as an advocate depends on whether policymakers can trust what you say. Don't exaggerate facts or statistics and don't make up information when you don't know the answer to a question. Be respectful of the policymaker and his or her time. Stay informed so that you can provide as much information to support your opinion as possible. And finally, be persistent. Changing policy takes time and it's important that you remind policymakers about your issue. Something as simple as a short email can serve as an important tool to keep your issue fresh in a policymaker's mind.

Writing Tips

Sending a letter or an email is a great way to communicate your thoughts and feelings to policymakers because it allows you to think about your message, write it down, and then edit it until you feel comfortable with what you are sending. It is also a good alternative to calling on the phone if you are concerned you may get "stage fright" or trouble understanding what is being said.

Here are some general guidelines for writing letters and emails to your representative:

- ❑ Your letter or email should address a single topic, issue, or bill.
- ❑ If you are mailing your letter, typed, one-page letters are best.
- ❑ The best letters and emails are courteous, to the point, and include specific supporting examples.
- ❑ Always say why you are writing and who you are. (If you want a response, you must include your name and address, even when using email.)
- ❑ Provide detail.
- ❑ Be factual not emotional.
- ❑ Provide specific rather than general information about how the topic affects you and others.
- ❑ If a certain bill is involved, cite the correct title or number whenever possible.
- ❑ Close by requesting the action you want taken: a vote for or against a bill, or change in general policy.
- ❑ As a general rule, emails are usually shorter and more to the point.
- ❑ ALWAYS THANK HIM OR HER FOR TAKING THE TIME TO READ THE LETTER/EMAIL.

Personalized letters and emails can have a big impact on policymakers. Whenever possible, write your own email or letter, even if you borrow points from a form letter. The message can be simple and to the point.

Appendix F – RID Views Article

A Monthly Publication of the Registry of Interpreters for the Deaf   Vol. 19, Issue 11, December 2002

Interactive Interpretation in African American Pentecostal Churches
By Myisha J. Blackman

Preacher: When you found Jesus…
Congregation: Yeah!
Preacher: You got Jesus. (pause)
Congregation: Amen!
Preacher: in the morning…in the noon day…Yes…when the sun goes down…
Congregation: (yelling, cheering, crying, jumping)
Preacher: It's Jesus…Jesus…Jesus…Jesus…Jeee!
Congregation: (yelling, cheering, crying, jumping)

Above is an excerpt from a sermon titled, "Wrong Focus" by Bishop T.D. Jakes. He preached it in 1998 at his annual singles conference called *No More Sheets*. Whereas sermons are conventionally monologic, they are necessarily interactive in African American Pentecostal churches. Following my discussion of what makes these church services interactive, I will, in this article, discuss what such interaction means for the ASL simultaneous interpreter.

Pentecostalism and African American Discourse

Pentecostalism is a branch of Christianity that places special emphasis on the Holy Spirit and values uninhibited expression of religious beliefs. The day of Pentecost (literally, the fiftieth day) is a celebration that takes place on the seventh Sunday after Easter. Today, it is celebrated by commemorating the day when the Holy Spirit descended on the apostles after the ascension of Christ. Among other things, the descent was characterized by a phenomenon known as "speaking in tongues." Pentecostal church services are seen as extremely emotional and often defiant of the strict customs of mainline Protestant services (Paris, 1982). Audience members may, as they will, communicate their sentiment to their God with reckless abandonment. They may show the preacher, making no small stir, how the sermon is affecting them.

African American discourse is not too far removed. As if the complexity of dealing with the emotive expressions in Pentecostal church services were not enough of a challenge for the ASL simultaneous interpreter, s/he is pitted against the indirect, metaphoric and implicit nature of African American discourse. Replete with "innuendo(s) and double meaning…" let the interpreter beware (Lee, 1993). In reviewing literature on African American discourse, the term *signifying* kept coming up. It is not evident who coined the term, yet it has been extensively defined. Signifying refers to a "form of social discourse within the African American community…(where speakers) play rhetorically upon the meaning and sounds of words, and…(are)…quick and…witty in (their responses" (lee, 1993). Although speakers may signify to insult one another, it always involves "a high use of figurative language" (Lee, 1993). Given the marriage of the soulful, unrestrained displays of worship typical in Pentecostal church services with the humorous, spontaneous circumlocution of African American discourse, one need not look too hard to see that an African American Pentecostal church service is a setting where interactive interpreting occurs.

Interactive Discourse

What are the characteristics of this interactive discourse? In order to answer this question, we must first look at what interactive means. Something (e.g. a computer game or discourse) is interactive if there exists a two-way communication between a source of information and a user (Random House, 2000). African American Pentecostal church services are filled with rich exchange between the minister and the congregation (Pasteur & Toldson, 1982). The minister both directly and indirectly seeks participation from the audience. Moreover, members of the audience are free to offer unsolicited responses. These responses may either be verbal or nonverbal.

Call-Response

Adjacency pairs are found in almost all interactive discourse (Metzger, 1999). They consist of two parts that usually occur together (e.g. "Hello" followed by "Hi" in a greeting)> Call-Response is an adjacency pair, exclusive to African American discourse, whereby the audience completes a speaker's thought or sentence out loud (Hill, 1998). Stepping to the podium, ministers often begin by saying "God is good." (Lewis, 2001). The audience, familiar with the service's proceedings and African American cultural norms, recognized the statement as an invitation to finish the sentence with "…all the time." If, on the other hand, the minister opens with "All the time…" the audience knows to say"…god is good." Moreover, the audience knows this statement to mean that the communication (the sermon) is about to start. A "call" therefore is what sociologist Erving Goffman refers to as the channel open signal (Goffman, 1976; Hatch, 1992).

Direct & Indirect Appeals for Participation

Ministers are constantly asking the audience to participate. These appeals are made directly and indirectly. For the sake of reciprocity, the audience must supply a quick response (Rickford & Rickford, 2000). By not responding in a timely manner, the minister will feel like s/he is out on a limb. Ministers will directly seek a response by asking questions such as *"Can I get a witness?"* or *"Ya'll gone help me preach?"* Besides questions, the minister will instruct audience members to act. They may say, *"Praise Him!"* or *"High-five your neighbor and tell them…!"*

Appeals for the audience's participation are indirect as well. When a minister says, "Amen, lights!" it is an indication that s/he is not getting enough feedback. S/he is saying, "Since, you are not responding, maybe the light bulbs will support me." Of course, this is said jokingly. The minister, in tune with the audience, has sensed that something has happened to quiet the audience. The statement, then, is an attempt to get them back on track.

Unsolicited Backchannel Signals

The minister must not always beseech the audience for support. Audience members may, at any time, offer backchannel signals, or show that the "message is getting through" (Goffman, 1976; Hatch, 1992). The minister may be at a point in the sermon where they can relate. They know what s/he is talking about. They are getting the answers they came for so, in exchange, they cheer or pat their feet (Perry, 1999). Some may cry and run around the church. Leaping from one's seat is not uncommon. They simply give back out a grateful heart. These unsolicited reactions come in many other forms. They may nod their heads, wave or clap their hands. Perhaps some will yell, "Gloray!" Others will dance (also called 'shouting')! Then again, some may elbow their neighbor proclaiming, "That's good!"

Interactive Interpreting

How must the interpreter handle all this interaction? Must every "Amen!" be interpreted? How can a Deaf audience member look at their neighbor, repeat the words of the minister while looking at the interpreter? How does the Deaf audience member interact with a hearing neighbor who does not sign? From the last two questions, it seems like the Deaf congregation has an isolated experience. However, there are strategies an interpreter can use to ensure that the Deaf congregant has a worship experience equivalent to that of a hearing congregant.

First, it is important that the interpreter be familiar with the traditions of the church (Sestak, 1996). An interpreter who is familiar with the proceedings of African American Pentecostal churches will recognize feedback from the audience as such and therefore not attempt to interpret them. In fact, I am sure that Deaf audience members who are familiar with the service may offer feedback of their own. It goes without saying, then, that interpreters must be able to convey the minister's message in ASL with the same equivalence so that Deaf congregants feel like leaping from their sets, too.

What does an interpreter do with "Amen, lights!"? For the most part, the interpreter must be cognizant of form versus meaning (Larson, 1998). The form, or grammatical make up (also called the surface structure) appears to be a simple declarative statement. However, closer scrutiny would reveal the speaker's intent and meaning also called the deep structure), which is a request. Having recognized and grasped the meaning of the statement, the interpreter must now explicate the meaning. That the statement is a request is implied by the minister's delivery and the hearing audience member's interpretation thereof. Their interpretation is based, in part, on the speaker-addressee relationship (Larson, 1998). What's more, the hearing audience members and the minister likely share a schema of the discourse of hearing African Americans as well as scripts relating to the protocol in African American Pentecostal churches. (Metzger, 1999). The interpreter may very well share the schema and scripts, too. Consequently, the implied information must be explicated, or made explicit, for the Deaf congregant who may not share the same framework (Metzger, 1999). Therefore, an equivalent interpretation might look like "LIGHT…HEY! THEY (the audience) NOT TELL ME 'AMEN' MABYE YOU HELP ME. AMEN?"

Second, the interpreter should, as part of the service, educate the congregation on deafness and the interpretation process (Bearden, 1975; Sampley, 1990; Godwin-Kogelschatz, 2000). By doing so, hearing members of the audience can become sensitive to the needs of the Deaf. In order for a Deaf congregation to interact with their neighbor (especially a hearing, non-signing one), it is the position of this paper that the interpreter conveys the minister's instructions. For example, "*Nudge your neighbor and tell them, 'You're in the right place today!'*" It is hoped that the hearing person will have seen that there is a time delay involved in interpretation and will wait until the message is given. When the hearing non-signing neighbor reports the words to the Deaf congregant, the Deaf congregant may choose to read his/her lips. The Deaf congregant has the option of mouthing or signing the words to the hearing neighbor.

Suggestions for the Future Research

To better understand the dynamics involved in interpreting in African American Pentecostal churches, there needs to be research on the interplay between culture and religious expression. As there exist all-Deaf congregations headed by a Deaf minister, the dynamics of their church services need to be explored. Herein lies tremendous insight for the interpreter. Furthermore, it would be worth examining what non-African American Pentecostal church services are like (i.e. Latino Pentecostal or Caucasian Pentecostal). For the religious interpreter, it would be beneficial to consider how the factor of ethnicity influences the dynamics of religious expression and therefore interpretation. In terms of interaction, are African American non-Pentecostal churches as interactive (e.g. Methodist, Catholic, Jehovah's Witness)? What would interpreting for these churches entail, given that explicit expression may not exist, yet African American discourse may be present?

Conclusion

The African American Pentecostal church is a setting in which interactive interpretation occurs. Services are highly interactive due to two aspects. First, there is rich interplay between the speaker (the minister) and the audience (the congregation). Ministers are constantly asking the audience for feedback, both directly and indirectly. Then again, the audience steadily offers unsolicited feedback to the minister. Responses from members of the congregation are both verbal and nonverbal.

Second, there is the factor of the African American discourse. It is indirect, high-context (much of the information is implicit) and tends to be exceptionally metaphorical. For the interpreter to do an effective job transmitting the interaction with equivalence, so that the Deaf congregant may participate fully, s/he has a great responsibility. S/he must be familiar with African American discourse, well-versed in the theory of interpretation, and well-informed about church protocol. (Note: s/he must also exercise self-restraint – s/he cannot dance and interpret at the same time!) If s/he loves what s/he is doing and knows what s/he is doing, then the interpreting in African American Pentecostal church can be most rewarding. Interpreting in this setting with skill and equivalence is a tough job. Most religious interpreters are stigmatized for not being skilled (Godwin-Kogelschatz, 2000). Some say "I do not need training because I am called by God. The Holy Spirit will cause me to do well." However, the interpreter who does their homework brings pride to their work and smiles to the faces of those they serve. Their work is important because it can bring prestige to the entire field. This alone is worth shouting about. Can I get an "Amen!"?

Works Cited

Bearden, C.E. (1975). *A handbook of religious interpreters for the Deaf*. Atlanta, GA: Home Mission Board of the Southern Baptist Convention.

Godwin-Kogelschatz, B. (2000). *Religious Interpreting: Perceptions and Realisms*. Working Paper, Gallaudet University, Department of ASL, Linguistics, and Interpretation.

Goffman, E. (1976). *Replies and responses*. Language in Society, 5,3, 254-313.

Hatch, E. (1992). *Discourse and Language Education*. Cambridge: Cambridge University Press.

Hill, P.L., et al. (Eds.) (1998) *Call and response the riverside anthology of the African American Literary Tradition*. Boston, MA: Houghton Mifflin Company.

Larson, M. (1998). *Meaning-Based Translation: A guide to cross-language equivalence*. Lanham, MD: University Press of America.

Lee, C. (1993). *Signifying as a scaffold for literary interpretations: the pedagogical implications of an African American discourse genre*. Urbana, IL: National Council of Teachers of English.

Metzer, M. (1999). *Sign language interpreting: deconstructing the myth of neutrality.* W

APPENDIX F – RID *VIEWS* ARTICLE

Paris, A. (1982). *Black Pentecostalism Southern religion in an urban world.* Amherst: University of Massachusetts Press.

Pasteur, A.B. & LL Toldson. (1982). *Roots of soul: the psychology of Black expressiveness.* Garden City, NY: Anchor Press.

Perry, M.V. (1999). *A heuristic investigation of the psychological benefits derived from participating in the African-American emotional church worship service.* Ohio: The Union Institute. Doctoral Dissertation.

Rickford, J. & Russell Rickford. (2000). *Spoken soul: The story of Black English.* New York, NY: John Wiley & Sons, Inc.

Sampley, DeAnn. (1990). *A Guide to Deaf Ministry: Let's Sign Worthy of the Lord.* Grand Rapids, MI: Zondervan Publishing House.

Sestak, C. (1996). *The dynamics of church interpretation.* Working Paper. Gallaudet University, Department of ASL, Linguistics and Interpretation.

Schegloff, E., and Harvey Sacks. (1973). *Opening up closings.* Semiotica 7, 4: 289-327.

Appendix G – RID Views Article #2

Team Interpreting in a Religious Setting
By Leo Yates, Jr., MDiv., CI & CT

Many of us have been in situations where we wish we had a co-interpreter, perhaps because we need a feed, we begin to feel fatigued or we want to learn from others. Working in teams can raise the expectation that interpreters can and do work in pairs. In most settings, team interpreting is preferable to interpreting alone. Many articles have been written in support of team interpreting, providing readers with good reason to use this approach.

Within the church setting, there are numerous ways to incorporate the concept of team interpreting. Teams of interpreters can share the responsibility of interpreting worship services, Sunday school lessons, Bible study sessions and other church-related activities. This article focuses primarily on strategies for team interpreting in worship services.

The worship service is the most common event in which an interpreter works within a church setting. When looking at the logistical aspects of the service, the interpreter will consider placement, lighting and language needs and distinguish between primary and secondary roles within the service. The following examples highlight typical mainline protestant worship services; however, these techniques can be adapted for services of varying styles of worship. Interpreting worship services can be a venue for interpreting students to work with a mentor, and the following strategies can be used by both learner and mentor as an effective way to introduce, rehearse and interpret the service. Worship services are not only conducive to mentoring, but they can also be a setting for working professionals to practice and work on goals such as increasing use of facial adverbs, expanding concepts or improving processing time.

It is helpful to know that most worship services have segments that originated from Jewish worship; the Early Church adapted the service for Christian worship.

Liturgy, a prescribed format for worship, guides the congregation in its praise and worship to God, with a liturgist (a minister or lay person) leading the service. Standard worship services include an opening with praise (hymn and/or prayer), a reading of the word (Scripture), a homily (the message), a sacrament (typically Holy Communion) and a closing with praise (hymn and/or prayer). The liturgy will vary depending on

* Special celebrations

* The service revolving around the Eucharist or the word (homily)

* Events of the liturgical calendar (i.e. Advent, Christmas, Lent, Easter, & Pentecost)

Opening/Closing

During the beginning of the service, some congregations begin with a litany or Call to Worship. Using the worship bulletin, team interpreters can divide the litany between them. For instance:

Interpreter 1: Leader: This is the day that the Lord has made.

Interpreter 2: All: (sign with me/copy me) Let us rejoice and be glad in it.

Some denominations such as the Episcopal Church use litanies more frequently than other denominations. Issuing interpreting roles for the litany reduces possible confusion so that deaf worshipers do not sign both parts, especially if the interpreter accidentally neglects body shifting (distinguishing roles).

Hymns and praise songs can be challenging for some interpreters, as some lyrics are abstract or use allegorical connotations, requiring extra preparation and rehearsal. Songs of praise are an integral part of worship for some congregations. Since contemporary praise worship services center the style of worship around song, it can be helpful if one interpreter interprets only the music, while the other interpreter focuses on the other aspects of the service. Working as a team, the second interpreter should observe and feed the first interpreter. This will benefit the interpreter signing the music, particularly if an extra song is unexpectedly added.

From time to time, a couple will sing an anthem (a duet). This provides the opportunity for the interpreters to shadow the two singers rather than remain in the typical interpreting location. Shadowing requires some coordination, as well as some rehearsal time; however, it will have an overall positive effect for those needing/viewing the interpreters.

The Word

Scripture can be the most enjoyable part of the service to interpret. Depending on the Scripture passage that is being read, interpreters can interpret biblical characters much like actors assuming roles. Sometimes there will be both a primary role and a secondary or supporting role. In some scenarios, one can interpret the narration, while the other interprets the verses spoken by a biblical character. This type of creativity enhances the dramatic effect when interpreting texts. For example:

Exodus 8:8 Interpreter 1 (Narrator): Pharaoh summoned Moses and Aaron and said, (pointing to the other interpreter)

Interpreter 2 (Pharaoh): "Pray to the Lord to take the frogs away from me and my people, and I will let your people go to offer sacrifices to the Lord."

There is a sense that the team using this strategy is leaning toward theatrical interpreting, but it can be quite effective to apply this technique to biblical discourse.

Interpreting Scripture (frozen text) will need some preparation beforehand, and a study Bible (a Bible with footnotes), Bible commentary and a Bible dictionary can help one to understand the historical context of the passage. There are other exceptional resources on the Internet, but these three references are a good start. Time permitting; it is helpful for both interpreters to study the Scripture reading so the team can discuss any text that appears challenging. In fact, this is how some ministers in a community study the text; by coming together in a cluster.

The Homily

Preaching styles are influenced by culture, tradition, denomination and expectations of the congregation. In a Catholic setting, a homily typically lasts five or ten minutes, whereas in some Hispanic settings, a homily may continue up to 45 minutes or longer. Team interpreters will need to discuss whether and how the sermon will be broken up if the homily goes beyond 20 minutes. There is no right answer to this, though it is critical that the interpreter does not look tired and worn out from interpreting for so long, thus not matching the effect of the speaker. If the preacher remains lively throughout the homily, then the interpreter must look lively as well, and team interpreting can help ensure this continuity of affect. The homily is the longest continuous amount of speech to interpret in a worship service. Unlike other parts of the service, which are short and sometimes interactive, the Homily can give the interpreter (whether practitioner or mentee) the opportunity to work on the National Interpreter Certification (NIC) performance test criteria or other skill areas that he or she wishes to improve (i.e. lag time, concept expansion, facial expression, etc.). As one interpreter is focusing on a particular goal, the second interpreter can observe to ensure the message is not diminished.

Conclusion

Promoting a team approach not only educates consumers and other participants that the integrity of the message will better remain intact (particularly when a service goes beyond an hour), but hopefully also influences those in charge (usually a coordinator or one who is paying for the service) that deaf ministry is an essential part of the overall mission of the church. Incorporating an interpreting team begins to open the door to understanding that the team approach is viable and indeed necessary, not only establishing an inclusive environment for all parties involved, but helping redefine standards of interpreting within religious settings to show that team interpreting renders professional services.

Leo Yates, Jr. is a freelance interpreter in the Baltimore-Washington, D.C. area who has over 13 years' experience. He specializes in religious interpreting and presents workshops on the topic. For further information, Mr. Yates can be reached at leoyjr@aol.com.

Appendix H – Wedding Liturgy

The following is a wedding liturgy for studying and practicing.

GREETING

Pastor to people:

Friends, we are gathered together in the sight of God to witness and bless the joining together of David and Lauren in Christian marriage.

The covenant of marriage was established by God, who created us male and female for each other. With his presence and power Jesus graced a wedding at Cana of Galilee, and in his sacrificial love gave us the example for the love of husband and wife. *Lauren and David* come to give themselves to one another in this holy covenant.

DECLARATION OF INTENTION

DECLARATION BY THE MAN AND THE WOMAN

Pastor to the persons who are to marry:

I ask you now, in the presence of God and these people, to declare your intention to enter into union with each other through the grace of Jesus Christ, who calls you into union with himself as acknowledged in your baptism.

Pastor to the woman:

Lauren, will you have David to be your husband, to live together in holy marriage?

Will you love him, comfort him, honor and keep him, in sickness and in health, and forsaking all others, be faithful to him as long as you both shall live?

Woman: I will.

Pastor to the man:

David, will you have Lauren to be your wife, to live together in holy marriage?

Will you love her, comfort her, honor and keep her, in sickness and in health, and forsaking all others, be faithful to her as long as you both shall live?

Man: I will.

RESPONSE OF THE FAMILIES AND PEOPLE

Pastor to people:

The marriage of Lauren and David unites their families and creates a new one. They ask for your blessing.

Parents come forward to light the unity candle and then take their seats.

Parents and other representatives of the families may respond in one of the following ways:

Do you who represent their families rejoice in their union and pray God's blessing upon them?

We do.

Pastor to people:

Will all of you, by God's grace, do everything in your power to uphold and care for these two persons in their marriage?

People: We will.

PRAYER

Let us pray.

God of all peoples, you are the true light illumining everyone. You show us the way, the truth, and the life. You love us even when we are disobedient. You sustain us with your Holy Spirit. We rejoice in your life in the midst of our lives. We praise you for your presence with us, and especially in this act of solemn covenant; through Jesus Christ our Lord. Amen.

PROCLAMATION AND RESPONSE

SCRIPTURE READING

Old Testament
Isaiah 62:5
For as a young man marries a young woman, so shall your

builder marry you, and as the bridegroom rejoices over the bride,
so shall your God rejoice over you.

New Testament
Galatians 5:22-25

22 By contrast, the fruit of the Spirit is love, joy, peace, patience,
kindness, generosity, faithfulness, 23 gentleness, and self-control.
There is no law against such things. 24 And those who belong to
Christ Jesus have crucified the flesh with its passions and desires.
25 If we live by the Spirit, let us also be guided by the Spirit.

SERMONETTE (a short sermon)

INTERCESSORY PRAYER

Eternal God, Creator and Preserver of all life, Author
of salvation, Giver of all grace: Bless and sanctify with
your Holy Spirit Lauren and David, who come now to
join in marriage. Grant that they may give their vows to
each other in the strength of your steadfast love. Enable
them to grow in love and peace with you and with one
another all their days that they may reach out in
concern and service to the world; through Jesus Christ
our Lord. Amen.

THE MARRIAGE

EXCHANGE OF VOWS

The woman and man face each other, joining hands.
The pastor may prompt them, line by line.

Man to woman:

In the name of God, I, David, take you, Lauren, to be my wife, to have and to hold from this day forward, for better, for worse, for richer, for poorer, in sickness and in health, to love and to cherish, until we are parted by death. This is my solemn vow.

 Woman to man:

 In the name of God, I, Lauren, take you, David, to be my husband, to have and to hold from this day forward, for better, for worse, for richer, for poorer, in sickness and in health, to love and to cherish, until we are parted by death. This is my solemn vow.

BLESSING AND EXCHANGE OF RINGS

The pastor, taking the rings, may say one of the following:

These rings (symbols) are the outward and visible sign of an inward and spiritual grace, signifying to us the union between God and his Church. These rings (symbols) are the outward and visible sign of an inward and spiritual grace, signifying to all the uniting of David and Lauren in holy marriage.

The pastor may bless the giving of rings or other symbols of the marriage:

Bless, O Lord, the giving of these rings (symbols), that they who wear them may live in your peace and continue in your favor all the days of their life; through Creator, Redeemer, and Sustainer. Amen.

While placing the ring on the third finger of the recipient's left hand, the giver may say (prompted, line by line, by the pastor):

Lauren/David, I give you this ring as a sign of my vow, and with all that I am, and all that I have, I honor you; in the name of our Creator, Redeemer, and Sustainer.

DECLARATION OF MARRIAGE

The wife and husband join hands. The pastor may place a hand on their joined hands.

Pastor to husband and wife:

You have declared your consent and vows before God and this congregation. May God confirm your covenant and fill you both with grace.

The couple may turn and face the congregation.

Pastor to people:

Now that David and Lauren have given themselves to each other by solemn vows, with the joining of hands, and the giving and receiving of rings, I announce to you that they are husband and wife. Those whom God has joined together, let no one put asunder. Amen. **David, you may kiss your bride.**

BLESSING OF THE MARRIAGE

The pastor prays:
O God, you have so consecrated the covenant of Christian marriage that in it is represented the covenant

between God and his dwelling place. Send therefore your blessing upon Lauren and David that they may surely keep their marriage covenant, and so grow in love and godliness together that their home may be a haven of blessing and peace. Amen.

SENDING FORTH

DISMISSAL WITH BLESSING

Pastor to wife and husband:

God the Eternal keep you in love with each other, so that the peace and grace may abide in your home. Go to serve God and your neighbor in all that you do.

Pastor to people:

Bear witness to the love of God in this world, so that those to whom love is a stranger will find in you generous friends. The grace of our Redeemer, and the love of God, and the communion of the Holy Spirit be with you all. Amen.

Glossary of Interpreting Terms

American Sign Language (ASL): a visual gestural language with its own linguistic structure and grammar; the language used by most Deaf people in the US and Canada.

audism: is the attitude or favor of those who are hearing.

code-switching: using more than one language during a dialogue or conversation.

Code of Professional Conduct: a core set of beliefs, values, and responsibilities fundamental to the interpreting profession that serve to define the exemplary practices of the profession.

Conceptually Accurate Signed English (CASE): Uses ASL features and conceptually accurate signs while following English grammar and structure.

communicative competence: a speaker's underlying knowledge of the linguistic system and the norms for the appropriate sociocultural use of language in particular situations; when someone knows a language, he/she knows how to use the forms of the language; knows the phonology, morphology, and syntax of the language; and knows how to use the language appropriately.

consecutive interpreting: a speaker's signed or spoken discourse into another language when the speaker pauses for the interpretation to occur.

culture: a group's beliefs, values, patterns of behavior, language, expectations, and achievements which are passed on from generation to generation.

Deaf: a particular group of Deaf people who share a language, ASL, and a culture; members of this group use ASL as a primary language among themselves and hold a set of beliefs about themselves and their connection to the larger society; self-identification with the group and native or acquired fluency in ASL, not hearing loss, often determines who is Deaf.

deaf: refers to the audiological condition of not hearing; deaf persons often do not identify with the knowledge, beliefs, and practices that make up the culture of Deaf people.

Deaf community: a cultural group comprised of persons who share similar attitudes towards deafness. The "core" Deaf community is comprised of those individuals who have a hearing loss and who share common language, values, and experiences, and a common way of interacting with each other, with non-core members of the Deaf community, and with the hearing community. The wider Deaf community is comprised of individuals (both deaf and hearing) who have positive, accepting attitudes toward deafness, attitudes which can be seen in their linguistic, social, and political behaviors.

Deaf interpreter: a Deaf professional, skilled in ASL, visual gestural communication, pantomime, and other non-conventional communication systems, who, in combination with an ASL-English interpreter, facilitates communication between a hearing consumer and a deaf consumer with minimal language skills or whose native language may be neither English nor ASL (e.g., Italian sign language). Sometimes called a CDI (certified).

Demand-Control Schema (DC-S): an ethical framework (schema), developed by Dr. Robert Pollard and Robyn Dean, where interpreters can assess the demands (problems or stresses) of a situation and utilize controls (solutions) for dealing with them.

discourse: in sociolinguistics, discourse refers to any use of language that goes beyond the sentence; how language is organized in conversations, how sentences in a written text are organized; the study of discourse involves the functions of language, the norms and structure of language use, and language as a signal of social identity.

dynamic equivalent: not a word-for-word translation, but a conceptual and culturally accurate interpretation.

feed: during team interpreting, team members provide support and assistance to each other, often referred to as 'feed' within the interpreting community; ideally, in team interpreting situations, while one interpreter is interpreting, the other interpreter "stands by" and provides assistance whenever needed; i.e., if the working interpreter misses or misunderstands any part of the source message or has difficulty expressing difficult concepts.

grammar: the mental system of rules and categories that allows humans to form and interpret the words and sentences of their language; the relevant components of grammar are phonology, syntax, and semantics.

interpreter: provides signed or spoken translation of a speaker's discourse from one language into another.

lag time: the time between delivery of the original message and the delivery of the interpreted version of that message.

language style: language use appropriate to a given register.

language variation: the differences in the pronuncia-tion/production, vocabulary and grammar of the people who use a particular language. Language variation develops because people have different ways of saying the same thing. Variation is often caused by such factors as age, sex, racial or ethnic background, geographic area, education, context, etc.

linguistic competence: the ability to produce and understand an unlimited number of utterances, includ-ing many that are novel and unfamiliar.

linguistics: The study of language. Some of the specialties within the field of linguistics are philology, semantics, grammar, phonology, morphology, compara-tive linguistics, and applied linguistics.

Manually Coded English (MCE): a form of signed English.

phonology: the study of the smallest contrastive units of a language. In sign language linguists use the term phonology to refer to the study of how signs are structured and organized. ASL signs have five basic parts: handshape, movement, location, palm orientation, and non-manual behaviors (facial expression, eye gaze, head tilt and body posture).

pragmatics: how the meaning conveyed by a word or sentence depends on aspects of the context in which it is used (such as time, place, social relationship between speaker and listener, and speaker's assumption about the listener's beliefs).

prosody: the study or discussion of linguistic structure, including its parts (e.g. a sign choice).

register: the situation within which the communication takes place; the relative level of formality or informality called for and used by a speaker in a particular situation; a range of language use that will be appropriate or acceptable in any given situation; register can be frozen (such as that used in courtroom or religious services), formal, consultative (used in everyday conversation between speakers who are strangers or do not know each other very well), casual and intimate (used by people who know each other very well and who interact on a regular basis). Contextual factors help determine register such as the physical setting and social activity, channel used, (e.g., written, spoken, or signed), purpose (e.g., lecture or interview), the participants, and the interpersonal dynamics involved.

register variation: the structure of a discourse may differ depending on the setting (i.e., where and when a conversation takes place; language appropriate for a certain occasion. In ASL, different signs are used in formal settings than those used in informal settings; the location of signs may also vary depending on the social setting.

semantics: the study of the system of meaning; how words and sentences are related to the objects (real or imaginary) they refer to and the situations they describe; the relationship between words/signs and concepts.

simultaneous interpreting: signed/spoken interpretation of a discourse into another language while the speaker is signing/speaking.

source language: the originating language of a discourse that will be interpreted (e.g. English [source language] into ASL [target language]).

syntax: the study of the way in which sentences are constructed; how sentences are related to each other; knowledge of the rules for making sentences; study of word order.

target language: the language into which a discourse is to be signed or spoken (e.g. English [source language] into ASL [target language]).

Glossary of Theological Terms

allegorical interpretation: Interpretation of a narrative in symbolic rather than literal terms. Allegorical interpretation is a product of the interpreter, rather than a property of the text itself; scholars often debate whether a particular text was intended by its original author to be read allegorically. For example, Galatians 4:21-31 interprets OT story of Abraham's two sons Ishmael and Isaac allegorically, representing Mount Sinai and Jerusalem respectively, slave and free.

allegory: Literary form in which plot, setting, characters etc. are meant to be interpreted symbolically or figuratively.

Ancient Middle East: Region of southwest Asia which today includes Saudi Arabia, Iran, Iraq, Jordan, Israel, Lebanon, Syria, and Turkey.

apocalyptic: Type of biblical and other literature in which a revelation is given through highly symbolic visions. The premier biblical examples are found in the books of Revelation and Daniel. From the Greek meaning "uncovering" or "revelation."

Apocrypha: Writings included in the Septuagint, Orthodox, and/or Roman Catholic canon, but not the Jewish Tanak or Protestant Old Testament. Some of the apocryphal books are Tobit, Judith, and Baruch. Members of the groups that accept these books as canonical tend to call them the deuterocanonical books; "Apocryphal" is considered derogatory and is mostly used in Protestant settings. More generally, "apocryphal" refers to writings of questionable authenticity.

Aramaic: Semitic language related to Hebrew in which some parts of the Old Testament were originally written. Thought to be the language Jesus spoke.

Babylonian Captivity: Biblical time period when the Israelites were deported to and exiled in Babylon by King Nebuchadnezzar. Also known as the Exile.

biblical criticism: Study of biblical texts using specified methods in an effort to make sound scholarly judgments about these texts and their meanings; from the Greek *krino*, to judge. Terms like "text criticism," "literary criticism," and "canonical criticism" each refers to a particular focus and method of biblical criticism.

canon: A fixed list of books or other works deemed authoritative in a particular community. In Biblical Studies, "the canon" usually means the Bible, but the Jewish canon is different from the Christian canon (e.g., the Christian canon includes the New Testament and the Jewish canon does not), and within the Christian community the Protestant canon is different from the Catholic canon (Catholic Bibles include some books not found in Protestant Bibles).

canonical: Belonging to some established official group, especially a book that is part of the accepted canon of the Bible. The "canonical" Gospels are Matthew, Mark, Luke and John. The "Gospel of Thomas" is a non-canonical Gnostic text that was not included in the Bible.

Dead Sea Scrolls: Ancient manuscripts written in Hebrew, Aramaic and Greek, found in 1947-56 at Qumran. The Dead Sea Scrolls date from around the time of Christ, and are an invaluable resource for biblical scholarship.

Deism: Belief system arising in the 17th and 18th century among "freethinkers." Included belief in God as creator and originator of the universal laws being discovered by science, but denied the possibility of miracles or divine intervention in the world. Deism was in part a response to the Enlightenment and an attempt to reconcile some belief in God with Enlightenment rationalism. Search the web for "deism" and you'll find plenty of fans.

deuterocanonical: "Second canon." The parts of some Christian versions of the Old Testament canon that are found neither in the Protestant Old Testament nor in the Jewish Tanak. Commonly called the apocrypha. The deuterocanon is contrasted to the protocanon, with the events and writing of the protocanon ("first canon") having preceded the "second canon." Here's an explanation of the Old Testament Canon from a Roman Catholic perspective.

Deuteronomist: According to the Documentary Hypothesis, one of four authors or authorial schools thought to be responsible for the text of Torah.

didactic: Text or discourse that is intended to provide instruction, information, or teaching.

dietary laws: Rules about what persons are permitted to eat, and under what circumstances. Examples include the modern-day Muslim and Jewish prohibition of pork, and regulations spelled out in Torah, such as the admonition not to "boil a kid in his mother's milk (Exodus 23:19, Exodus 34:26, Deuteronomy 14:21).

Enlightenment: 18th century period of European intellectual history based in rationalism and empiricism, often seen as trying to supplant religion with science and secular philosophy. Also known as the Age of Reason.

exegesis: Critical interpretation of a text, especially a biblical text; from the Greek *ex-* + *egeisthai* meaning "to lead out. Sometimes it seems the terms "exegesis" and "hermeneutics" are used interchangeably; "exegesis" properly refers to the act or process of actually inter-preting texts, whereas "hermeneutics" refers to the theory of how one interprets."

Exile: Biblical time period when the Israelites were deported to and exiled in Babylon by King Nebuchad-nezzar. Also known as the Babylonian Captivity.

First Temple: The temple built by Solomon. Some-times the term "First Temple Judaism" is used to denote the religious and cultural practices of the biblical Israelites prior to the Babylonian Captivity.

genre: A category of oral or written literature defined by style, content, and/or forms. The biblical books can be categorized by genre, e.g. Judges is narrative, Psalms is poetry, Mark is a gospel, Romans is a letter, and Revelation is an apocalypse. Within these broad categories, scholars have identified many more specific genres include proverbs, parables, "hero" tales, and many others.

Gnosticism: Religious and philosophical movement from about the 1st century BCE through the 3rd century CE. Its name derives from the Greek word *gnosis*, "knowledge" because it claimed secret knowledge that ensured salvation.

Hebrew Bible: The collection of texts traditionally called Tanak by Jews and the Old Testament by Christians, written mostly in Hebrew. The term "Hebrew Bible" was constructed in order to avoid the Christian bias present in the term "Old Testament" (to Jews Tanak is the Bible; the concept of Old and New Testament is from a different religion).

Hellenistic age: The period when Greece dominated the ancient Near East, from the death of Alexander the Great to the beginning of the Roman Empire (323-30 B.C.). Sometimes in biblical studies the Hellenistic age is considered to be the period when Greece dominated Palestine, from the surrender of Jerusalem to Alexander in 333 B.C. until the conquest of Jerusalem by the Romans under Pompey in 63 B.C.

interpretive (or interpretative) community: The group of people with whom one reads and interprets a text, (e.g. the Bible. Religious denominations and congregations can be seen as interpretive communities; so can college classes, or the scholarly "Academy"). One's view of what scripture means is largely a function of one's interpretive community and what it thinks.

J, E, D, and P (or JEDP): Four hypothetical documents or possibly authors or authorial schools that many scholars believe represent distinct sources of the Pentateuch. J is the "Yahwist" (J from the German "Jahwist"), so called because of the use of the name

YHWH or Yahweh; E is the Elohist, using the name Elohiym for God; D is the Deuteronomist, from which the laws in Deuteronomy 12-26 are thought to have come; and P is the Priestly source, thought to be responsible for the genealogies, laws and temple rituals pertaining to priestly functions. J, E, D, and P are thought to have dated from around 850 B.C., 750 B.C., 621 B.C. (cf. 2 Kings 22-23), and 450 B.C. respectively, and combined by a series of redactors ending in about 400 B.C. This theory is called the Documentary Hypothesis.

justifying grace describes the work of the Holy Spirit at the moment of conversion in the lives of those who say yes to the call of prevenient grace by placing their faith and trust in Jesus Christ.

LXX: The Septuagint, so-called because of the tradition that it was translated by seventy scholars working independently, who all came up with exactly the same Greek wording for the original Hebrew text. "LXX" is the Roman numeral for seventy.

Markan priority: Commonly accepted theory that the Mark was the first of the Synoptic Gospels to be written, and that Matthew and Luke used Mark as a source. One common version of the theory holds that Matthew and Luke also used another common source, known as Q.

Masoretic Text (MT): Text of the Hebrew Bible/Old Testament produced by the Masoretes, Jewish scholars in the 5th to 10th century. The MT establishes both the consonantal text and the vowel "pointings" provided by the Masoretes to indicate pronunciation. The present-day edition of the MT most widely viewed as authoritative is the BHS.

messianic secret: Recurrent feature of the Gospels, particularly Mark, in which Jesus attempts to keep secret his miraculous deeds and his identity as Messiah. Scholars believe that the messianic secret was a product of early Christians' attempt to explain why Jesus' messiahship was not more broadly known.

metaphor: Figure of speech in which one word or phrase substitutes for another in order to make an analogy between them; e.g., "The Lord is my shepherd."

midrashic interpretation: Method of Jewish biblical interpretation; sometimes used quite broadly of imaginative storytelling only loosely based on the original text. From a Hebrew word meaning "investigation," "treatise," or "story" (2 Chron 13:22, 24:27).

ontology: Branch of philosophy concerned with the study of the nature of being. Ontology can be thought of as a description of the nature of some aspect of being or being in general.

parable: A story meant to teach a religious lesson, illustrate a point, or elucidate a principle.

Pentateuch: The first five books of the Bible: Genesis, Exodus, Leviticus, Numbers, and Deuteronomy. Means "five books" or "five tools." Also known as Torah.

pericope: A defined selection or passage from a larger literary work. In form criticism, a pericope is considered to have been passed down as a unit within the oral tradition prior to the "redaction" (compilation and editing) of the complete written biblical book. Pronounced pe-RIH-ko-pe.

prevenient grace or preventing grace for Wesley describes the universal work of the Holy Spirit in the hearts and lives of people between conception and conversion.

prophets: The second part of the Tanak, in Hebrew *nevi'im*. Comprises the following books: Joshua, Judges, Samuel and Kings; Isaiah, Jeremiah, Ezekiel and the Twelve (Hosea, Amos, Joel, Obadiah, Jonah, Micah, Nahum, Habakkuk, Zephaniah, Haggai, Zechariah, and Malachi).

Q ("Sayings Gospel"): Hypothetical source document for the Synoptic Gospels, sometimes called the "Sayings Gospel" because it is thought to consist mainly of Jesus' speeches, with little or no narrative. Q is one component of the usual version of the theory of Markan priority, which holds that Mark was the first gospel, and that Matthew and Luke were written with Mark as one source and Q as another.

Qumran: Site of the caves where the Dead Sea Scrolls were discovered, just northwest of the Dead Sea in the West Bank.

Reformation: Short for "Protestant Reformation," the 16th century European Christian movement which sought initially to reform the church but which eventually led to a split between the Roman Catholic Church and the "Protestants."

sanctifying grace described the work of the Holy Spirit in the lives of believers between conversion and death.

Second Temple: The temple re-built after the Babylonian Captivity, in the time of Ezra and Nehemiah. Sometimes the term "First Temple Judaism" is used to denote the religious and cultural practices of the biblical Israelites from the time of the Babylonian Captivity until the destruction of the Second Temple by the Romans in 70 A.D.

setting: The place, time, and general background circumstances of a narrative text (story).

Septuagint: Greek translation of the Hebrew Bible completed approximately 2nd century B.C.E. Thought to be the primary version of scripture known to Jesus and the authors of the New Testament. Also known as the LXX.

source: A hypothetical document or oral tradition believed to have been used in the production of a "final form" document such as a biblical book.

Synoptic Gospels: Matthew, Mark and Luke; so called because they "see together" or take a common view, that is, they basically tell the same story in much the same way, unlike John, with which they have much less in common.

syntax: From the Greek *syn-taxis*, to "put together." The system or rules according to which a particular language arranges words to make meaningful sentences.

Tanak: The Jewish Bible, also called the Hebrew Bible. The word Tanak is an acronym: TaNaK, for the three major types of writing in the Hebrew Bible, arranged in order: Torah, Nevi'im (the Prophets) and Ketuvim (the Writings).

text: A piece of writing or speech that is being studied or discussed; often used of a passage from the Bible. Can also be used far more broadly, as when writers refer something other than writing or speech -- even all of life - as a "text."

theodicy: An attempt to answer the question "How could an all-good and all-powerful God allow evil?" An attempt to defend God's goodness and power in the face of evil. From the Greek, "justification of God."
theology: Set of beliefs about or study of the nature of God and God's relationship to humanity and the world.

translate: Render a source language sentence, phrase, or word in a target language.

Torah: Hebrew word meaning "teaching." Usually refers to the first five books of the Hebrew Bible (the Christian Old Testament), or Tanak, but can also be used for other types of religious teaching.

versions: Translations of the Bible from one language into another. In Old Testament text criticism, the "primary versions" which translated the Hebrew into Greek, Syriac, Latin, and Coptic are particularly important.

Victorian period: The period from about the 1830's through 1900 (Victoria was Queen of England 1837-1901). A pivotal time for the field of Biblical Studies.

Vulgate: Ancient translation of the Bible into Latin, traditionally ascribed to Jerome (c.347-420). The word is from the Latin *vulgata editio* meaning "common edition."

Writings: The third part of the Tanak, in Hebrew *ketuvim*. Comprises the following books: Psalms, Proverbs, Job, the Song of Songs, Ruth, Lamentations, Ecclesiastes, Esther, Daniel, Ezra-Nehemiah, and Chronicles.

Yahweh: One of the names of God found in the Hebrew Bible; like "Jehovah" it is formed from the Tetragrammaton YHWH, with vowels added. In many English language Bibles it is written LORD (all capital letters). In OT source criticism, Yahweh is distinguished from another common name for God, "Elohihm," and considered as a marker of which hypothetical source each part of the Pentateuch comes from.

Glossary of Church Terms

acolyte: An acolyte is a lay person, often a child or a teenager, who performs minor duties during the worship service to assist the ministers, such as lighting candles, carrying books, directing traffic during communion, and so forth. Acolyte comes from a Greek word for follower.

archbishop: The word *archbishop* is Greek for *chief overseer*. Therefore, *archbishop* is not a separate order of clergy, it is just a bishop who has administrative duties over fellow bishops in a geographical region. In some areas, bishops elect one of their number to be the archbishop; in other areas, the bishops rotate the office. The head of the Episcopal Church of the USA is called a *presiding bishop* rather than an *archbishop*, but the meaning is the same.

bishop: *Bishop* is the English version of the Greek word επισκοπος (episkopos), which means overseer or supervisor. In the historic church, a bishop is a regional minister, a priest with administrative duties over a group of churches in a territory called a diocese. Only bishops can preside at the rite of ordination. An individual bishop can ordain a deacon or a priest, but it takes three bishops to consecrate a new bishop.

cardinal: Cardinals are bishops who serve as advisers to the pope. The pope can make any priest or bishop a cardinal; however, when a priest becomes a cardinal, he is consecrated a bishop.

catechumen: *Catechumen* is an ancient term, not often used as often, for a person who is taking instruction in Christianity, but is not yet baptized. In the ancient Church, catechumens were dismissed from the service between the Service of the Word and the Eucharist.

cathedral: The term *cathedral* refers to the function of a church, not its architectural style. A cathedral is a church that serves as a bishop's headquarters (or where he/she serves from).

celebrant: A term for the minister who is the moderator of a worship service that includes communion. In most cases, only a member of the ordained clergy can be a celebrant.

chancel: the chancel is the front part of the church from which the service is conducted, as distinct from the nave, where the congregation sits. The chancel is usually an elevated platform, usually three steps up from the nave. The words *chancel* and *sanctuary* are often synonyms.

chapel: A chapel can either be an alcove with an altar in a large church, or a separate building that is smaller than a full-sized church. Chapels have the same function as church buildings and are equipped the same way, but they are usually dedicated for special use.

clergy: The word clergy comes from a Latin word that means "office holder." It refers to ordained ministers who are authorized to conduct the rites and sacraments of the church. Some clergy may have administrative duties at various regional and national levels of a church.

congregation: The people who have gathered for worship. The term has two meanings: (1) Those presently assembled for worship. (2) All of the people who make up the local church's constituency. In some churches the word *congregation* is only used in the first meaning, and the word *parish*
is used for the second meaning.

crucifer: *Crucifer* is a Latin word meaning cross-bearer, used for the acolyte who carries the cross in a church procession. It is an ancient custom for the clergy and the other ministers to enter the church after the worshipers have already assembled. When this is done in a procession, the procession is led by the crucifer, usually a young person, bearing the cross. The crucifer is followed by the choir, the acolytes, the lay ministers, and finally the clergy; the highest-anking clergy last.

cu-rate: *Curate* is an Anglican term for assistant pastor.

deacon: The word *deacon* comes from the Greek word διακονος (diakonos), which means servant. The New Testament records the appointment of the first deacons in Acts 6 and lists their qualifications for office in 1 Timothy 3. Depending on the church, a deacon can be any of the following: a member of the clergy; a lay minister; or a lay administrator.

diocese Modern churches generally follow political boundaries when they set up ecclesiastical regions, even if they don't call them dioceses. In Orthodoxy, a *diocese* is called an *eparchy*. In the United Methodist Church, the word *conference* is used instead of diocese.

elder: *Elder* is the English word which translates the Greek word *presbuteros* (or presbyter), which translates into English as priest.

father: In Roman Catholicism, in Orthodoxy, and to some degree in Anglicanism, people often address priests as *father*.

kneeler: In churches where it is customary to kneel for prayer, there is often a long, narrow padded bar at the base of pew in front of you, which can be tilted down for kneeling and tilted up to make it easier to get in and out of the pew.

lay reader: A *lay reader* is a lay person who is authorized to read the scripture lessons and lead the congregation in certain parts of the worship service. It is not uncommon to refer to the lay reader as a *liturgist*.

lectern: There are generally two speaker's stands in the front of the church. The one on the right (as viewed by the congregation) is called the *lectern*.

minister: *Minister* is the Latin word for doer of little deeds, as opposed to a magistrate, who is a doer of great deeds. In some churches, the word *minister* denotes a person who is charged with the spiritual care of a church. In most churches, *minister* is a generic term that includes all who assist in worship, whether clergy or lay. The following are ministers: bishops, priests, deacons, acolyte, lay readers, and crucifers.

narthex: The term for what might otherwise be called the foyer or entry way of the church.

nave: The architectural term for the place where the congregation gathers for worship, as opposed to the front part of the church from which the service is led.

Many churches use the term 'sanctuary,' which is often to mean both chancel and nave.

officiant: A term for the minister who is the moderator of a worship service. This term is most often used when the service does not include communion. Depending on circumstances, the officiant may be an ordained minister, a lay minister, or a lay person.

parish: In some churches, the geographical territory of a local church. In general, the constituency of a local church; that is, all the people who are members or who informally consider it to be their church.

pastor: Pastor is the Latin word for shepherd. This word refers to the ordained minister who is charged with the primary spiritual care of a local church.

pew: Originally, Christians stood for worship, and that is still the case in many eastern churches. The pew, a long, backed bench upon which congregants sit.

pope: The term *pope* or *papa* originated as a term of endearment for bishops and sometimes even priests. It is a form of the word *father*. The pope is the only member of the Roman Catholic clergy who always wears white vestments and clericals.

presbyter: The Greek word πρεσβυτερος (presbyteros) is used in the New Testament for people who perform the functions of clergy in the Church. It means elder.

priest: *Priest* is the English word that originated from the Greek word *πρεσβυτερος* (presbyteros), which means elder. Roman Catholic priests must be unmarried at the time of their ordination and they must remain that way.

In the Eastern Church, a priest must remain in the state in which he was ordained. If he was single when he was ordained a priest, he must remain unmarried. If he was married when he was ordained a priest, he may remained married, but he is not permitted to remarry if he is widowed. Anglican and Lutheran priests can marry after ordination.

priesthood: *Priesthood* is a synonym for clergy in Anglican, Catholic, and Orthodox churches. The phrase *priesthood of all believers* comes from 1 Peter 1:4-10 and refers to all baptized believers work in God's kingdom.

pulpit: It is used by clergy to read the gospel and preach the sermon.

rector: Rector is the Anglican word for the elected pastor of a financially self-supporting congregation. The term derives from the fact that if there are multiple clergy on staff in a church, the pastor has primary responsibility for directing the worship.

Reverend: The term *reverend* is an adjective that simply indicates that a person is a member of the clergy.

sacristy: In historic church architecture, the sacristy is the room or closet in which communion equipment, linen, and supplies are kept. It is usually equipped with a sink.

sanctuary: In historic church architecture, the front part of the church from which the service is conducted, as distinct from the nave, where the congregation sits. The term 'sanctuary' is often used to mean both chancel and nave because the two are not architecturally distinct.

shrine: A shrine is a building or a place that is dedicated to one particular type of devotion that is limited to commemorating an event or a person.

thurifer: A thurifer is a person who carries and swings the thurible in a worship service. The thurible (or censer) is the device in which incense is burnt.

vestry: In the Anglican Communion, the vestry corresponds to the board of directors of a secular organization. The vestry elects the rector of the church and conducts its secular business.

Religious Sign Dictionary

ABRAHAM

1   2

DESCRIPTION: This sign represents an angel stopping Abraham from slaying (sacrificing) his son, Isaac.

TIP: Read Genesis 22:1-19 to read about the story.

ADULTERY / AFFAIR

1   2

DESCRIPTION: This sign describes an intimate encounter behind a closed door.

AMEN

1   2

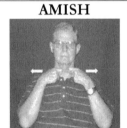

DESCRIPTION: "Amen" is signed with the initialized "A." When using the initialized "A," it changes the sign "stop" to "amen" (e.g., The prayer has stopped / concluded.)

AMISH

DESCRIPTION: The sign represents the tying of a female bonnet, a common Amish head covering.

TIP: The Amish faith is from the Anabaptist tradition; it was established in 1693. Jacob Amman is considered to be their founder. Amman's group separated from the Swiss Mennonites.

ANGEL

1   2

DESCRIPTION: This sign models the flapping of an angel's wings.

ANGLICAN CHURCH

1   2

CHURCH   ENGLAND

DESCRIPTION: This is a compound sign of CHURCH + ENGLAND.

TIP 1: The term "Anglican Church" is interchangeable with "The Church of England."

TIP 2: The Church of England was established in 1534 when King Henry VIII had England separate from the Catholic Church because of the Pope's refusal to grant the king a divorce. King Henry appointed himself as the head of the Church.

ANOINT

DESCRIPTION: This sign refers to the pouring of oil, which symbolizes the act of consecrating (e.g., 1 Samuel 6:12). Another version for "anoint" is signed by using the thumb and making the sign of the cross on the forehead (see the images on the following page).

TIP: This sign represents a different meaning from the term "anointed" (e.g., He is anointed.). To interpret, "He is anointed," one choice is to sign GOD FAVORS HIM.

APOSTLE / DISCIPLE / FOLLOWER

 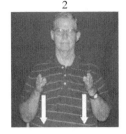

DESCRIPTION: This is a compound sign of FOLLOW + PERSON.

ALTERNATIVE: Using an initialized "D," in place of the sign "follow," can represent the sign "disciple."

TIP: "Apostle" means one of the elected 12 by Jesus.

ASH WEDNESDAY

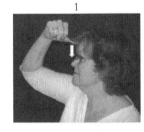 

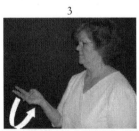

WEDNESDAY (LETTER "W")

Continued

DESCRIPTION: The sign of the cross is formed on the forehead. This sign describes the act of putting ashes on the forehead (a sign of penance) during an Ash Wednesday service.

TIP 1: Ash Wednesday is the first day of the season of Lent (40 days before Easter, but not including Sundays).

TIP 2: The cross formation on the forehead can be signed to represent "anoint" (with oil) that might be done during a healing service or for the purpose of consecrating.

BAPTISM
(immersion)

1

2

3

DESCRIPTION: This sign symbolizes the act of immersing (dipping) a person into water.

TIP 1: The rite of baptism represents a birth to a new life as a Christian.

TIP 2: Baptism and the Eucharist / Holy Communion are two sacraments (or ordinances) practiced by all Christian traditions (The Catholic Church, The Orthodox Church, and the Protestant Church).

BAPTISM / BAPTIST

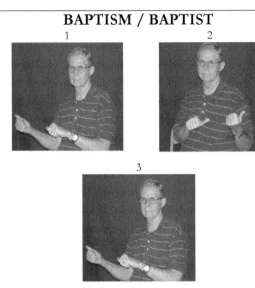

DESCRIPTION: This is a modified sign of baptism by immersion.

TIP 1: Baptist denominations evolved from Anabaptist reformers of the sixteenth century. These reformers are known for their stance of a believer's baptism and their opposition to infant baptism.

TIP 2: According to one's faith tradition, the Sacrament of Baptism is done by sprinkling of water, pouring of water, or by immersion. It is a public ritual of a person's acceptance of faith and entrance into a covenant with God. (Reference: Matthew 28:19)

BAPTISM / CHRISTENING
(sprinkling)   (Catholic term) .

Continued

DESCRIPTION: This sign describes the act of sprinkling water on an infant's head.

TIP: Denominations that perform infant baptisms are The A.M.E. Church, The Catholic Church, The Episcopal Church, The Lutheran Church, The Presbyterian Church, and the United Methodist Church. (Reference: Acts 2:38, 39)

BETHLEHEM

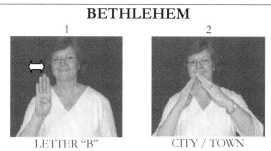

LETTER "B"   CITY / TOWN

DESCRIPTION: This is a compound sign of B + TOWN.
TIP: Spell the name of the town first, and then set up the sign "Bethlehem." The same suggestion applies to "Jerusalem" and "Nazareth."

BIBLE

JESUS   JESUS

BOOK   BOOK

DESCRIPTION: A compound sign of JESUS + BOOK.

Continued

TIP: Bible translations recommended by denomination:

NRSV	**NAB / NJB**	**KJV / NKJV**
United Methodist	Catholic	Baptist
A.M.E.		Pentecostal
Evangelical Lutheran		Charismatic
Presbyterian		Evangelical
Episcopal		

* The NIV translation is a popular choice for many
pastors. Translation preferences vary by congregation.

BISHOP

DESCRIPTION: This sign represents the bishop's mitre
(head garment).

TIP: A few denominations that have bishops are
The African Methodist Episcopal Church, The Anglican
Church, The Catholic Church, The Episcopal Church, The
Orthodox Church, and The United Methodist Church.

BLESS / BLESSING

DESCRIPTION: The sign represents the breathing out
the Holy Spirit, like Jesus did (see John 20:22).

TIP: This sign can be used for the term "consecrate."

BLOOD

TIP: This sign can be moved to specific areas of the body to indicate the location of the bleeding. In order to sign "bleeding," repeat the sign two or three times.

BURIAL / BURY / GRAVE

DESCRIPTION: This sign describes the placement of a deceased in a crypt (e.g., A burial vault in the ground).

CARE

VERSION 1   **VERSION 2**

Example: I care for you.   Example: Take care of it.

CATHOLIC

1   2

DESCRIPTION: Using the index and middle finger together, the sign of the cross is made on the forehead. ..

TIP: When professing the Apostles' Creed or the Nicene Creed* at a Protestant church, instead of signing "catholic" church, the sign "Christian" church or "universal" church will want to be signed. These images represent the Roman Catholic Church.

*The creed states, "I believe in the Holy Spirit, the holy catholic church."

CELEBRATE / CELEBRATION / ANNIVERSARY / HALLELUJAH

1   2

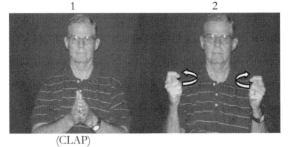

(CLAP)

DESCRIPTION: A compound sign of "applause" and "flag waiving". The second sign emulates one waiving a small handheld flag during national celebrations.

TIP: In order to accentuate the sign "hallelujah," the sign "happy" (used as an adjective) can go before "hallelujah" (e.g., HAPPY HALLELUJAH).

CHOIR

1	2
SING	SING

3	4
GROUP	GROUP

DESCRIPTION: This is a compound sign of SING + GROUP.

ALTERNATIVE: You can sign CHURCH + SING + GROUP.

CHRIST

DESCRIPTION: When using the initialized "C," it changes the meaning of "king" to "Christ."

CHRISTIAN (version 1)

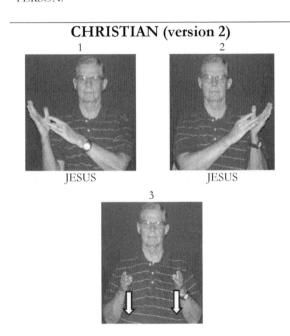

DESCRIPTION: This is a compound sign of CHRIST + PERSON.

CHRISTIAN (version 2)

JESUS   JESUS

DESCRIPTION: A compound sign of JESUS + PERSON.

TIP: The sign for "Christianity" is a compound sign of CHRISTIAN + RELIGION.

CHRISTMAS

1   2

DESCRIPTION: This is signed with the initialized "C," represnting a wreath.

CHURCH / PARISH

DESCRIPTION: The sign for "rock" is changed to "church" when using an initialized "C." It references Jesus' statement that the church is to be built on this rock (Matthew 16:18).

TIP: "Temple" is signed this way with the initialized "T."

COFFIN

1   2

DESCRIPTION: This sign describes a closed coffin.

COMMANDMENT

1   2

Continued

DESCRIPTION: "Commandment" is signed with the initialized "C," changing the meaning of "Law" to "Commandment."

TIP: This sign for "Commandment" is used as a noun. In order to use the verb "command," the sign "order" can be used.

CONFESS / CONFESSION

1   2

DESCRIPTION: This sign shows the expression of a person getting something off his or her chest.

CONGREGATION

1   2

 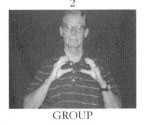

CHURCH   GROUP

3

GROUP

DESCRIPTION: The sign for "congregation" is a compound sign of "church" and "group."

COVENANT (version 1)

1   2

DESCRIPTION: Using the sign for "agreement" also represents the word "covenant."

COVENANT (version 2)

1   2

DESCRIPTION: Using the sign "promise" also represents the word "covenant."

CREATION

DESCRIPTION: This sign is the same sign as "earth."

ALTERNATE: Some users change the sign for "make" to "Creation" when using an initialized "C."

CROSS

DESCRIPTION: Using a classifier (letter C), make the sign of a cross.

CRUCIFIXION / CRUCIFY

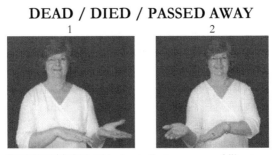

DESCRIPTION: This sign models Jesus' crucifixion (nails going into the palm of his hands).

DEAD / DIED / PASSED AWAY

DESCRIPTION: This sign indicates a person falling to the ground.

DEMON

1

EVIL / SATAN

2   3

SPIRIT   SPIRIT

DESCRIPTION: This is a compound sign of "evil" and "spirit."

DENOMINATION

1   2

DESCRIPTION: This is signed with the initialized "D."

TIP 1: When forming the initialized "R," the meaning changes and becomes the sign "religion."

TIP 2: Since the sign "denomination" is not always a recognized sign, the sign "church" might be substituted.

TIP 3: When forming the initialized "T," one version for the sign "theology" is made.

EASTER

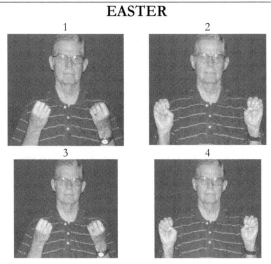

DESCRIPTION: Changing the sign "party" with the initialized P, this will sign will be signed with the initialized "E."

EPISCOPAL

DESCRIPTION: This models the sleeve of a priest's robe.

TIP: The Episcopal Church (in the U.S.) was established in 1789. It is part of the Anglican Communion.

EUCHARIST / HOLY COMMUNION

Continued:

DESCRIPTION: This sign is in the form of a cross in front of the mouth.

TIP: The Eucharist is a celebration of the Lord's Supper. It is the feast of bread and wine (for some, grape juice), which has been consecrated by pastor or priest.

FAITH (version 1)

1   2

DESCRIPTION: This is signed with an initialized "F," and modifies the sign "trust."

FAITH (version 2)

1   2

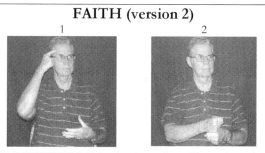

DESCRIPTION: Using the sign as "trust" is an alternative for signing "faith."

FELLOWSHIP

VERSION 1   **VERSION 2**

 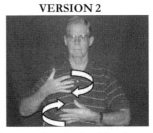

DESCRIPTION: These are the same signs for "socialize."

FORGIVE / FORGIVENESS

1   2

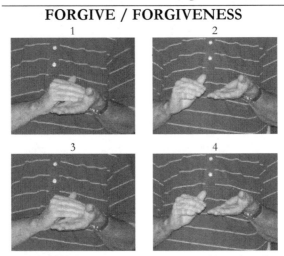

3   4

DESCRIPTION: This sign indicates something released.
TIP: This is the same sign for "justified" (forgiven).

FUNERAL

1   2

Continued

DESCRIPTION: This sign represents people walking to a grave site.

TIP: "Home Going Service" (or homegoing) is the phrase sometimes used at an African American funeral.

GIFT / SKILL

DESCRIPTION: This is the standard sign for "skill."

TIP: The Holy Spirit gives us "gifts" (skills) for ministry. (Reference: 1 Corinthians 12)

GLORIFY / GLORY

DESCRIPTION: One definition of glory is the manifestation of God's presence. With this in mind, this sign represents the "shining" light from God's presence. (Reference: Exodus 33:22 & 34:29)

TIP: The term "glory" has various connotations and differs from the term "glorification."

GOD

DESCRIPTION: This is a modified sign of the sign "honor." (Reference: Isaiah 26:13)

TIP: This sign can be a substitute for "Jehovah."

GOSPEL

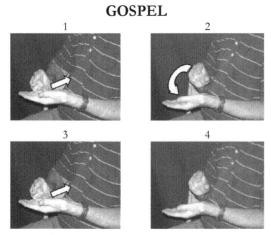

DESCRIPTION: "Gospel" is signed with the initialized "G," changing the sign for "dictionary" ('D") to "Gospel."

TIP: Gospel means "Good News."

GRACE

1   2

DESCRIPTION: This symbolizes divine inspiration of love onto the heart.
TIP: Grace means God's love freely given without merit.

GUIDE / LEAD

1   2

DESCRIPTION: This sign describes the one hand taking the other and taking it forward.

GUILT

DESCRIPTION: This sign shows an action plaguing the heart.

HEAL / HEALTHY

1   2

DESCRIPTION: This sign models an individual who is strong or physically able.

HEAVEN

DESCRIPTION: This sign symbolizes entering a transcendent place, locating heaven above the earth. (Reference: Psalm 103:11)

TIP: This sign can be used for the word "paradise."

HELL

1   2

LETTER "H"   LETTER "H"

DESCRIPTION: Using the initialized "H," this sign indicates hell is below/downward.

TIP: "Damnation" is signed with the initialized "D."

HOLY GHOST / HOLY SPIRIT

1

2

HOLY (LETTER "H")

HOLY

3

HOLY

4

5

GHOST / SPIRIT

GHOST / SPIRIT

DESCRIPTION: Holy - With your right hand making the letter H, make a circular motion above the left palm. Proceed to drop the H and sign clean. Spirit – Signing an iconic sign for apparition.

HOSANNA IN THE HIGHEST

1

2

GOD   GOD

3   4

HIGH   HIGH

DESCRIPTION: This sign for "high" indicates that the person (e.g., Jesus) is omnipotence (authoritative and supreme).

TIP: The phrase "Hosanna in the Highest" is commonly used in a Eucharist / Holy Communion service. Also, the phrase will be used if a congregation reads Matthew 21:9 (Jesus entering Jerusalem) on Palm Sunday.

HYMN / SING / SONG

1   2

TIP: If "hymn" and "song" are used in the same sentence, sign "church" before the sign "song." This becomes a compound sign and emphasizes the concept of hymn (e.g., CHURCH + SONG).

INSPIRATION / INSPIRE

1   2

DESCRIPTION: This sign shows a person being filled with a thought or an emotion.

TIP: The sign "inspiration" can be used when the message references a person filled with the Holy Spirit (e.g., Like at the day of Pentecost).

ISRAEL

1

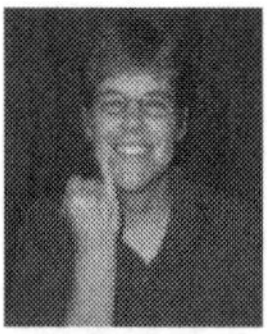

2

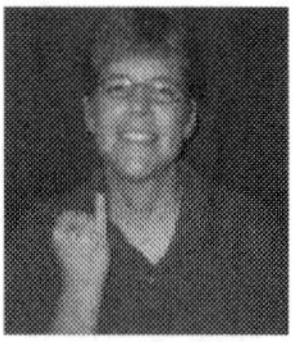

3

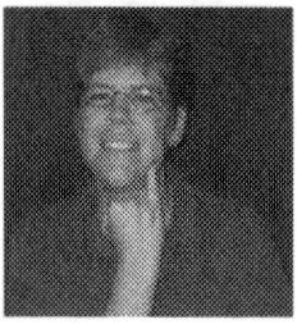

4

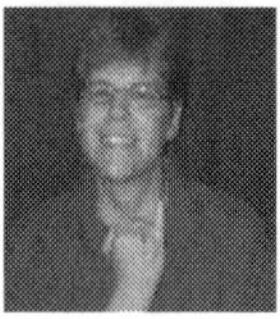

DESCRIPTION: "Israel" is signed with the initialized "I," outlining a Jewish man's beard. (Reference: Genesis 35:10)

JERUSALEM (version 1)

1

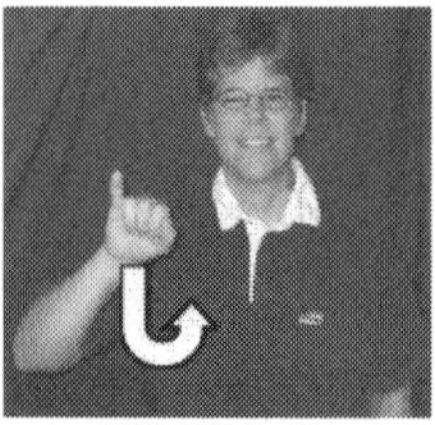

LETTER "J"

2

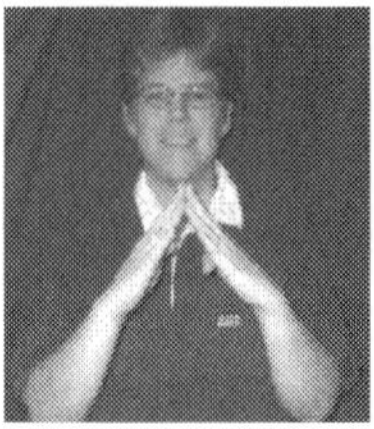

TOWN

DESCRIPTION: A compound sign for J + TOWN.

JERUSALEM (version 2)

1

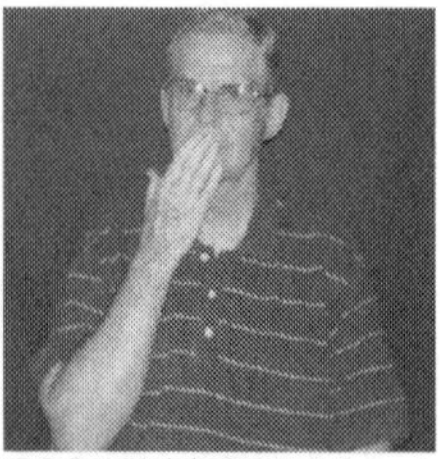

2

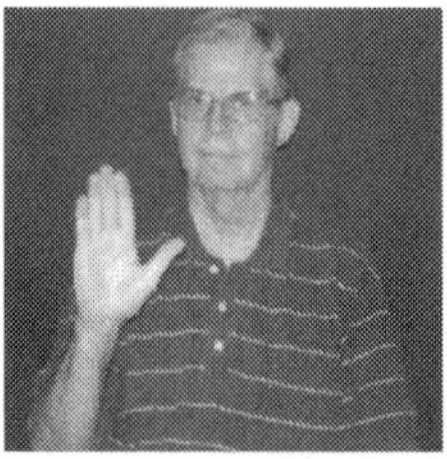

DESCRIPTION: This sign represents a person kissing the Jerusalem wall (the Western Wall).

JESUS

DESCRIPTION: This sign represents the nail marks (crucifixion) on Jesus' hands.

TIP: The name, Jesus, means "Lord Saves." (Reference: Matthew 1:21)

JEWISH / HEBREW

DESCRIPTION: This sign describes a light pulling of a Jewish man's beard. (Reference: Leviticus 19:27)

TIP 1: The sign for "Judaism" is JEWISH + RELIGION.

TIP 2: The sign for "Israelites" is JEWISH + PEOPLE.

JUSTICE

Continued
DESCRIPTION: The sign "justice" is a circular motion and is the same sign as "equality" and "fairness."
TIP: This sign is different from the judicial / legal meaning (court or trial).

KINGDOM

1

KING

2

KING

3

AREA

DESCRIPTION: "King" is made with the initialized "K" and the sign "area" references his dominion..

TIP 1: A suggestion for signing the phrase "the kingdom of God" is to sign GOD KINGDOM.

TIP 2: The phrase "kingdom of God" (the reign of God) has three connotations: 1) it is a future kingdom, 2) it is a kingdom already here, and 3) it is within you.

LEPROSY

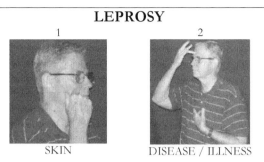

SKIN   DISEASE / ILLNESS

DESCRIPTION: A compound sign for SKIN + ILLNESS.

TIP: Leprosy is a communicable disease that causes a person to live in isolation. One symptom is skin lesions.

LITANY

INTERACTIVE   INTERACTIVE   INTERACTIVE

READING   READING

DESCRIPTION: A compound sign of INTERACTIVE + READING.

LITURGY

WORSHIP   OUTLINE / LIST

DESCRIPTION: This sign represents practices listed in a worship bulletin (an order of worship).

TIP: Liturgy is the ritual or worship format performed by a congregation (e.g., prayer, singing, Scripture reading).

LORD (version 1)

DESCRIPTION: This is signed with the initialized "L." It changes the sign "king" to "Lord."

LORD (version 2)

1

2

3

DESCRIPTION: When ... using an initialized "L" and directing the sign upward (in image 3), it references a divine entity.

LOVE

DESCRIPTION: This models a hug between people, an expression of affection/love.

LUTHERAN

DESCRIPTION: This sign is made with the initialized "L." It symbolizes the hammering of Luther's 95 Theses.

TIP: Martin Luther is the founder of the Lutheran Church. It separated from the Catholic Church in 1517.

MANGER

DESCRIPTION: This sign represents the trough in which feed for livestock is placed.

TIP: If a location is referenced (e.g., Away in a manger.), then FARM + HOUSE (indicating a barn) might be used.

MARGINALIZE

1   2

DESCRIPTION: This sign represents a person or persons pushed to the margins (e.g., People who are disenfranchised by a society or government.).

MARRIAGE / MATRIMONY

1   2

DESCRIPTION: This symbolizes the joining of a couple by holding hands.

MARY

DESCRIPTION: Referencing Jesus' mother, "Mary" is signed with the initialized "M." This sign models a nun's habit.

ALTERNATIVE: VIRGIN MARY

MESSIAH

DESCRIPTION: "Messiah" is signed with the initialized "M." It changes the sign "king" to "Messiah."

TIP: The term Messiah and the term Christ have the same meaning (The Anointed One). Messiah comes from the Hebrew translation and Christ comes from the Greek translation.

METHODIST

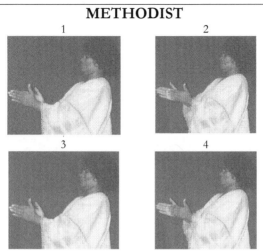

DESCRIPTION: This is the same sign as "enthusiastic" and "motivated" in which early Methodists were known for.

TIP: John Wesley is the founder of Methodism. The first denomination was established in the U.S. in 1784.

MINISTER / PASTOR / PREACHER

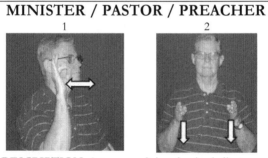

DESCRIPTION: A compound sign, the sign indicates an individual providing spiritual advice **along with the sign for person.**

TIP: There are distinctions between the three roles; however, this is the standard sign.

MINISTRY (version 1) / SERVE

1  2

3

DESCRIPTION: The sign for ministry emphasizes the service aspect of its meaning.
TIP: Using the initialized "M" is signed by some users.

MINISTRY (version 2)

DESCRIPTION: This is signed with an initialized "M," which changes the sign "work" to "ministry."

MIRACLE

1

2

AMAZING

AMAZING

3

4

BLESSING

BLESSING

DESCRIPTION: A compound sign of AMAZING + BLESSING. It is describing the outcome of a miracle.

TIP: Fingerspelling the word "miracle" is also a good alternative.

MISSION

DESCRIPTION: This is signed with the initialized "M" in a circular motion over the heart.

MOSES (version 1)

1   2

 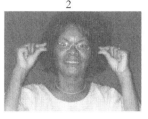

DESCRIPTION: This sign portrays Michael Angelo's sculpture "Moses." The sign references "horns," which is sculpted on the figure (a likely mistranslation from Hebrew to Latin by Angelo for the meaning "ray of light").

TIP: Moses is a major Jewish leader who is highly revered because he had a close relationship with the Lord and he helped the Hebrews leave the land of Egypt.

MOSES (version 2)

1   2

DESCRIPTION: "Moses" is signed with the initialized M," changing the meaning of "Law" to "Moses."

TIP: In American Sign Language, a sign name will usually represent some type of characteristic of the person. Since Moses brought down the 10 Commandments from Mt. Sinai, this sign name is fitting.

MYSTERY

DESCRIPTION: Using the same sign as "puzzled," this sign emphasizes one aspect of the meaning of mystery.

TIP: Occasionally, this is signed with the sign "holy" for the concept of "holy mystery." HOLY + MYSTERY

NAZARETH

LETTER "N"   TOWN

DESCRIPTION: A compound sign, signing the letter "N" with the sign "town."

TIP 1: Spell the name of the town first, and then set up the sign "Nazareth." The same suggestion applies to "Bethlehem" (using the letter "B") and "Jerusalem" (using the letter "J").

TIP 2: Nazareth is Jesus' hometown. (Reference: Matthew 2:23)

NEW TESTAMENT

1

NEW

2

NEW

3

TESTAMENT

4

TESTAMENT

DESCRIPTION: "Testament" is signed with the initialized "T," changing the meaning of "Law" to "Testament."

ALTERNATIVE: Fingerspell the letters N.T.

TIP: The New Testament consists of 27 books, which are grouped as (1) Gospels, (2) Epistles (3) general letters, and (4) Revelation (apocalyptic writing).

OFFERING

1

MONEY

2

COLLECT

3

COLLECT

DESCRIPTION: This is a compound sign of "money" and "collection."

ALTERNATIVE: DONATE + MONEY + COLLECT

TIP: Occasionally, the term "tithe" is used in place of the term "offering."

OLD TESTAMENT

1   2

OLD   OLD

3   4

TESTAMENT   TESTAMENT

DESCRIPTION: "Testament" is signed with the initialized "T," changing the meaning of "Law" to "Testament."

ALTERNATIVE: Fingerspell the letters O.T. or HEBREW + BIBLE (used by some Christians)

TIP: The Old Testament consists of 39 books, which have three parts: the Law (Torah), the Prophets & the Writings.

OPPRESS / OPPRESSION

1   2

DESCRIPTION: This sign describes the suppression (pushing down) of those who are economically, emotionally, ethnically, physically, and o/r politically burdened by society or some other entity.

ORDAIN / LAYING ON OF HANDS

1   2

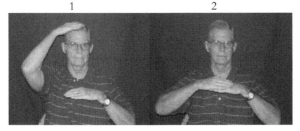

DESCRIPTION: This sign references laying hands on an individual's head, symbolizing consecration.

TIP: The phrase "laying on of hands" means one or more persons (typically clergy) putting their hands on a person's head or shoulders and praying for him or her.
(Reference: Genesis 48:14)

PEACE / PEACEFUL / SHALOM

1   2

 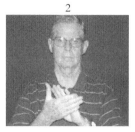

3

DESCRIPTION: This is a compound sign by using the sign "become" and "silent" together.

POOR / POVERTY

1   2

DESCRIPTION: With your right palm on your left elbow, gently squeeze the elbow and pull downward.

PRAISE (version 1)

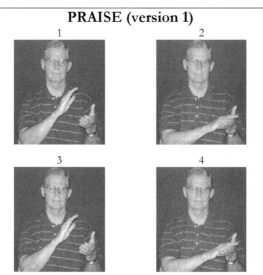

DESCRIPTION: This represents the concept of applause.

PRAISE (version 2)

DESCRIPTION: This models a visual applause.

PRAY / PRAYER

DESCRIPTION: This sign references a common prayer posture.

PREACH / SERMON

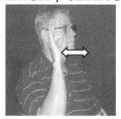

DESCRIPTION: This sign describes someone influencing his or her beliefs (e.g., The gospel).

PRESBYTERIAN

DESCRIPTION: This is signed with the initialized "P." It changes the meaning of "stand" to "Presbyterian."

TIP 1: Early Calvinists (Presbyterians) partly expressed their Christian reform from the Catholic Church by standing instead of kneeling during worship.

TIP 2: John Calvin is considered the spiritual father of this denomination. It was established during the 16th century.

PRESENCE

1   2

DESCRIPTION: This sign symbolizes a transcendent God approaching.

PRIEST / CHAPLAIN / CLERGY

1   2

DESCRIPTION: This signs represents the clerical collar.

TIP: The Anglican Church, The Catholic Church, The Episcopal Church, and The Orthodox Church have clergy referred to as "priests."

PROMISED LAND

1   2

PROMISE   PROMISE

3   4

LAND   LAND

DESCRIPTION: A compound sign of PROMISE + LAND.

TIP: The "Promised Land" is the land of Israel that was given to the Jews during biblical times. (Reference: Exodus 3:17)

PROPHECY / PREDICT

1   2

DESCRIPTION: A person looking into the future.

PROTESTANT

DESCRIPTION: This is the sign for "keeling," an early common liturgical practice for Protestant denominations (e.g. Lutherans and Congregationalists).

PUNISH / PUNISHMENT

1   2

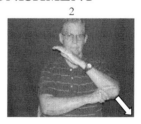

DESCRIPTION: Making the #1 sign with your right hand, gently brush your left elbow.

RABBI

1   2

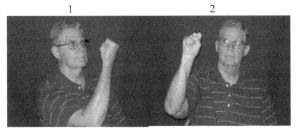

DESCRIPTION: This is signed with the initialized "R." The sign represents the tallit (a shawl like garment) worn by many rabbis during a service.

TIP: From a biblical perspective, rabbi means teacher.

REBEL / REBELLIOUS / REVOLT

1   2

DESCRIPTION: This is the same sign for "protest."

RESURRECTION

1   2

DESCRIPTION: This sign describes Jesus getting up from where he was laid (in the tomb).

ALTERNATIVE: ALIVE + AGAIN

RIGHTEOUSNESS

1

2

APPROPRIATE

APPROPRIATE

3

4

WAY

WAY

DESCRIPTION: A compound sign, combining the sign "appropriate" and the sign "way."

ALTERNATIVE: The sign "clean" can substitute the sign "way." APPROPRIATE + CLEAN.

TIP: "Righteousness" means someone who is morally right. From a biblical perspective, "righteous" and "righteousness" means someone who is observant to God.

SACRAMENT

DESCRIPTION: This is signed with the initialized "S" in the form of a cross in front of the face.

TIP: A sacrament is an outward sign of faith that initiates an inward, spiritual grace. Baptism and the Eucharist / Holy Communion are considered sacraments.

SACRIFICE

DESCRIPTION: This sign represents "giving up."

TIP: This sign does not mean the sacrifices at an altar. The sign "animals" can be signed to represent the meaning for burnt sacrifices (animals). This sign for "sacrifice" represents "to give up" something.

SANCTUARY

1   2

WORSHIP   ROOM

3

ROOM

DESCRIPTION: This sign describes walls of a room. If the size of the sanctuary is large, show that by spacing the hands further apart.

ALTERNATIVE: WORSHIP + AUDIENCE
or
WORSHIP + PLACE

SATAN / DEVIL / EVIL

DESCRIPTION: Referencing reformation theology, this sign describes the devil's horns.

SAVIOR

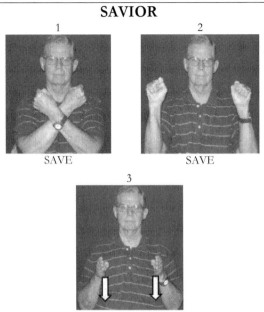

DESCRIPTION: A compound sign, combining the sign "save" and the sign "person." This describes a person releasing someone from bondage. (Reference: Isaiah 14:3)

SCRIPTURE / VERSE

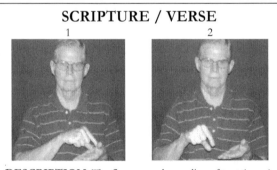

DESCRIPTION: The fingers go along a line of text (verse).

SCROLL / TORAH

DESCRIPTION: This sign models a scroll being opened.
TIP: The Torah is the first 5 books of the Old Testament.

SHEPHERD

Continued
DESCRIPTION: The sign "sheep" describes sheers cutting off wool.
TIP: The sign "supervisor" can substitute the sign "caretaker."

SIN

DESCRIPTION: This sign portrays spoken hurtful words that are contrary to God. It modifies the sign "offensive."

SLAVE / SLAVERY / BONDAGE

DESCRIPTION: This sign describes a person bound by chains.

SOUL

DESCRIPTION: This sign references the soul being part of the heart.

ALTERNATIVE: The sign "spirit" is used by some users.

STRENGTH / POWER

DESCRIPTION: This sign emphasizes muscle strength.

TIP: Inserting the sign "all" makes it "Almighty." ALL + STRENGTH

SUFFER

DESCRIPTION: With your thumb on your chin, twist your fist to the left.
TIP: This is the same sign for "misery" and "miserable."

TEACH

DESCRIPTION: This sign represents knowledge being passed from one individual to another.

TEMPT / TEMPTATION

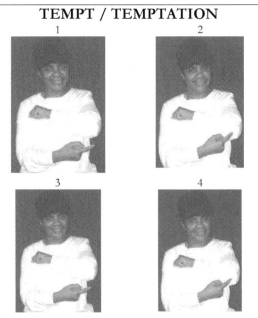

DESCRIPTION: Use the index finger to tap the elbow.

TESTIMONY / EVANGELIZE / SPEECH

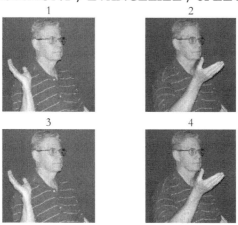

DESCRIPTION: This sign represents someone speaking.

TIP: The initialized "E" is sometimes used for the sign "evangelize." Also, the initialized "T" is sometimes used for the sign "testimony."

THEOLOGY

FAITH   FAITH

3

DESCRIPTION: This is a compound sign of FAITH + OPINION.

TIP: Theology is the study of religious faith, practice, and experience.

OPINION (LETTER "O")

ALTERNATIVE: FAITH + PERSPECTIVE

TRADITION / CUSTOM

1   2

DESCRIPTION: The sign for "habit" is used for the sign "tradition."

ALTERNATIVE: Sometimes users will sign tradition with an initialized "T".

TRINITY

1   2

DESCRIPTION: This sign represents the 3-in-1 concept of the Trinity.

TIP: The concept of the Trinity is a Triune God: Father, Son, and Holy Spirit - three persons, yet one God.

VISION / DREAM

1   2

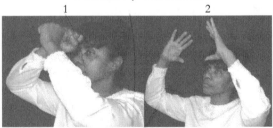

DESCRIPTION: The sign "vision" models a thought balloon, as seen in cartoon illustrations.

WATER

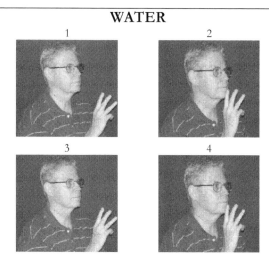

DESCRIPTION: When using the initialized "W," it changes the sign "drink" to "water."

WEDDING

DESCRIPTION: This sign describes the joining of two hands (two persons) in holy matrimony.

WINE

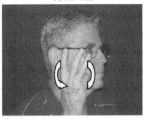

DESCRIPTION: This sign uses an initialized "W" and is signed in a circular motion. This sign indicates the blush of color the wine brings to the cheek.

WORSHIP / DEVOTION

DESCRIPTION: This is a modified sign of a prayer posture.

TIP: This sign can be used for the term "adoration."

Index

Abraham (sign), 277

adultery (sign), 277

affair (sign), 277

amen, 278

American with Disabilities Act (ADA), 8

Amish (sign), 278

angel (sign), 278

Anglican Church (sign), 279

anniversary (sign), 286

anoint (sign), 279

Apostle (sign), 280

Apostle's Creed, 165

Ash Wednesday (sign), 280

assistive listening devices (ALDs), 56

Associate Continuing Education Tracking (ACET), 3

attire, 26, 46, 185

baptism (sign), 281, 282

Baptist (sign), 282

Bethlehem (sign), 283

Bible (sign), 283

bishop (sign), 284

bless (sign), 284

blessing (sign), 284

blood (sign), 285

boundaries, 18, 20, 195

burial (sign), 285

bury (sign), 285

care (sign), 285

categories of Christianity, 66

Catholic (sign), 286

celebrate (sign), 286

celebration (sign), 286

certification, 4, 5, 6, 7, 11, 13, 47, 95, 129

chaplain (sign), 324

choice of language, 102

choir (sign), 287

Christ (sign), 287

Christian (sign), 288

Christian worship, ii, 65

church (sign), 289

classifiers, 110

cochlear implant, 103

Code of Professional Conduct, 7, 9, 10, 15, 28, 43, 46, 251

coffin (sign), 289

commandment (sign), 289

commentaries, 140, 141

Communion (sign), 294

compensation, 24, 36, 55

Computerized Access Realtime Translations (CART), 58

confess (sign), 290

confession (sign), 290

congregation (sign), 290

consecutive interpreting, 118, 252

contact signing, 111

context, 50, 68, 82, 102, 114, 120, 122, 132, 141, 142, 169, 183, 193, 254, 255

covenant (sign), 291

CPC, 10, 15, 18, 27, 41

creed, 164, 165

cross (sign), 292

cross-cultural, 67, 79

crucifixion (sign), 292

crucify (sign), 292

custom (sign), 336

dead (sign), 292

Deaf congregations, iv

Deaf church, v, vi, 217

Deaf congregations, iv, v

Deaf empowerment, 53

Deaf worship services, iv

deaf-blind individual, 59

Department of Rehabilitation Services (V.R.), 53

devil (sign), 329

died (sign), 292

disciple (sign), 280

dream (sign), 336

dynamics, v, 46, 49, 52, 66, 82, 103, 177, 255

Easter (sign), 294

Eastern Orthodoxy, 68

Education Interpreting Performance Assessment (EIPA), 13

Episcopal (sign), 294

ethical dilemmas, 18, 32, 195

Ethical Practice System (EPS), 10

Eucharist (sign), 294

evangelize (sign), 335

evil (sign), 329

exegesis, 140, 142, 160, 260

expansion techniques, 123

faith (sign), 295

fee, 55, 98, 132, 173, 184

fellowship (sign), 296

follower (sign), 280

forgive (sign), 296

forgiveness (sign), 296

frozen text, 139, 166, 197

funeral, 8, 156, 169, 171, 172, 173, 175, 176, 177, 179, 197, 296 (sign)

generalist, 3, 5

gift (sign), 297

glaucoma, 63

glorify (sign), 297

glory (sign), 297

goals, 2, 7, 28, 131

God (sign), 298

gospel (sign), 298

grace (sign), 299

grave (sign), 285

group settings, 64

guilt (sign), 299

guilty (sign), 299

hallelujah (sign), 286

heal (sign), 299

healthy (sign), 299

Heaven (sign), 300

Hebrew (sign), 305

Hell (sign), 300

helpful tips, 59

Holy Communion (sign), 294

Holy Ghost (sign), 301

Holy Spirit (sign), 301

Hosanna in the Highest (sign), 302

hymn (sign), 303

Individuals with Disabilities Education Act (IDEA), 9

inspiration (sign), 303

inspire (sign), 303

interpreter participation, 27

Interpreter Training Program, 95

interpreting philosophies, 113

interpreting training programs, 1, 153

interview, vi, 5, 6, 7, 10, 95, 255

Israel (sign), 304

Jerusalem (sign), 304

Jesus (sign), 305

Jewish (sign), 305

justice (sign), 305

kingdom (sign), 306

language fluency, 107, 215

language register, 119

laying of hands (sign), 320

leprosy (sign), 307

litany (sign), 307

liturgy, iv, 103, 147, 171, 179, 181, 183, 190, 193, 308

loan signs, 110

logistics, 54

Lord (sign), 309

love (sign), 309

Lutheran (sign), 309

macular degeneration, 62

manger (sign), 310

marginalize (sign), 310

marriage (sign), 310

married (sign), 310

Mary (sign), 311

mentor, 28, 33, 129, 130, 131, 191

Messiah (sign), 311

Methodist (sign), 312

minister (sign), 312

ministry (sign), 313

miracle (sign), 314

mission (sign), 314

Moses (sign), 315

multiple roles, 22

music, iv, 66, 98, 99, 103, 117, 118, 130, 139, 153, 154, 155, 156, 157, 174, 184, 192, 213, 214 (sign)

music stand, 98, 99, 174

mystery (sign), 316

National Interpreting Certification (NIC), 5, 11

Nazareth (sign), 316

New Testament (sign), 317

Nicene Creed, 164, 165

non-denominational, 69

offering (sign), 318

Old Testament (sign), 319

oppress (sign), 320

oppression (sign), 320

ordain (sign), 320

parallel Bible, 141, 143, 148, 149, 150, 151

parameters, 108

parish (sign), 289

passed away (sign), 292

pastor (sign), 312

payment, 23, 25, 48, 55

peace (sign), 321

peaceful (sign), 321

Pidgin Signed English (PSE), 111

poor (sign), 321

poverty (sign), 321

power (sign), 333

praise (sign), 322

pray (sign), 322

prayer (sign), 322

preach (sign), 323

preacher (sign), 312

predict (sign), 325

preparation materials, 6, 98, 213

Presbyterianv, 323

presence (sign), 323

priest (sign), 324

professional liability insurance, 51

Promised Land (sign), 324

prophecy (sign), 325

Protestant (sign), 325

Psalm 23, 175

punish (sign), 325

punishment (sign), 325

Quality Assurance Screening (QAS), 12

rabbi (sign), 326

rebel (sign), 326

rebellious (sign), 326

resources, 15, 29, 45, 52, 58, 61, 80, 104, 107, 108, 139, 141, 142, 166, 169

Resurrection (sign), 326

Revised Common Lectionary, 140

revolt (sign), 326

rhetorical questions, 109

RID, 1, 2, 3, 4, 6, 7, 10, 11, 13, 16, 19, 23, 28, 29, 41, 43, 51, 52, 90, 96, 113, 116, 117, 129, 130, 133, 191, 193, 195, 202, 216

righteousness (sign), 327

sacrament (sign), 328

sacrifice (sign), 328

sanctuary, 52, 54, 56, 89, 99, 101, 329 (sign)

Satan (sign), 329

Savior (sign), 330

Scripture (sign), 330

scroll (sign), 331

self-monitoring, 127, 128

semantics, 254

sermon, iv, 56, 66, 98, 99, 113, 119, 127, 135, 159, 160, 161, 173, 193, 213, 323 (sign)

shalom (sign), 321

shepherd (sign), 331

signer, ii, 124, 125

simultaneous interpreting, 118, 256

sin (sign), 332

sing (sign), 303

slave (sign), 332

slavery (sign), 332

song (sign), 303

soul (sign), 333

source language, 118, 119, 121, 167, 256, 266

Standard Practice Paper, 19, 23, 52, 90, 133

strength (sign), 333

study Bible, 148, 150

suffer (sign), 333

syntax, 102, 111, 251, 254, 256, 265

target language, 118, 119, 121, 139, 160, 256, 266

tempt, temptation (sign), 334

tenets, 7, 9, 10, 18, 27

TENETS, 9

tensions, 81

testimony (sign), 335

theology (sign), 335

topicalization, 109

tradition (sign), 336

Transliterating, 10

Trinity (sign), 336

Usher syndrome, 63

V.R., 53

verse (sign), 330

Video Remote Interpreting (VRI), 16

vision (sign), 336

water (sign), 337

wedding, 169, 181, 182, 183, 184, 185, 186, 197, 337 (sign)

Western Church, 65, 66, 67, 164

Wh-question, 109

wine (sign), 338

Made in the USA
Columbia, SC
17 September 2020